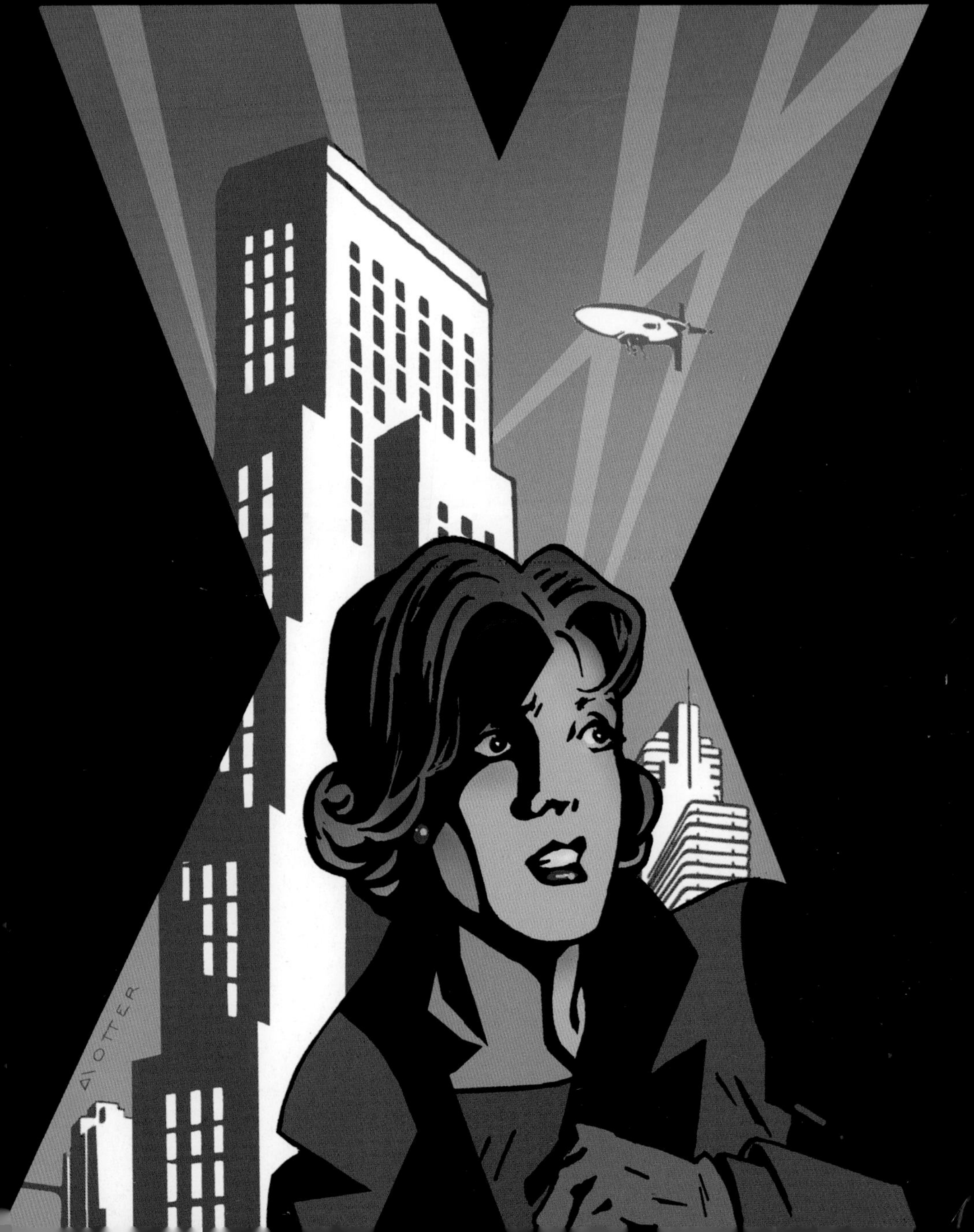

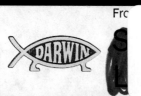

DEAN MOTTER's

MISTE

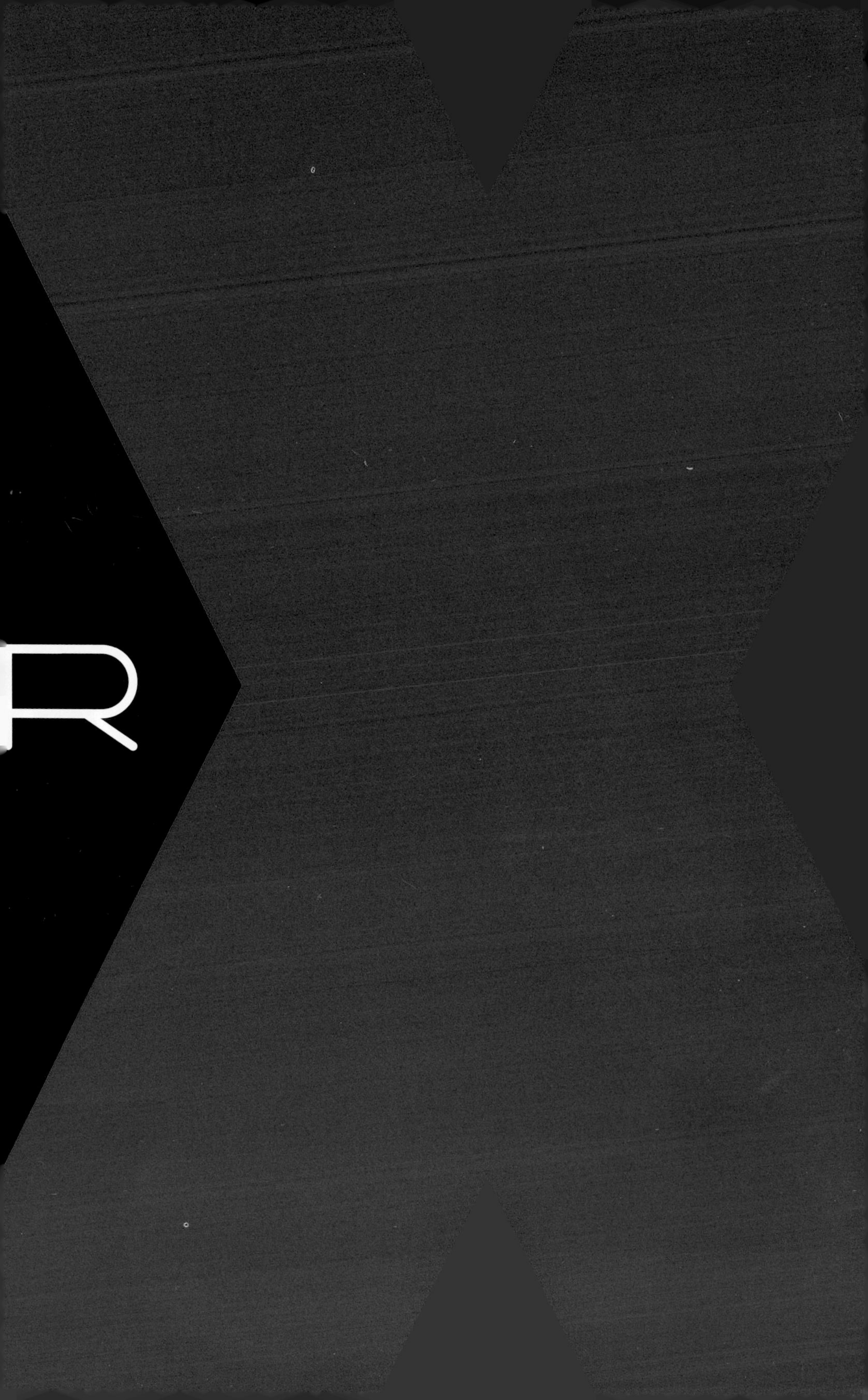

CONDE

EMNED

DARK HORSE BOOKS®

MISTER X CREATED BY DEAN MOTTER

Publisher...MIKE RICHARDSON
Editor...DAVE MARSHALL
Assistant Editor ....BRENDAN WRIGHT
Design......................... DEAN MOTTER & JOSH ELLIOTT
Digital Production.......................................MATT DRYER

Color and art assist by HAMID BAHRAMI

Special thanks to Cliff Biggers (*CSN*), Heather Brown, Paul
Gravett, Los Bros. Hernandez, William P. Marks, Philip Nutman,
Katie Ryle, Cara Sanders, Diana Schutz, Seth, Paul Rivoche, Ken
Steacy, David Terrien (*Art Review*), and the Dark Horse crew.

Dedicated to J. G. Ballard

Published by
Dark Horse Books
A division of
Dark Horse Comics, Inc.
10956 SE Main Street
Milwaukie, OR 97222

darkhorse.com
First edition: November 2009
ISBN 978-1-59582-359-5

10 9 8 7 6 5 4 3 2 1
Printed in China

This volume collects #1 through #4 of the Dark Horse comic-
book series *Mister X: Condemned*, a story from #13 of the
online comic-book anthology *MySpace Dark Horse Presents*,
and a story from the comic-book anthology *Noir*, all published
by Dark Horse Comics.

Library of Congress Cataloging-in-Publication Data

Motter, Dean.
Mister X : condemned / Dean Motter. -- 1st ed.
   p. cm.
ISBN 978-1-59582-359-5
1. Graphic novels. I. Title.
PN6727.M68M57 2009
741.5'973--dc22
                                                  2009023817

INTRODUCTION BY HOWA

It's always a pleasure to sit back and spend a little quality time in Radiant City and the world of Mister X. It's a familiar cityscape, since Dean and I—along with all of his collaborators—seem to share a deep affection for our parents' and grandparents' idea of how our world of the twenty-first century would look, feel, and sound.

Call it retro future, heightened reality, future past, or whatever—this chiaroscuro, high-light-and-deep-shadow urban landscape holds an enormous fascination for those of us who remain disappointed at the lack of personal jetpacks, flying cars, and atomic-powered zeppelins in our lives.

From the first time I saw *Metropolis*, *Things to Come*, and *Just Imagine*, I've wanted to live in a world that combined John Alton's cinematography in Anthony Mann's noir universe with the future as visualized by Frank R. Paul on those fantastic covers for *Amazing Stories*.

Guys like Dean and me were alone in our obsessions with this particularly urban, seamy, and sexy strain of science fiction for a long time, wandering, lost and alone like the Israelites in the desert . . .

. . . And then along came *Blade Runner*.

Ridley Scott's brilliant cinematic imagining of Philip K. Dick's *Do Androids Dream of Electric Sheep?* was nothing more than all of my retro-future obsessions brought to life. From then on, my and Dean's private obsession became public domain—and, almost instantly, a cliché.

A critic, whose name unfortunately escapes me, once said that *Blade Runner*, although far from a critical or commercial success when it arrived, remains a vastly more important film than the big blockbusters of its time, in that it completely changed the way we visualize the future.

ARD CHAYKIN

Sorry, pal, but Dean and I were already there, waiting for the atomic-powered dirigible—he in Radiant City, I in *Time*[2]. It didn't come as a surprise to either of us that the future was a dark, wet, and scary place—Murnau and Lang had hipped us to this when we were boys, for heaven's sake.

Dean and I also share a love of puns, wordplay, and cryptic references to the bulwarks of our magnificent obsessions—from Rand and Reinhardt, from Howard Roark and Eric Blair, to our love for naming drugs. I have to assume he loves those drug commercials on *Jeopardy* and the nightly news as much as I do, assuming he's reached that point in his life where he watches those television series that run ads intended to reach the aging freak in all of us.

Dean's a crackerjack designer, too—again, delivering work that demonstrates an awareness of a lost world that seems merely to have been misplaced or forgotten, as opposed to never having existed at all.

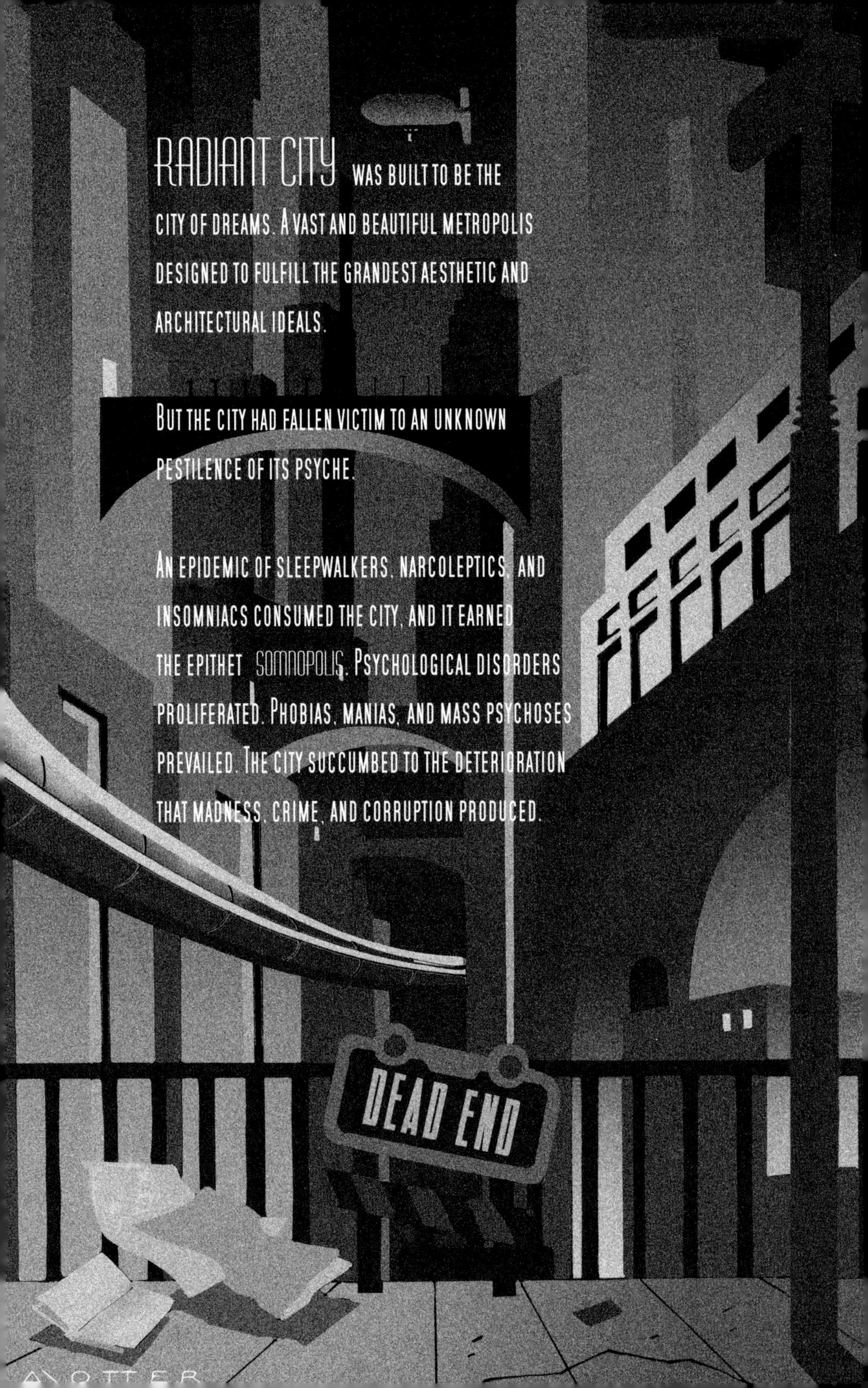
DEAD END

RADIANT CITY WAS BUILT TO BE THE CITY OF DREAMS. A VAST AND BEAUTIFUL METROPOLIS DESIGNED TO FULFILL THE GRANDEST AESTHETIC AND ARCHITECTURAL IDEALS.

BUT THE CITY HAD FALLEN VICTIM TO AN UNKNOWN PESTILENCE OF ITS PSYCHE.

AN EPIDEMIC OF SLEEPWALKERS, NARCOLEPTICS, AND INSOMNIACS CONSUMED THE CITY, AND IT EARNED THE EPITHET SOMNOPOLIS. PSYCHOLOGICAL DISORDERS PROLIFERATED. PHOBIAS, MANIAS, AND MASS PSYCHOSES PREVAILED. THE CITY SUCCUMBED TO THE DETERIORATION THAT MADNESS, CRIME, AND CORRUPTION PRODUCED.

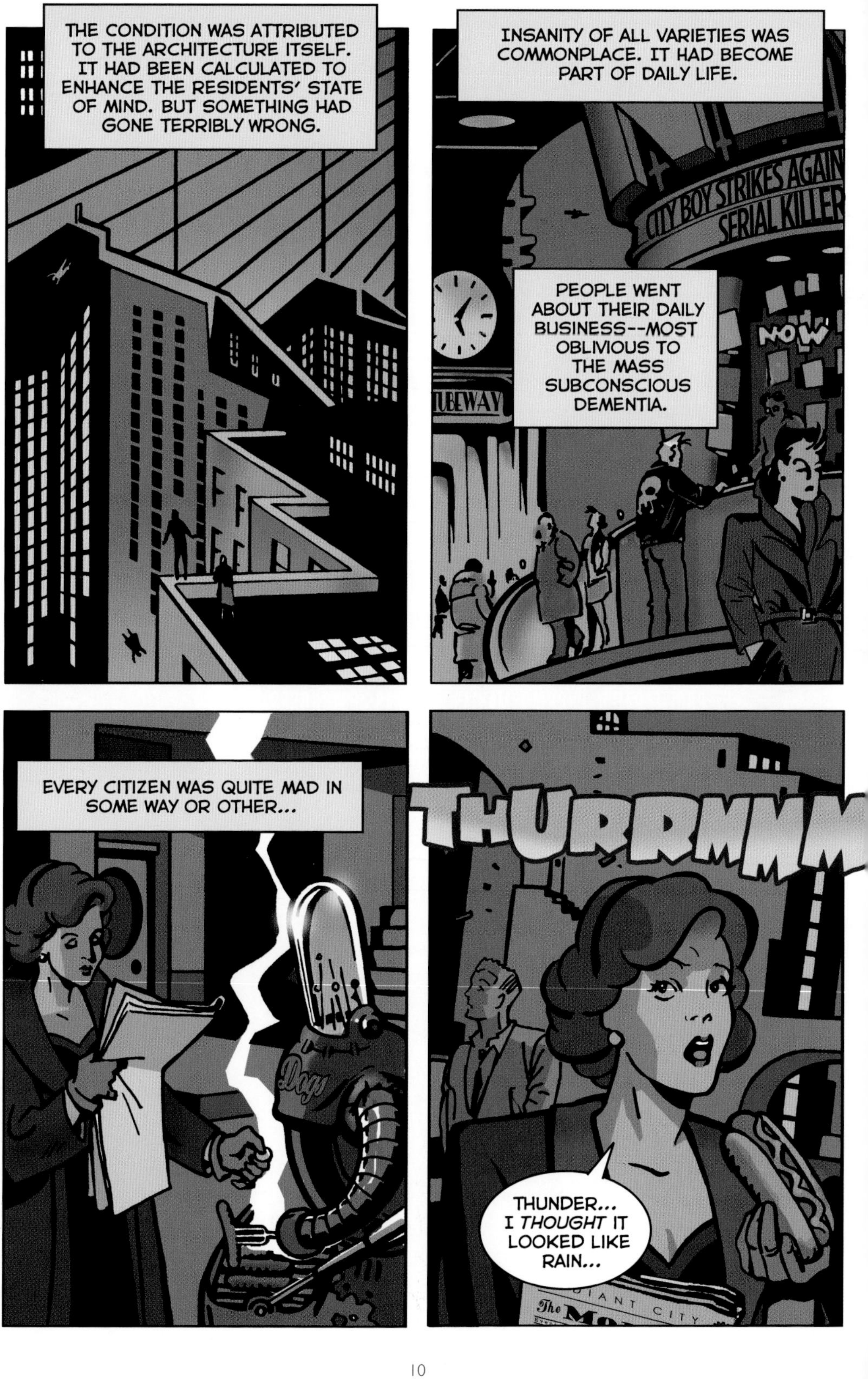
THE CONDITION WAS ATTRIBUTED TO THE ARCHITECTURE ITSELF. IT HAD BEEN CALCULATED TO ENHANCE THE RESIDENTS' STATE OF MIND. BUT SOMETHING HAD GONE TERRIBLY WRONG.
INSANITY OF ALL VARIETIES WAS COMMONPLACE. IT HAD BECOME PART OF DAILY LIFE.
CITY BOY STRIKES AGAIN
SERIAL KILLER
PEOPLE WENT ABOUT THEIR DAILY BUSINESS--MOST OBLIVIOUS TO THE MASS SUBCONSCIOUS DEMENTIA.
TUBEWAY
NOW
EVERY CITIZEN WAS QUITE MAD IN SOME WAY OR OTHER...
Dogs
THURRMMM
THUNDER... I *THOUGHT* IT LOOKED LIKE RAIN...

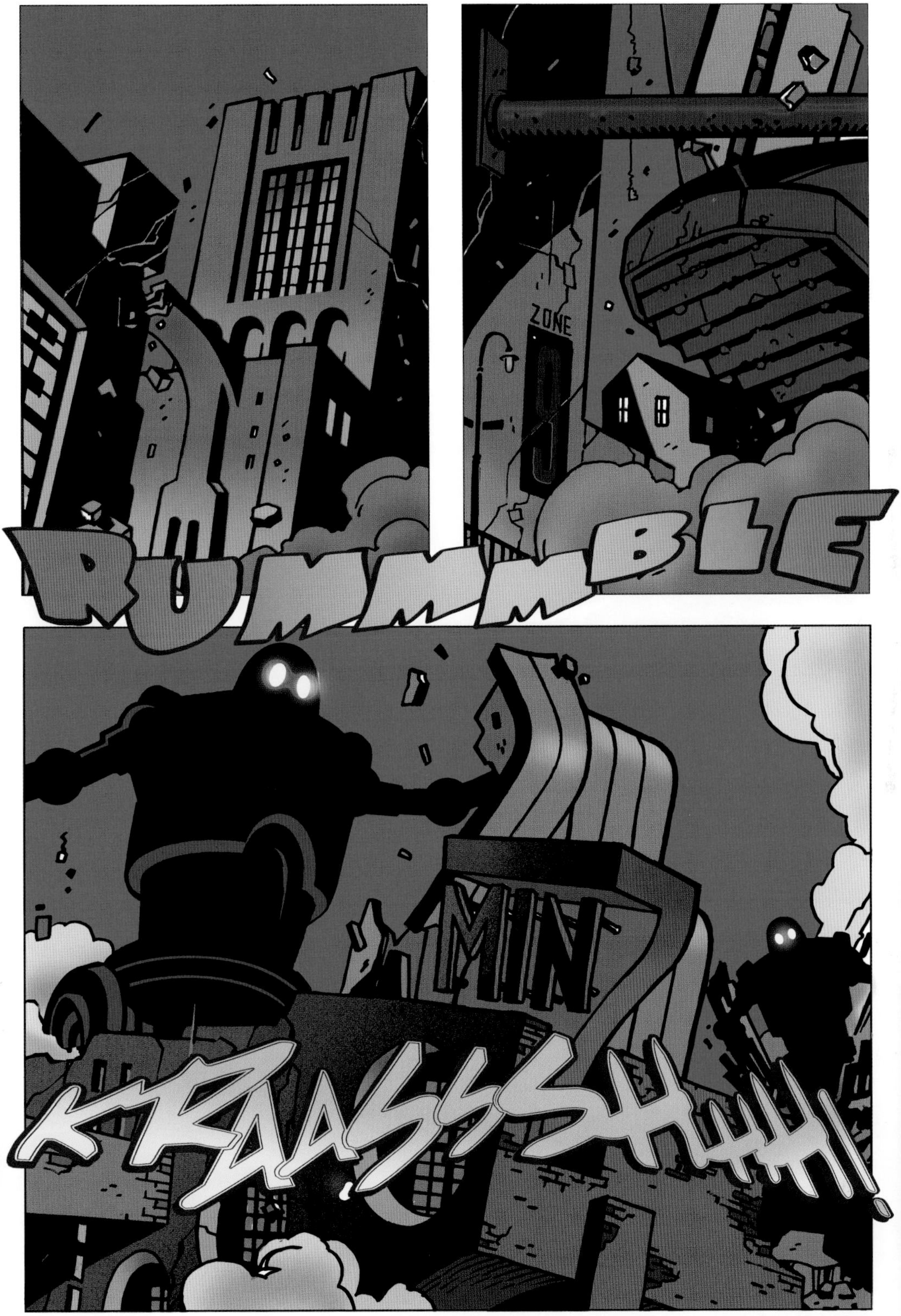
ZONE
RUMMMBLE
MIN
KRAASSSHHH!

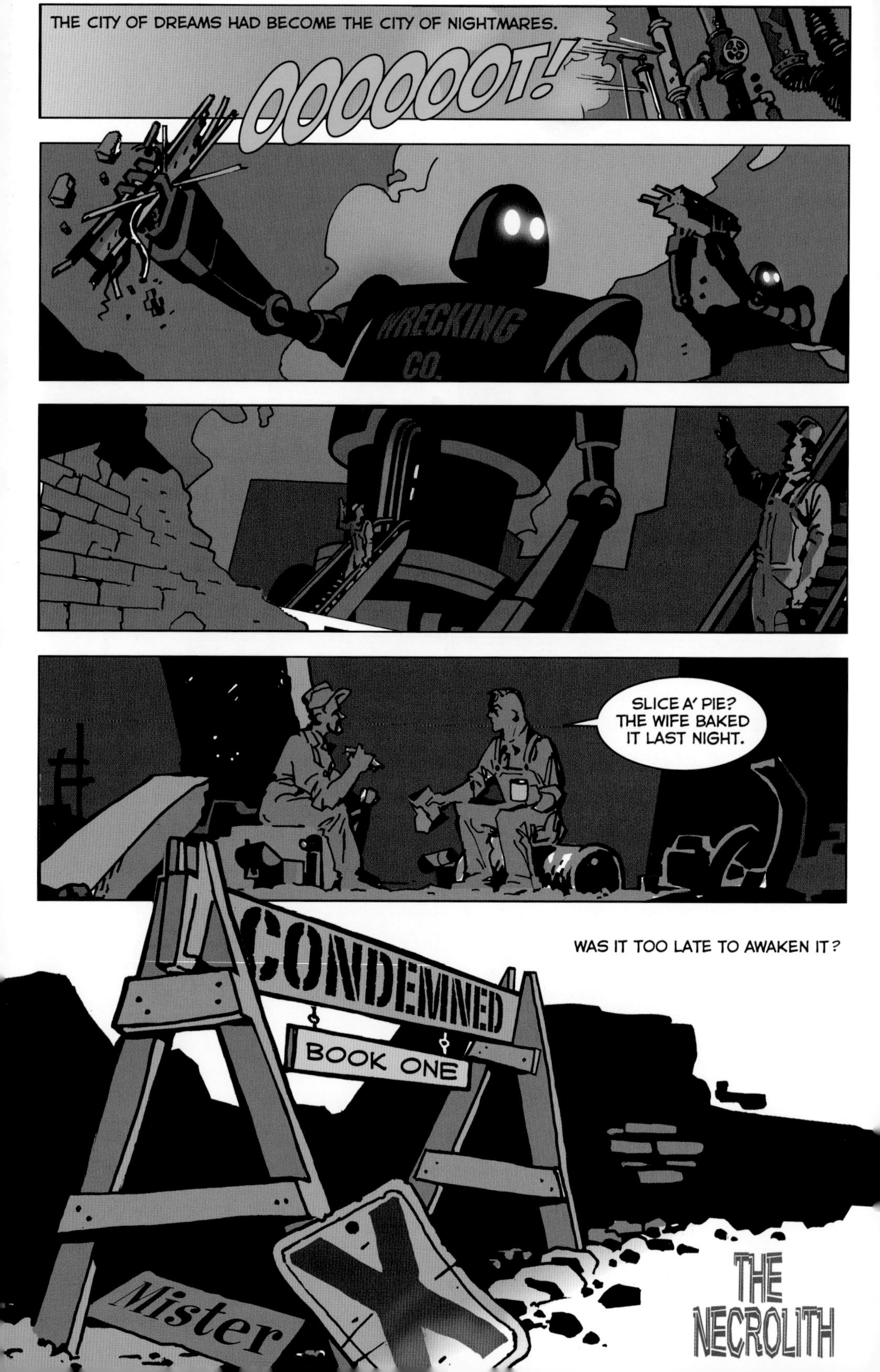
THE CITY OF DREAMS HAD BECOME THE CITY OF NIGHTMARES.
OOOOOOOT!
WRECKING CO.
SLICE A' PIE? THE WIFE BAKED IT LAST NIGHT.
WAS IT TOO LATE TO AWAKEN IT?
CONDEMNED
BOOK ONE
Mister X
THE NECROLITH

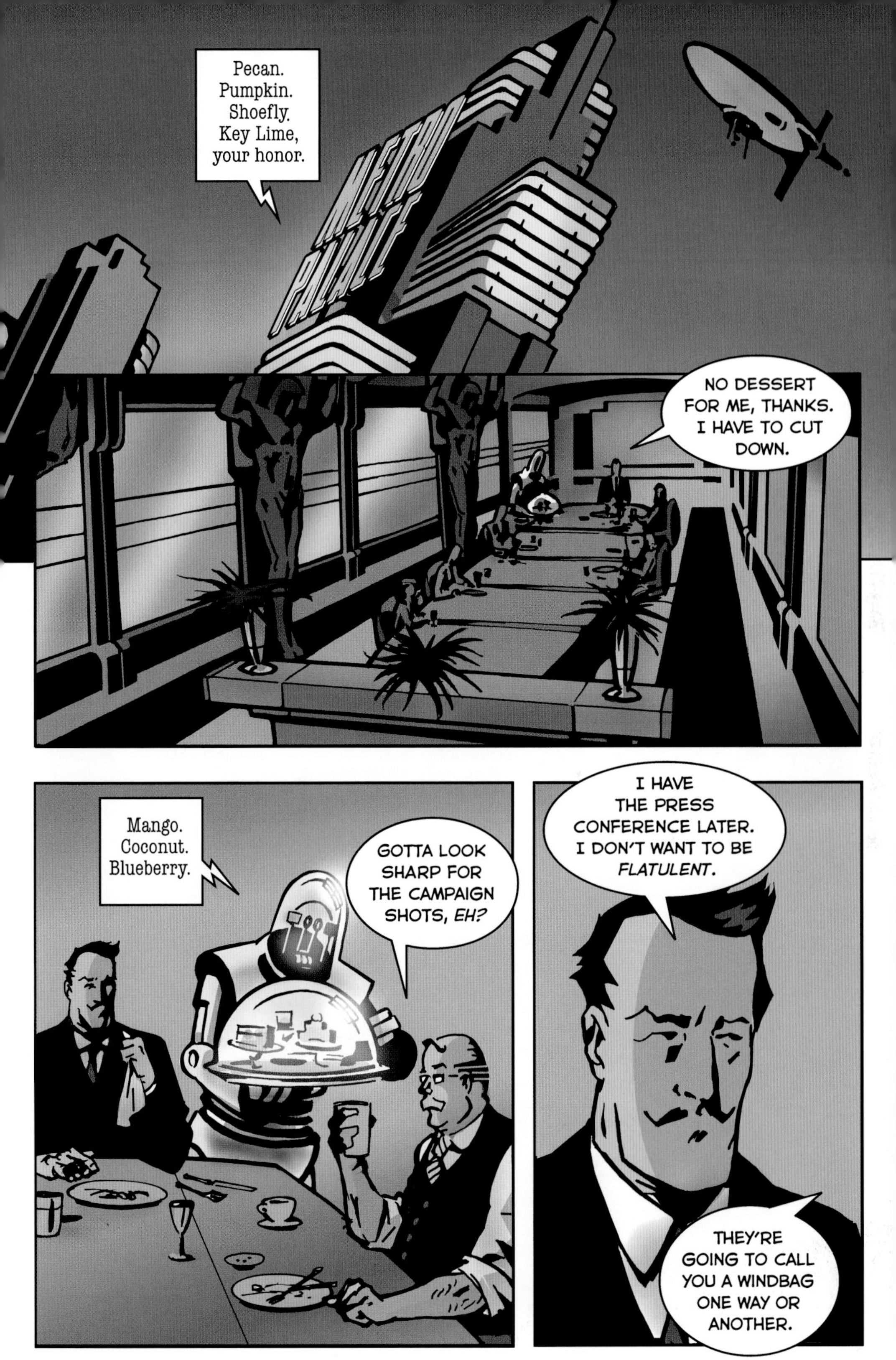
Pecan. Pumpkin. Shoefly. Key Lime, your honor.
METRO PALACE
NO DESSERT FOR ME, THANKS. I HAVE TO CUT DOWN.
Mango. Coconut. Blueberry.
GOTTA LOOK SHARP FOR THE CAMPAIGN SHOTS, *EH?*
I HAVE THE PRESS CONFERENCE LATER. I DON'T WANT TO BE *FLATULENT*.
THEY'RE GOING TO CALL YOU A WINDBAG ONE WAY OR ANOTHER.

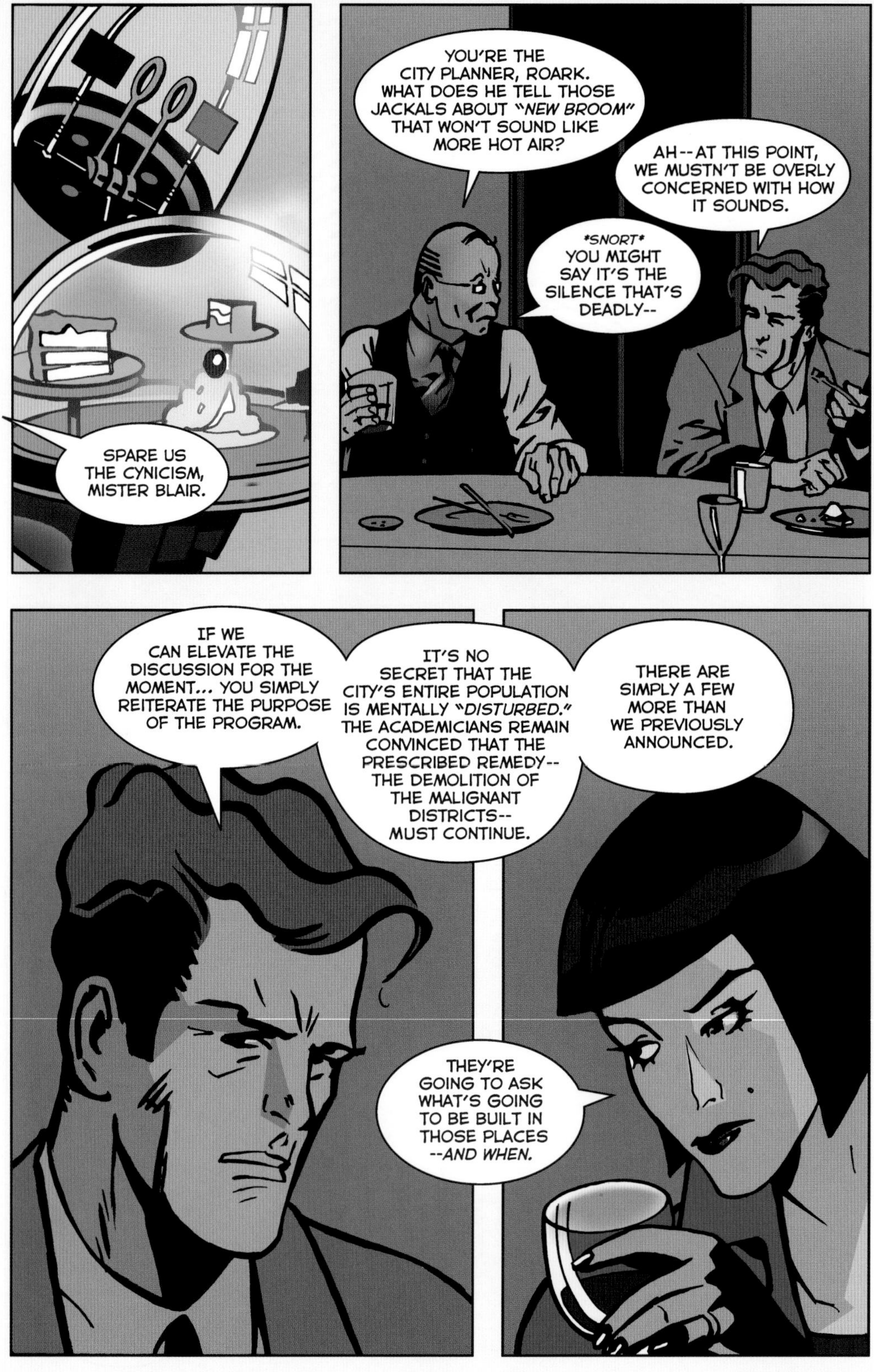
SPARE US THE CYNICISM, MISTER BLAIR.
YOU'RE THE CITY PLANNER, ROARK. WHAT DOES HE TELL THOSE JACKALS ABOUT "NEW BROOM" THAT WON'T SOUND LIKE MORE HOT AIR?
AH--AT THIS POINT, WE MUSTN'T BE OVERLY CONCERNED WITH HOW IT SOUNDS.
SNORT YOU MIGHT SAY IT'S THE SILENCE THAT'S DEADLY--
IF WE CAN ELEVATE THE DISCUSSION FOR THE MOMENT... YOU SIMPLY REITERATE THE PURPOSE OF THE PROGRAM.
IT'S NO SECRET THAT THE CITY'S ENTIRE POPULATION IS MENTALLY "DISTURBED." THE ACADEMICIANS REMAIN CONVINCED THAT THE PRESCRIBED REMEDY-- THE DEMOLITION OF THE MALIGNANT DISTRICTS-- MUST CONTINUE.
THERE ARE SIMPLY A FEW MORE THAN WE PREVIOUSLY ANNOUNCED.
THEY'RE GOING TO ASK WHAT'S GOING TO BE BUILT IN THOSE PLACES --AND WHEN.

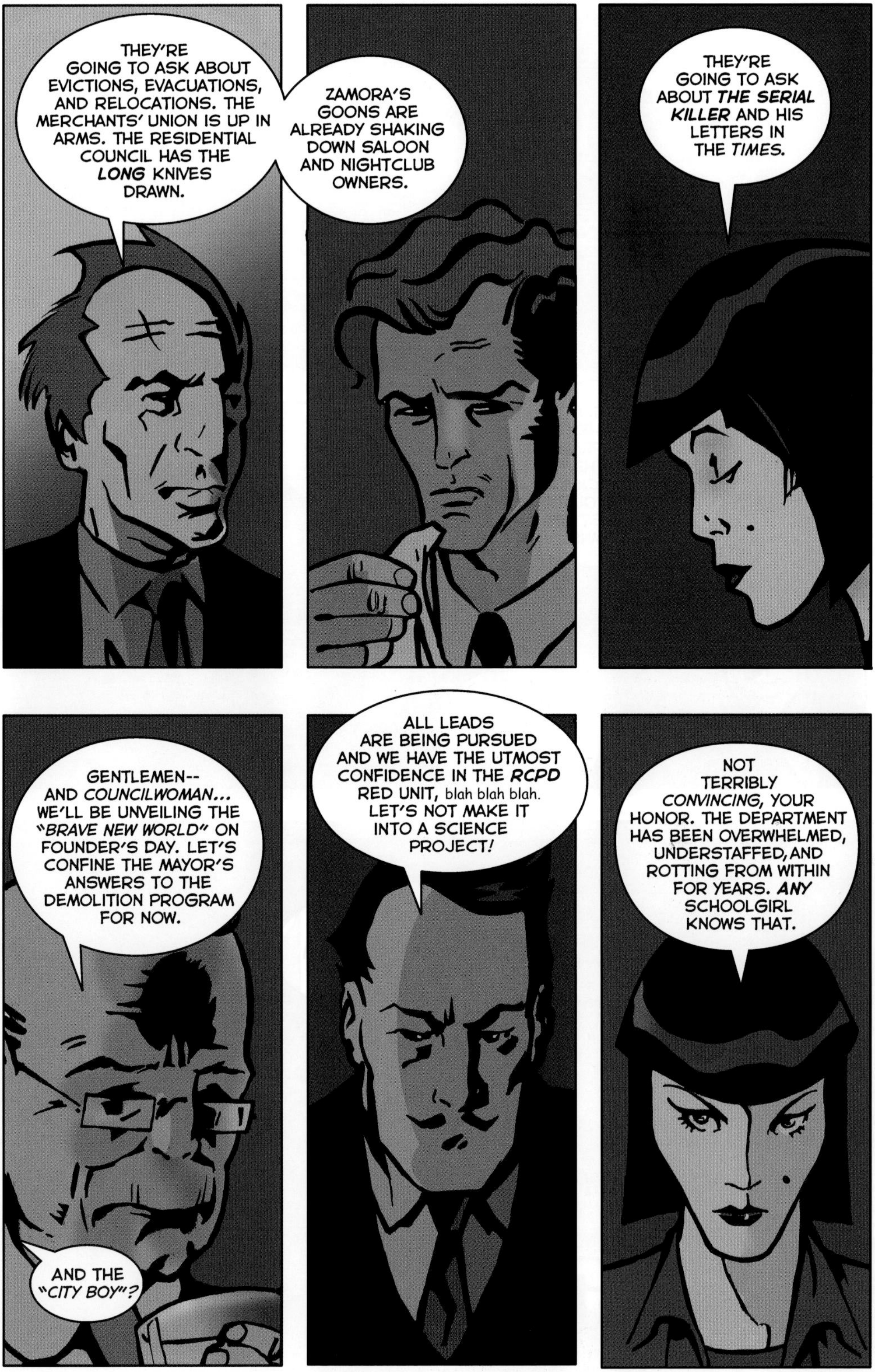
THEY'RE GOING TO ASK ABOUT EVICTIONS, EVACUATIONS, AND RELOCATIONS. THE MERCHANTS' UNION IS UP IN ARMS. THE RESIDENTIAL COUNCIL HAS THE *LONG* KNIVES DRAWN.
ZAMORA'S GOONS ARE ALREADY SHAKING DOWN SALOON AND NIGHTCLUB OWNERS.
THEY'RE GOING TO ASK ABOUT *THE SERIAL KILLER* AND HIS LETTERS IN THE *TIMES.*
GENTLEMEN-- AND *COUNCILWOMAN...* WE'LL BE UNVEILING THE *"BRAVE NEW WORLD"* ON FOUNDER'S DAY. LET'S CONFINE THE MAYOR'S ANSWERS TO THE DEMOLITION PROGRAM FOR NOW.
AND THE *"CITY BOY"*?
ALL LEADS ARE BEING PURSUED AND WE HAVE THE UTMOST CONFIDENCE IN THE *RCPD* RED UNIT, blah blah blah. LET'S NOT MAKE IT INTO A SCIENCE PROJECT!
NOT TERRIBLY *CONVINCING,* YOUR HONOR. THE DEPARTMENT HAS BEEN OVERWHELMED, UNDERSTAFFED, AND ROTTING FROM WITHIN FOR YEARS. *ANY* SCHOOLGIRL KNOWS THAT.

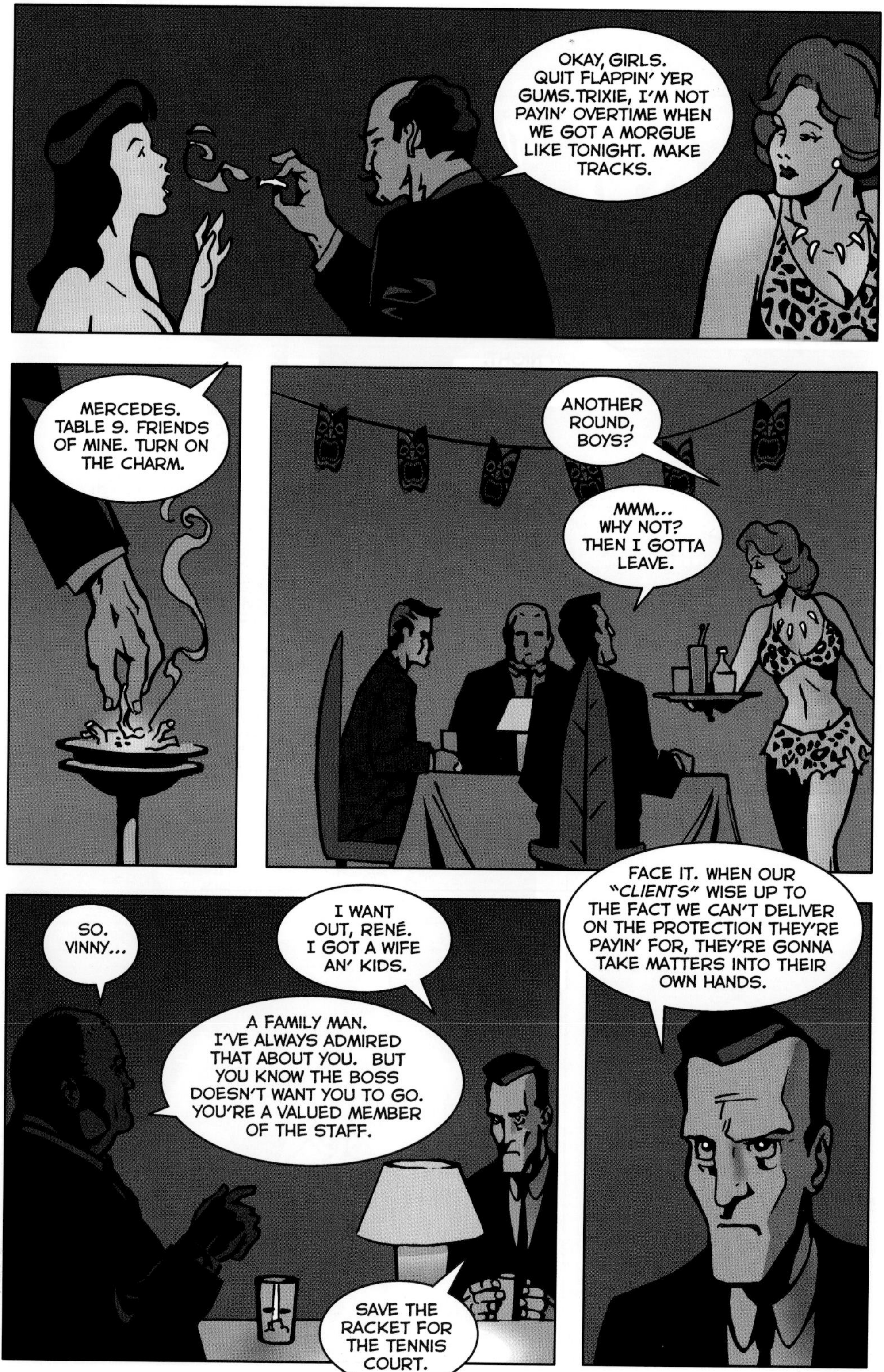
OKAY, GIRLS. QUIT FLAPPIN' YER GUMS. TRIXIE, I'M NOT PAYIN' OVERTIME WHEN WE GOT A MORGUE LIKE TONIGHT. MAKE TRACKS.
MERCEDES. TABLE 9. FRIENDS OF MINE. TURN ON THE CHARM.
ANOTHER ROUND, BOYS?
MMM... WHY NOT? THEN I GOTTA LEAVE.
SO. VINNY...
I WANT OUT, RENÉ. I GOT A WIFE AN' KIDS.
A FAMILY MAN. I'VE ALWAYS ADMIRED THAT ABOUT YOU. BUT YOU KNOW THE BOSS DOESN'T WANT YOU TO GO. YOU'RE A VALUED MEMBER OF THE STAFF.
SAVE THE RACKET FOR THE TENNIS COURT.
FACE IT. WHEN OUR *"CLIENTS"* WISE UP TO THE FACT WE CAN'T DELIVER ON THE PROTECTION THEY'RE PAYIN' FOR, THEY'RE GONNA TAKE MATTERS INTO THEIR OWN HANDS.

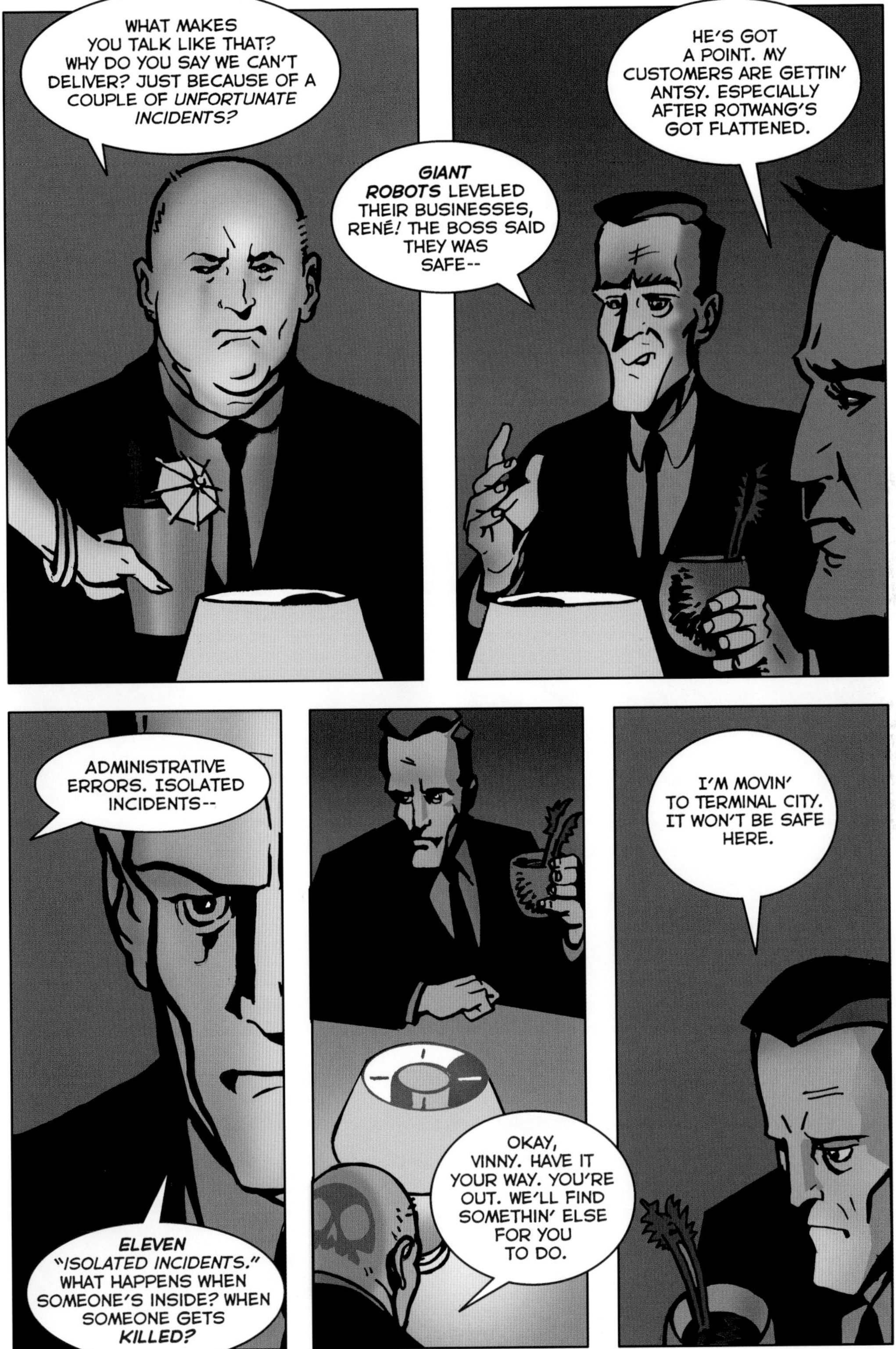
WHAT MAKES YOU TALK LIKE THAT? WHY DO YOU SAY WE CAN'T DELIVER? JUST BECAUSE OF A COUPLE OF *UNFORTUNATE INCIDENTS?*
GIANT ROBOTS LEVELED THEIR BUSINESSES, RENÉ! THE BOSS SAID THEY WAS SAFE--
HE'S GOT A POINT. MY CUSTOMERS ARE GETTIN' ANTSY. ESPECIALLY AFTER ROTWANG'S GOT FLATTENED.
ADMINISTRATIVE ERRORS. ISOLATED INCIDENTS--
ELEVEN "ISOLATED INCIDENTS." WHAT HAPPENS WHEN SOMEONE'S INSIDE? WHEN SOMEONE GETS *KILLED?*
I'M MOVIN' TO TERMINAL CITY. IT WON'T BE SAFE HERE.
OKAY, VINNY. HAVE IT YOUR WAY. YOU'RE OUT. WE'LL FIND SOMETHIN' ELSE FOR YOU TO DO.

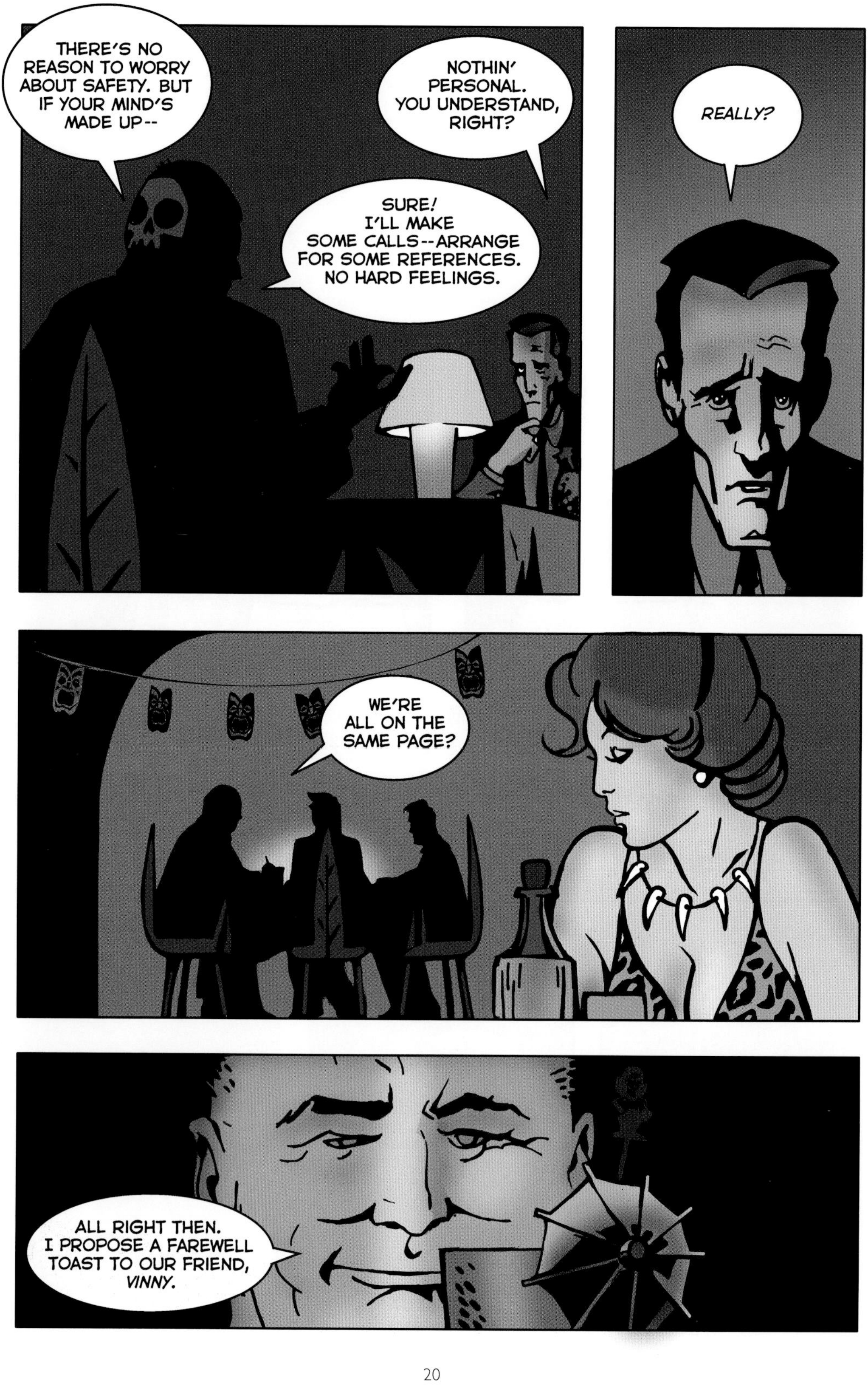
THERE'S NO REASON TO WORRY ABOUT SAFETY. BUT IF YOUR MIND'S MADE UP--
NOTHIN' PERSONAL. YOU UNDERSTAND, RIGHT?
SURE! I'LL MAKE SOME CALLS--ARRANGE FOR SOME REFERENCES. NO HARD FEELINGS.
REALLY?
WE'RE ALL ON THE SAME PAGE?
ALL RIGHT THEN. I PROPOSE A FAREWELL TOAST TO OUR FRIEND, *VINNY*.

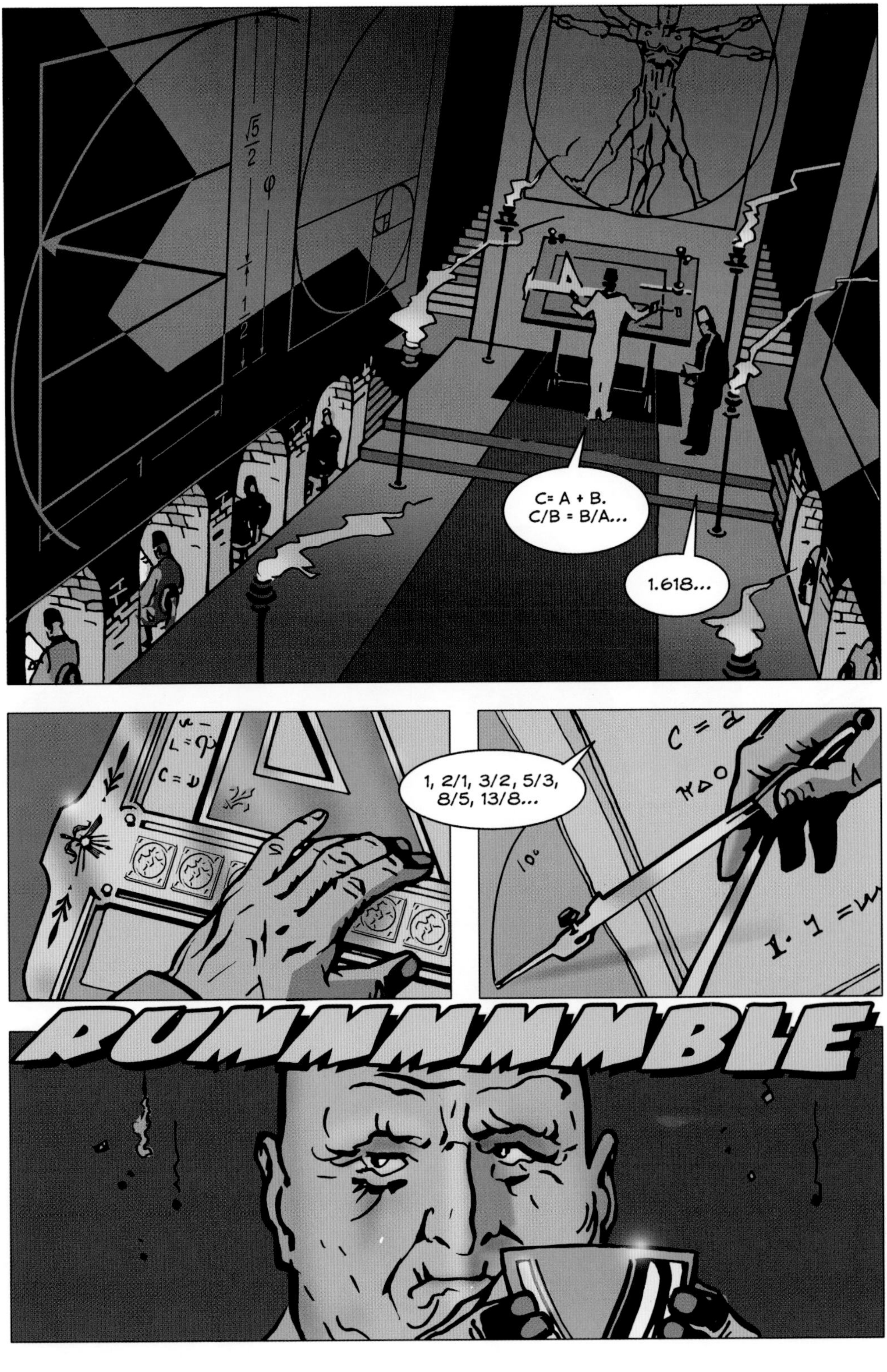

C= A + B.
C/B = B/A...
1.618...
1, 2/1, 3/2, 5/3, 8/5, 13/8...
RUMMMMMMBLE

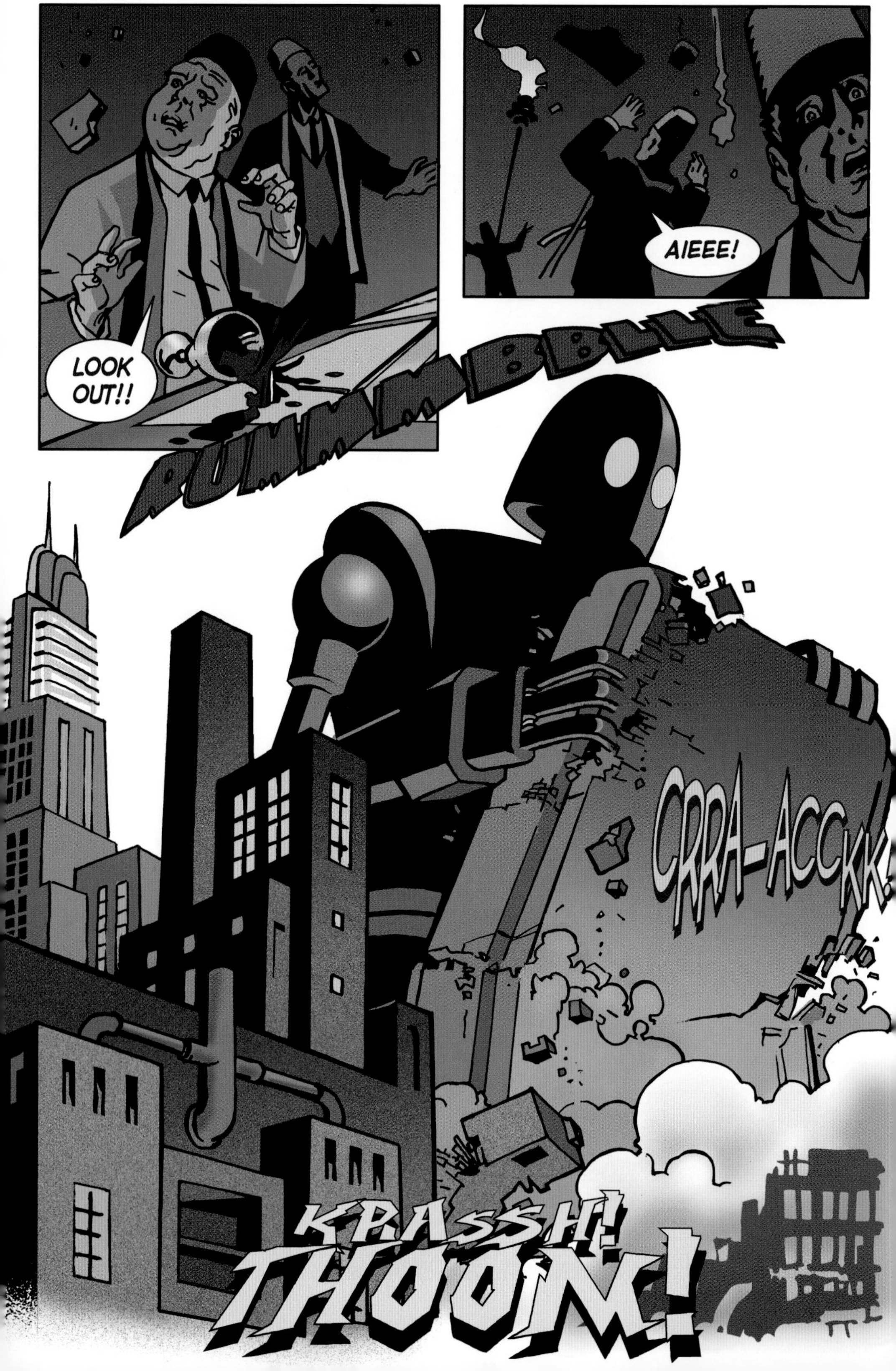
LOOK OUT!!
AIEEE!
RUMMMBBLLE
CRRA-ACCKK!
KRASSH!
THOOM!

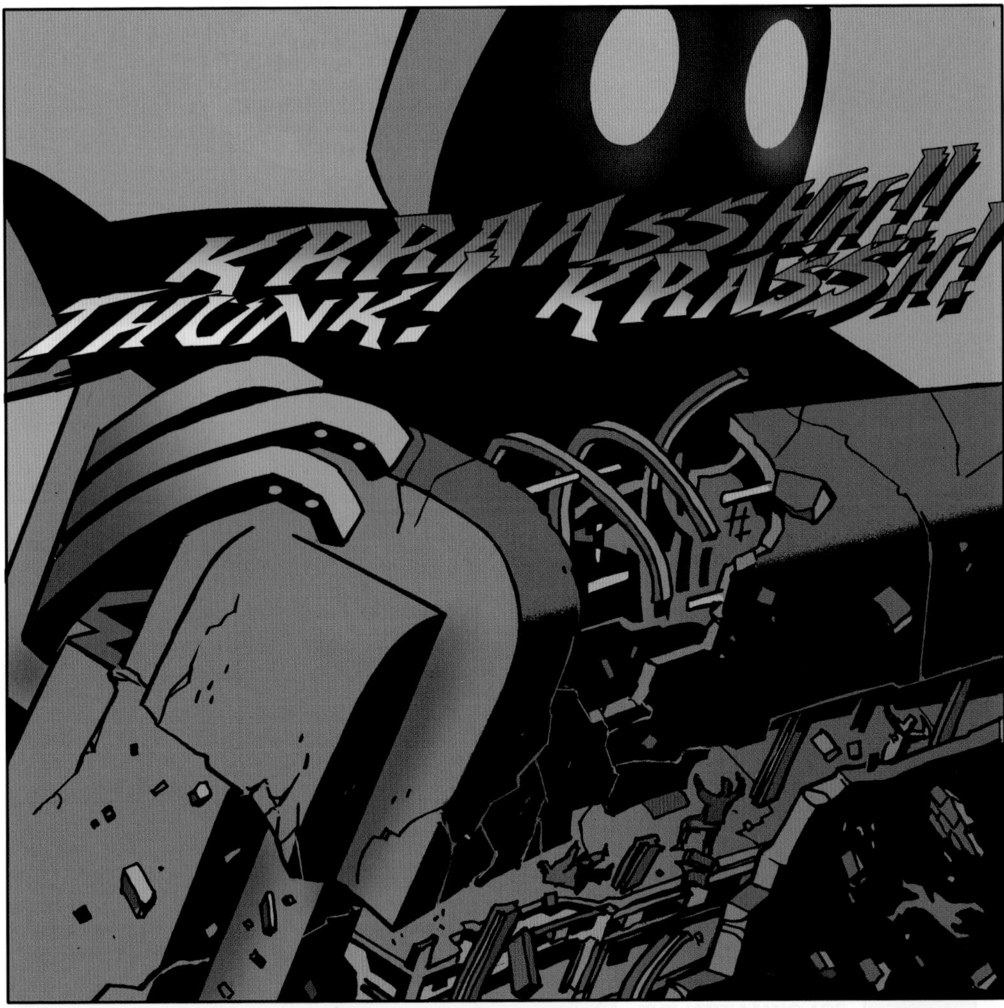
KRRAASSHH!!
THUNK! KRASSH!!

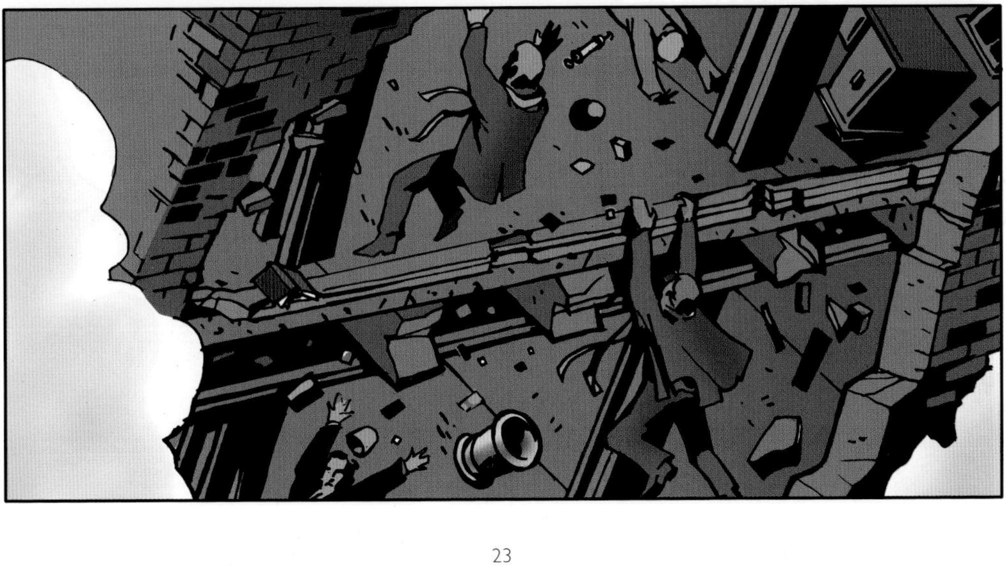

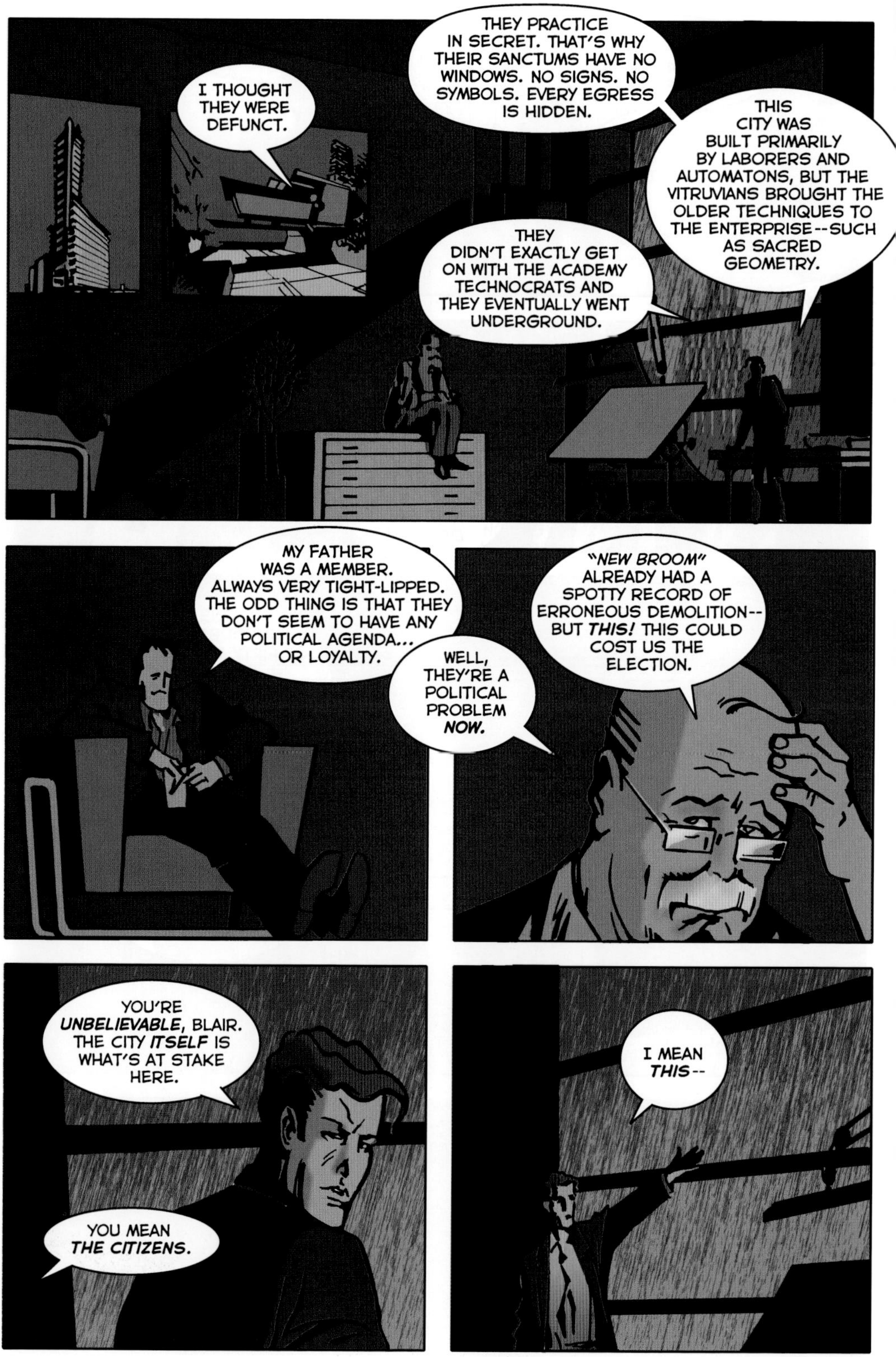
I THOUGHT THEY WERE DEFUNCT.
THEY PRACTICE IN SECRET. THAT'S WHY THEIR SANCTUMS HAVE NO WINDOWS. NO SIGNS. NO SYMBOLS. EVERY EGRESS IS HIDDEN.
THIS CITY WAS BUILT PRIMARILY BY LABORERS AND AUTOMATONS, BUT THE VITRUVIANS BROUGHT THE OLDER TECHNIQUES TO THE ENTERPRISE--SUCH AS SACRED GEOMETRY.
THEY DIDN'T EXACTLY GET ON WITH THE ACADEMY TECHNOCRATS AND THEY EVENTUALLY WENT UNDERGROUND.
MY FATHER WAS A MEMBER. ALWAYS VERY TIGHT-LIPPED. THE ODD THING IS THAT THEY DON'T SEEM TO HAVE ANY POLITICAL AGENDA... OR LOYALTY.
WELL, THEY'RE A POLITICAL PROBLEM *NOW.*
"NEW BROOM" ALREADY HAD A SPOTTY RECORD OF ERRONEOUS DEMOLITION-- BUT *THIS!* THIS COULD COST US THE ELECTION.
YOU'RE *UNBELIEVABLE*, BLAIR. THE CITY *ITSELF* IS WHAT'S AT STAKE HERE.
YOU MEAN *THE CITIZENS.*
I MEAN *THIS*--

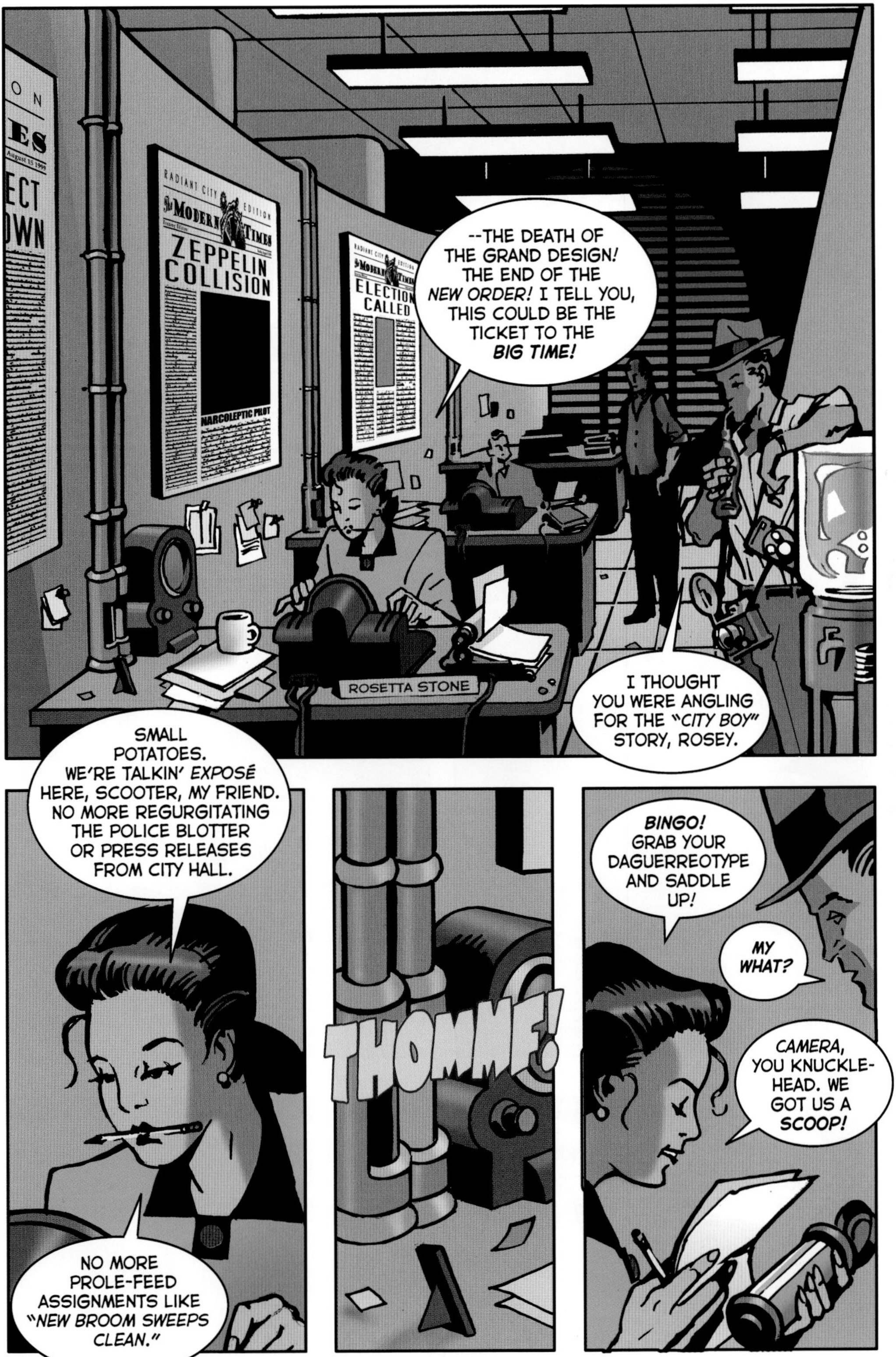
RADIANT CITY EDITION
The MODERN TIMES
ZEPPELIN COLLISION
NARCOLEPTIC PILOT
ELECTION CALLED
--THE DEATH OF THE GRAND DESIGN! THE END OF THE NEW ORDER! I TELL YOU, THIS COULD BE THE TICKET TO THE BIG TIME!
ROSETTA STONE
I THOUGHT YOU WERE ANGLING FOR THE "CITY BOY" STORY, ROSEY.
SMALL POTATOES. WE'RE TALKIN' EXPOSÉ HERE, SCOOTER, MY FRIEND. NO MORE REGURGITATING THE POLICE BLOTTER OR PRESS RELEASES FROM CITY HALL.
NO MORE PROLE-FEED ASSIGNMENTS LIKE "NEW BROOM SWEEPS CLEAN."
THOMMF!
BINGO! GRAB YOUR DAGUERREOTYPE AND SADDLE UP!
MY WHAT?
CAMERA, YOU KNUCKLE-HEAD. WE GOT US A SCOOP!

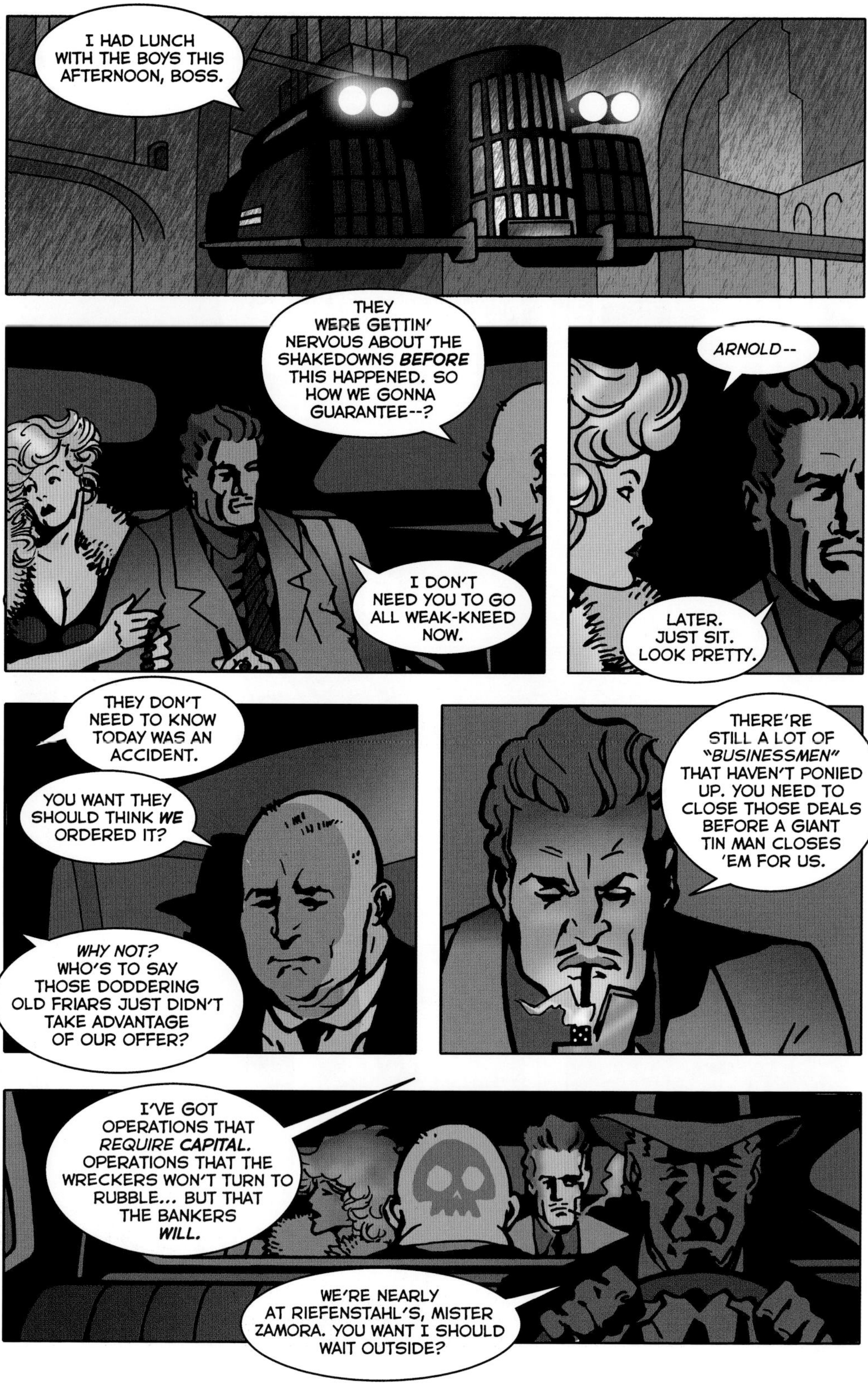

I HAD LUNCH WITH THE BOYS THIS AFTERNOON, BOSS.
THEY WERE GETTIN' NERVOUS ABOUT THE SHAKEDOWNS *BEFORE* THIS HAPPENED. SO HOW WE GONNA GUARANTEE--?
I DON'T NEED YOU TO GO ALL WEAK-KNEED NOW.
ARNOLD--
LATER. JUST SIT. LOOK PRETTY.
THEY DON'T NEED TO KNOW TODAY WAS AN ACCIDENT.
YOU WANT THEY SHOULD THINK *WE* ORDERED IT?
WHY NOT? WHO'S TO SAY THOSE DODDERING OLD FRIARS JUST DIDN'T TAKE ADVANTAGE OF OUR OFFER?
THERE'RE STILL A LOT OF *"BUSINESSMEN"* THAT HAVEN'T PONIED UP. YOU NEED TO CLOSE THOSE DEALS BEFORE A GIANT TIN MAN CLOSES 'EM FOR US.
I'VE GOT OPERATIONS THAT *REQUIRE CAPITAL.* OPERATIONS THAT THE WRECKERS WON'T TURN TO RUBBLE... BUT THAT THE BANKERS *WILL.*
WE'RE NEARLY AT RIEFENSTAHL'S, MISTER ZAMORA. YOU WANT I SHOULD WAIT OUTSIDE?

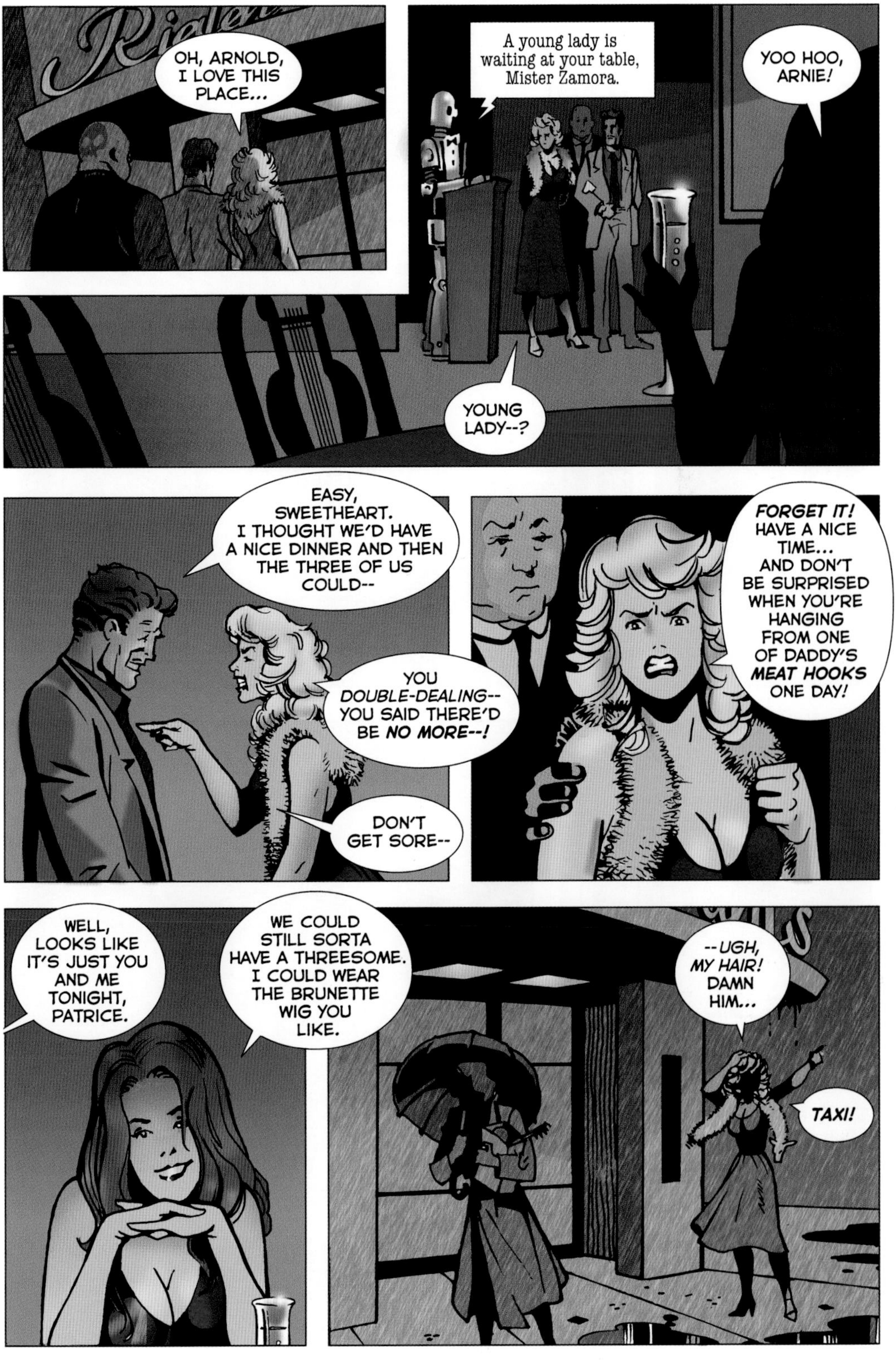
OH, ARNOLD, I LOVE THIS PLACE...
A young lady is waiting at your table, Mister Zamora.
YOO HOO, ARNIE!
YOUNG LADY--?
EASY, SWEETHEART. I THOUGHT WE'D HAVE A NICE DINNER AND THEN THE THREE OF US COULD--
YOU DOUBLE-DEALING-- YOU SAID THERE'D BE NO MORE--!
DON'T GET SORE--
FORGET IT! HAVE A NICE TIME... AND DON'T BE SURPRISED WHEN YOU'RE HANGING FROM ONE OF DADDY'S MEAT HOOKS ONE DAY!
WELL, LOOKS LIKE IT'S JUST YOU AND ME TONIGHT, PATRICE.
WE COULD STILL SORTA HAVE A THREESOME. I COULD WEAR THE BRUNETTE WIG YOU LIKE.
--UGH, MY HAIR! DAMN HIM...
TAXI!

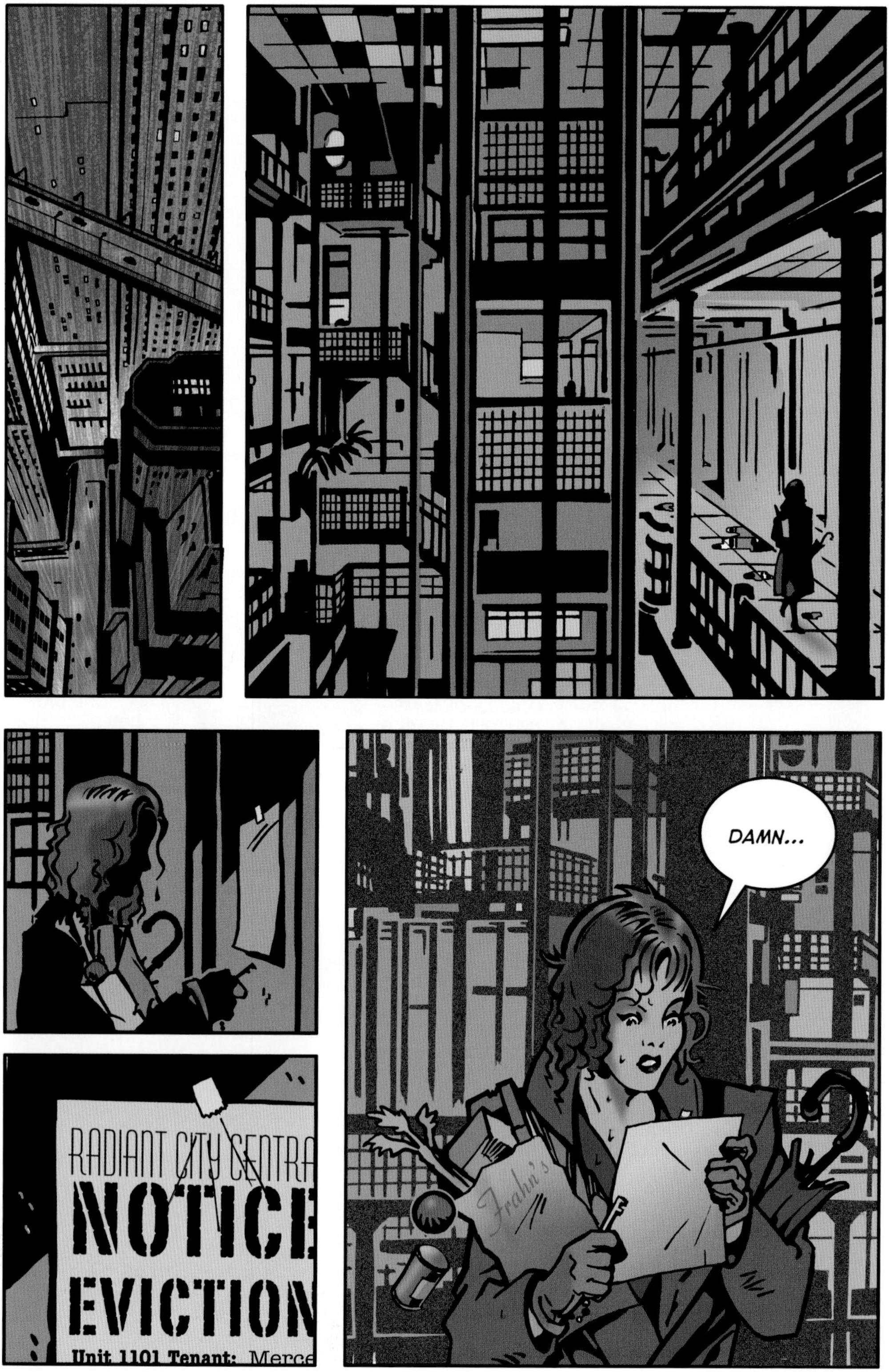
RADIANT CITY CENTRA
NOTICE
EVICTION
Unit 1101 Tenant: Merce
DAMN...
Frahn's

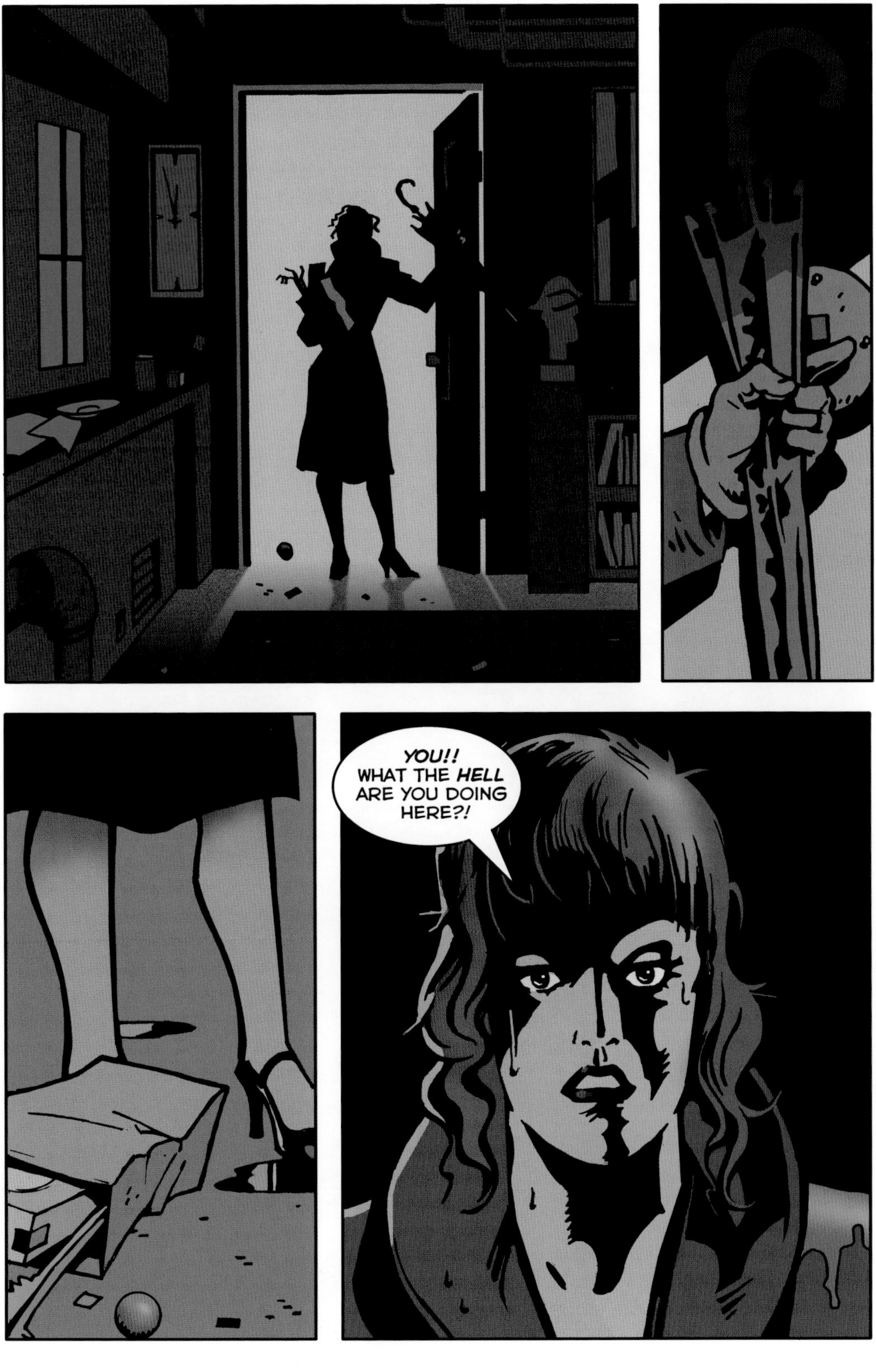
YOU!! WHAT THE HELL ARE YOU DOING HERE?!

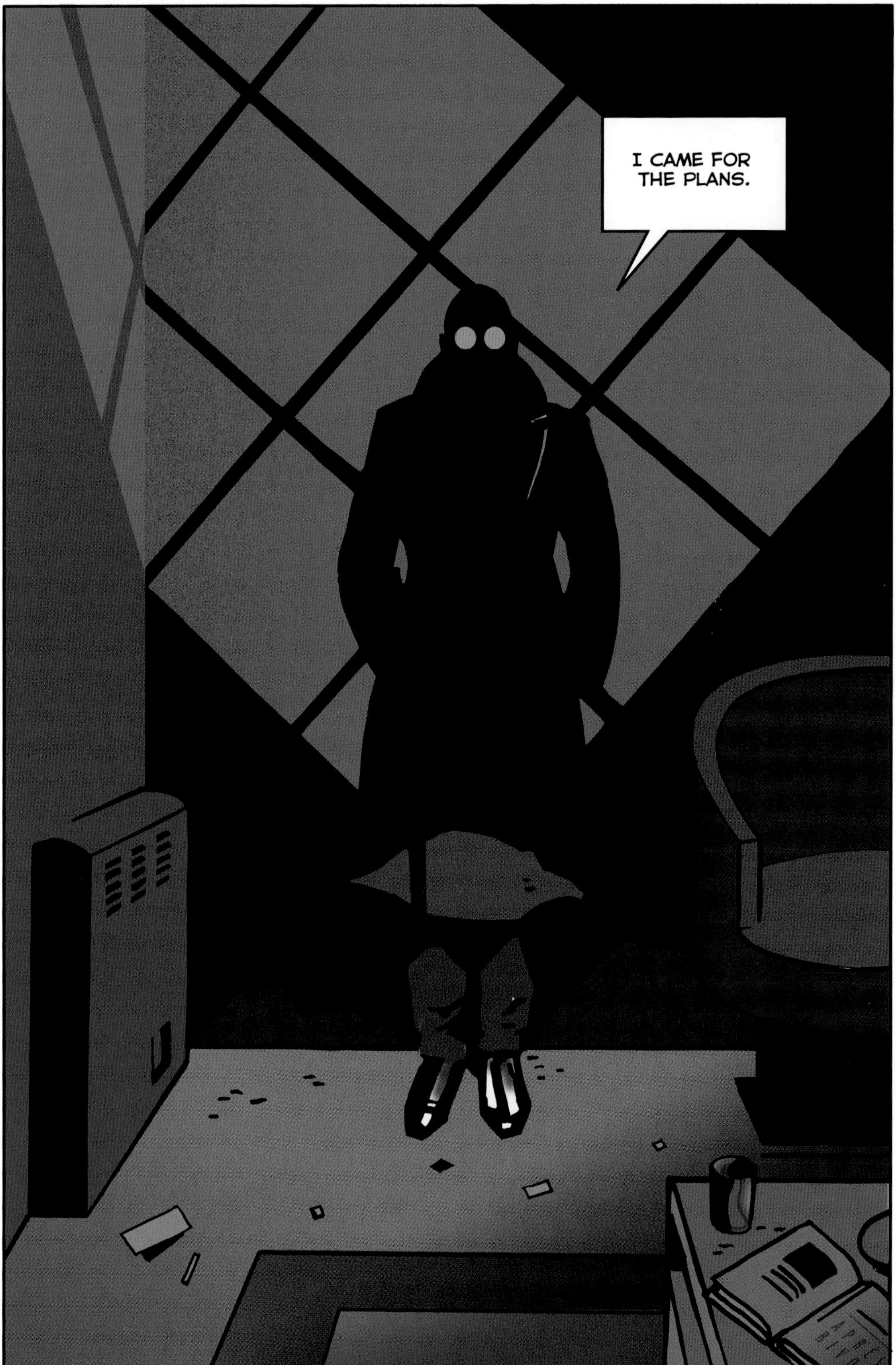
I CAME FOR THE PLANS.

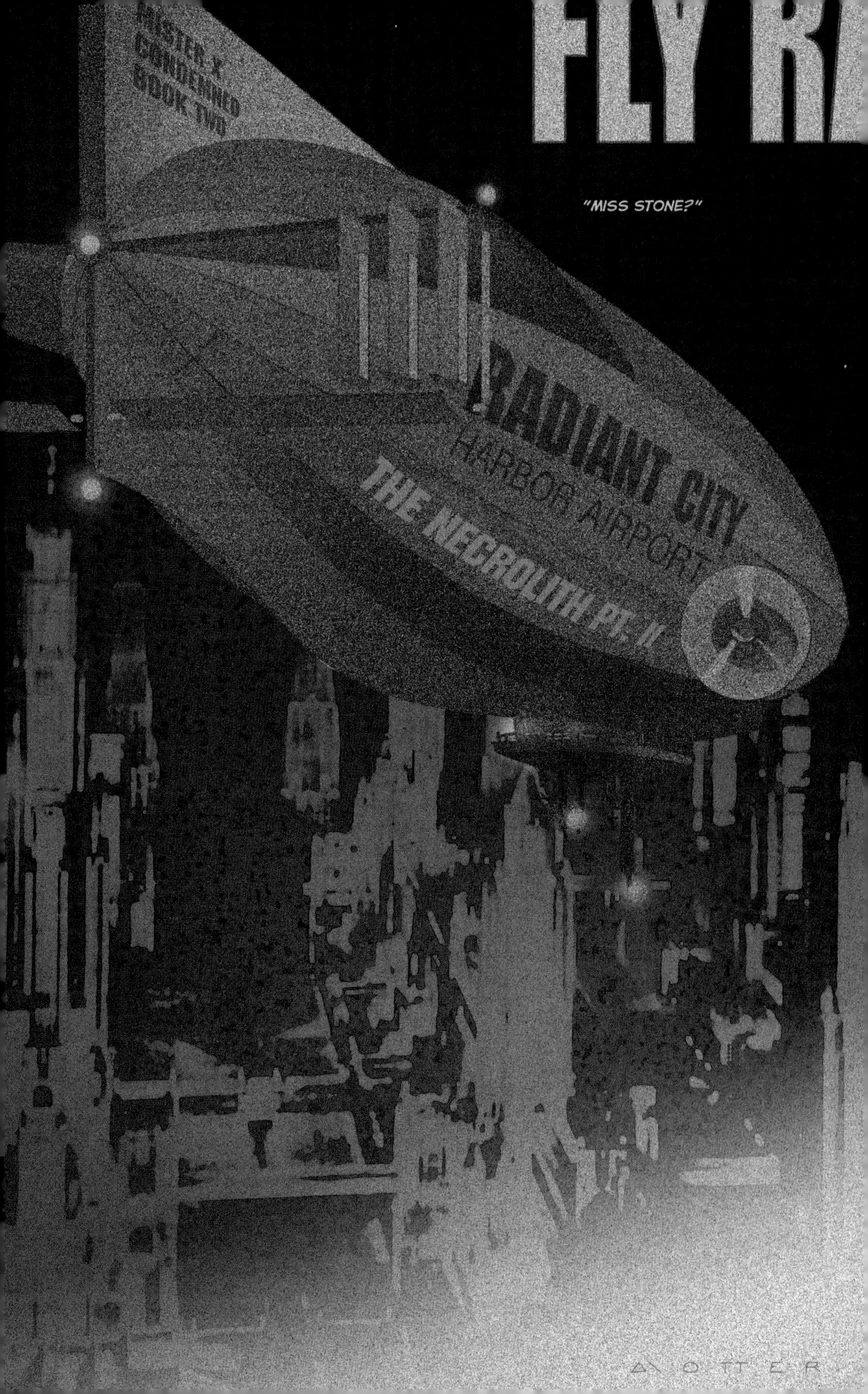
MISTER X
CONDEMNED
BOOK TWO
FLY RA
"MISS STONE?"
RADIANT CITY
HARBOR AIRPORT
THE NECROLITH PT. II
OTTER

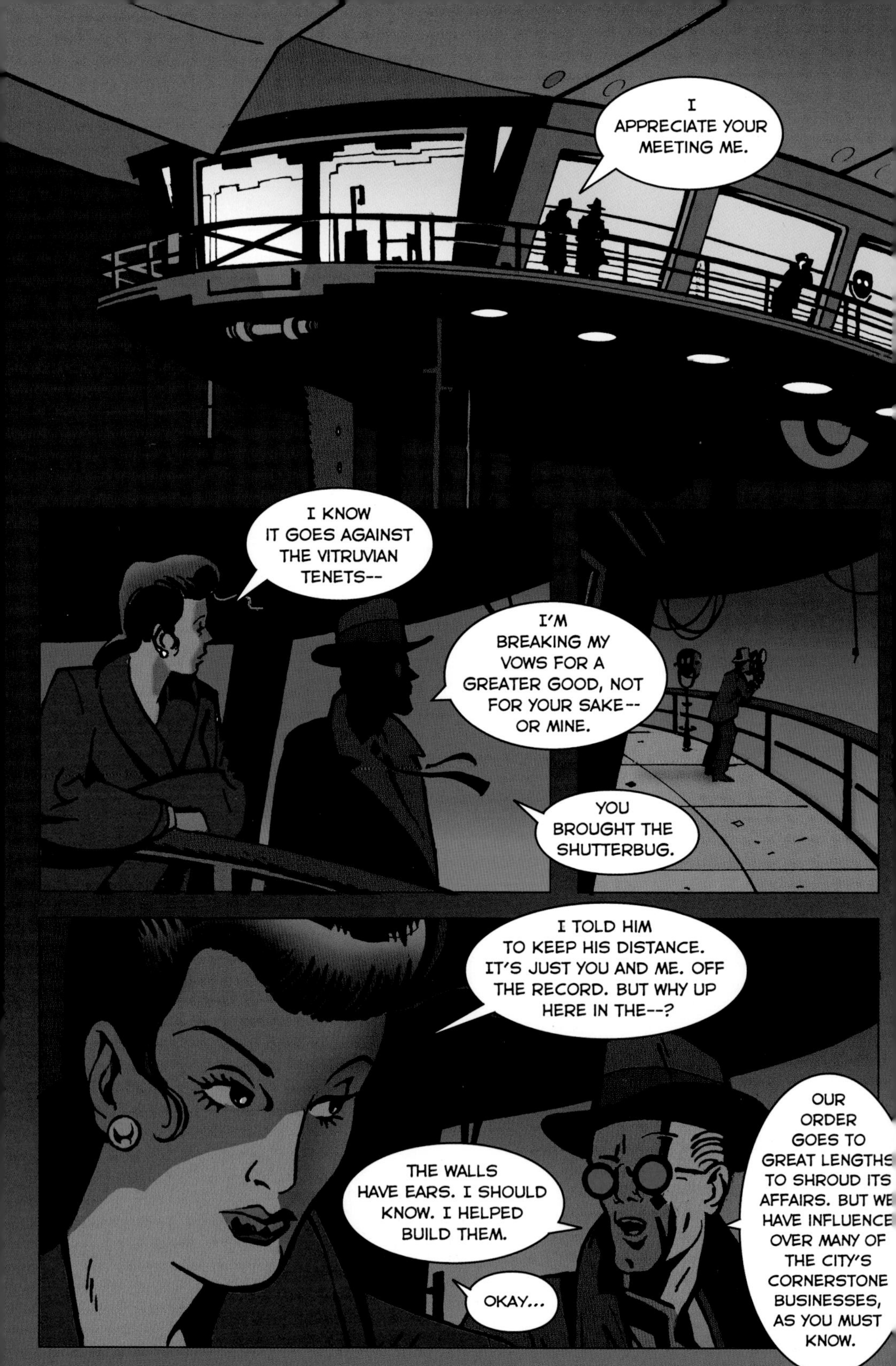
I APPRECIATE YOUR MEETING ME.
I KNOW IT GOES AGAINST THE VITRUVIAN TENETS--
I'M BREAKING MY VOWS FOR A GREATER GOOD, NOT FOR YOUR SAKE-- OR MINE.
YOU BROUGHT THE SHUTTERBUG.
I TOLD HIM TO KEEP HIS DISTANCE. IT'S JUST YOU AND ME. OFF THE RECORD. BUT WHY UP HERE IN THE--?
THE WALLS HAVE EARS. I SHOULD KNOW. I HELPED BUILD THEM.
OKAY...
OUR ORDER GOES TO GREAT LENGTHS TO SHROUD ITS AFFAIRS. BUT WE HAVE INFLUENCE OVER MANY OF THE CITY'S CORNERSTONE BUSINESSES, AS YOU MUST KNOW.

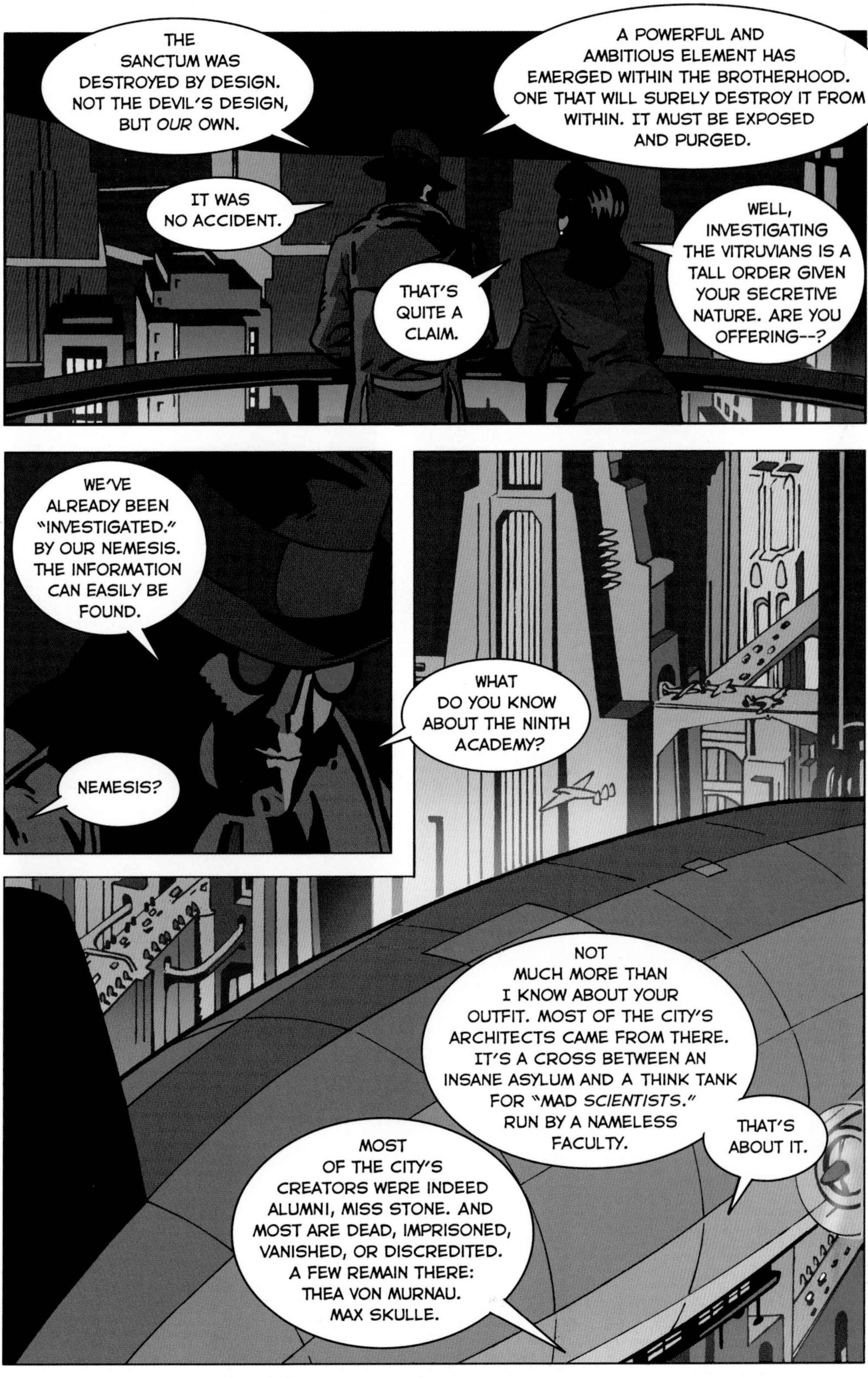
THE SANCTUM WAS DESTROYED BY DESIGN. NOT THE DEVIL'S DESIGN, BUT *OUR* OWN.
IT WAS NO ACCIDENT.
A POWERFUL AND AMBITIOUS ELEMENT HAS EMERGED WITHIN THE BROTHERHOOD. ONE THAT WILL SURELY DESTROY IT FROM WITHIN. IT MUST BE EXPOSED AND PURGED.
THAT'S QUITE A CLAIM.
WELL, INVESTIGATING THE VITRUVIANS IS A TALL ORDER GIVEN YOUR SECRETIVE NATURE. ARE YOU OFFERING--?
WE'VE ALREADY BEEN "INVESTIGATED." BY OUR NEMESIS. THE INFORMATION CAN EASILY BE FOUND.
NEMESIS?
WHAT DO YOU KNOW ABOUT THE NINTH ACADEMY?
NOT MUCH MORE THAN I KNOW ABOUT YOUR OUTFIT. MOST OF THE CITY'S ARCHITECTS CAME FROM THERE. IT'S A CROSS BETWEEN AN INSANE ASYLUM AND A THINK TANK FOR "MAD *SCIENTISTS.*" RUN BY A NAMELESS FACULTY.
THAT'S ABOUT IT.
MOST OF THE CITY'S CREATORS WERE INDEED ALUMNI, MISS STONE. AND MOST ARE DEAD, IMPRISONED, VANISHED, OR DISCREDITED. A FEW REMAIN THERE: THEA VON MURNAU. MAX SKULLE.

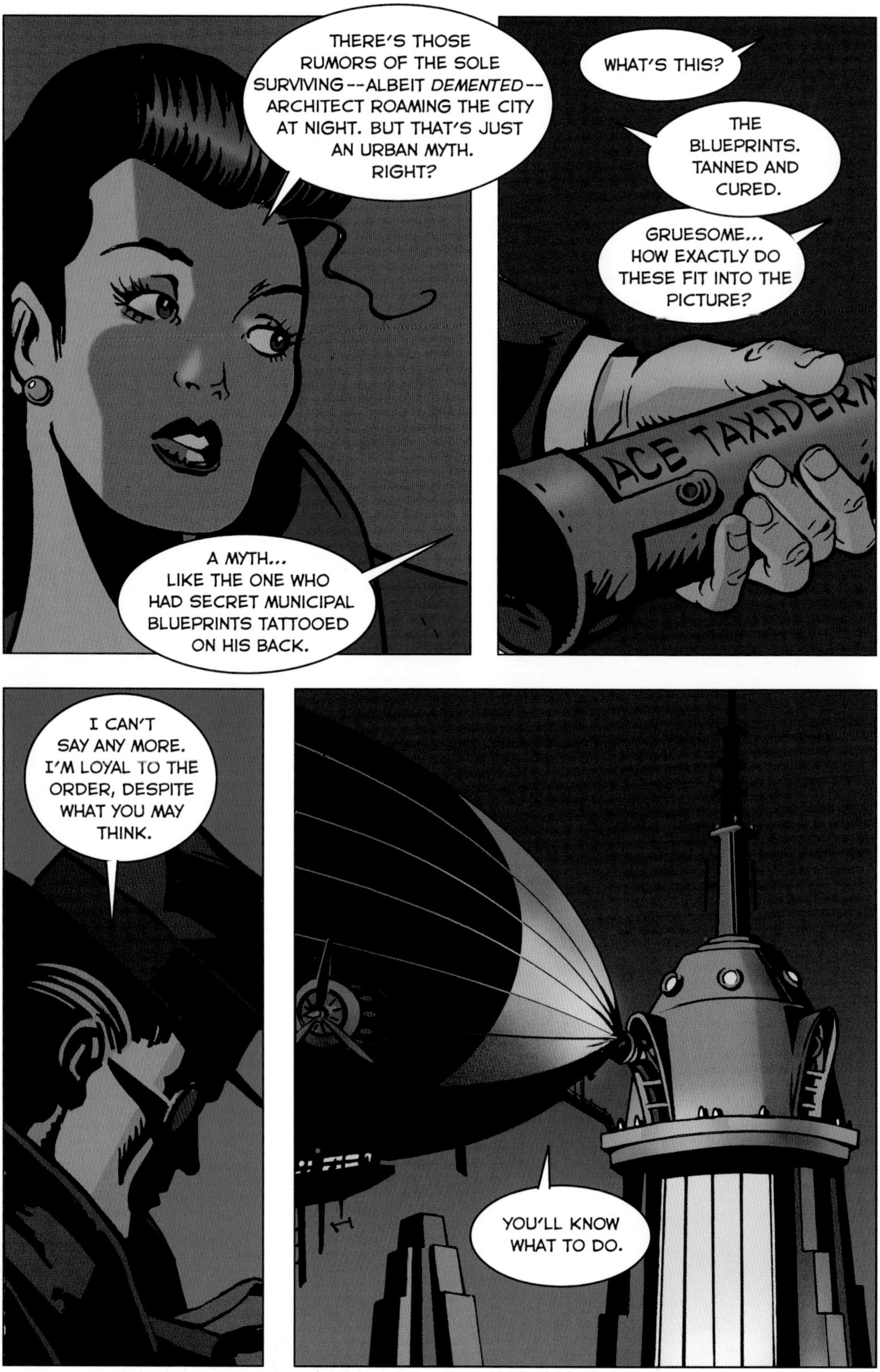
THERE'S THOSE RUMORS OF THE SOLE SURVIVING--ALBEIT *DEMENTED*--ARCHITECT ROAMING THE CITY AT NIGHT. BUT THAT'S JUST AN URBAN MYTH. RIGHT?
A MYTH... LIKE THE ONE WHO HAD SECRET MUNICIPAL BLUEPRINTS TATTOOED ON HIS BACK.
WHAT'S THIS?
THE BLUEPRINTS. TANNED AND CURED.
GRUESOME... HOW EXACTLY DO THESE FIT INTO THE PICTURE?
I CAN'T SAY ANY MORE. I'M LOYAL TO THE ORDER, DESPITE WHAT YOU MAY THINK.
YOU'LL KNOW WHAT TO DO.

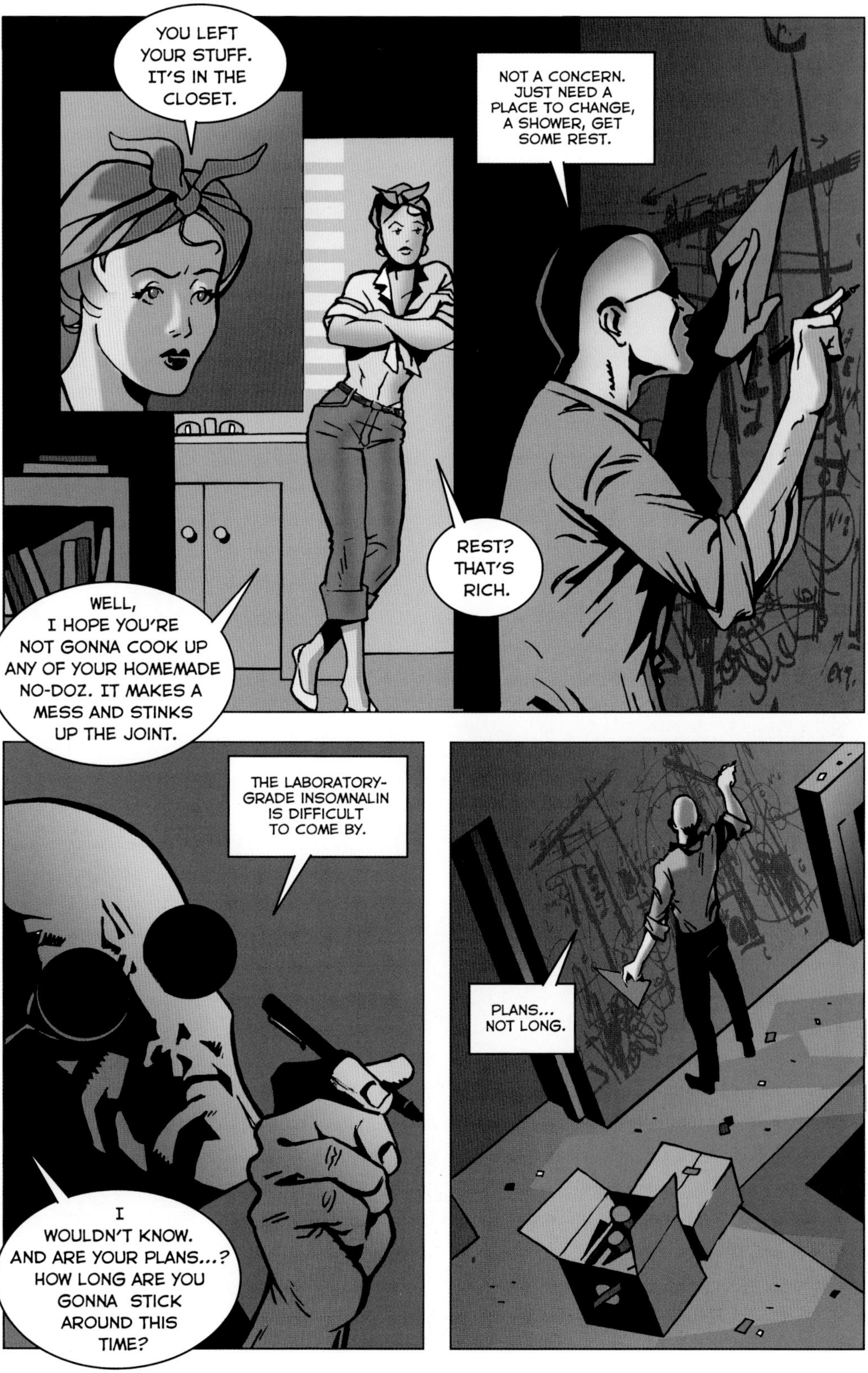
YOU LEFT YOUR STUFF. IT'S IN THE CLOSET.
NOT A CONCERN. JUST NEED A PLACE TO CHANGE, A SHOWER, GET SOME REST.
REST? THAT'S RICH.
WELL, I HOPE YOU'RE NOT GONNA COOK UP ANY OF YOUR HOMEMADE NO-DOZ. IT MAKES A MESS AND STINKS UP THE JOINT.
THE LABORATORY-GRADE INSOMNALIN IS DIFFICULT TO COME BY.
I WOULDN'T KNOW. AND ARE YOUR PLANS...? HOW LONG ARE YOU GONNA STICK AROUND THIS TIME?
PLANS... NOT LONG.

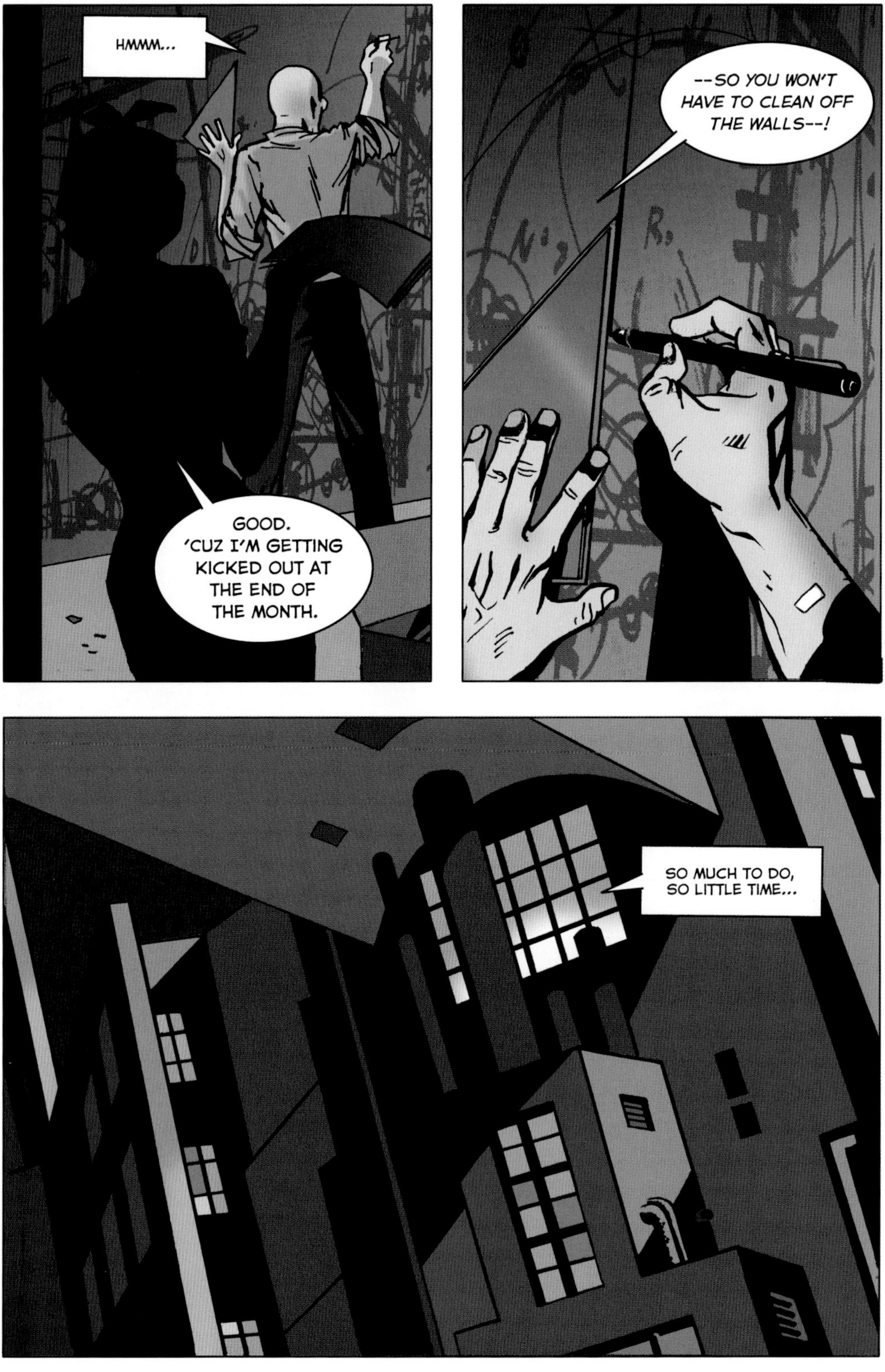
HMMM...
GOOD. 'CUZ I'M GETTING KICKED OUT AT THE END OF THE MONTH.
--SO YOU WON'T HAVE TO CLEAN OFF THE WALLS--!
SO MUCH TO DO, SO LITTLE TIME...

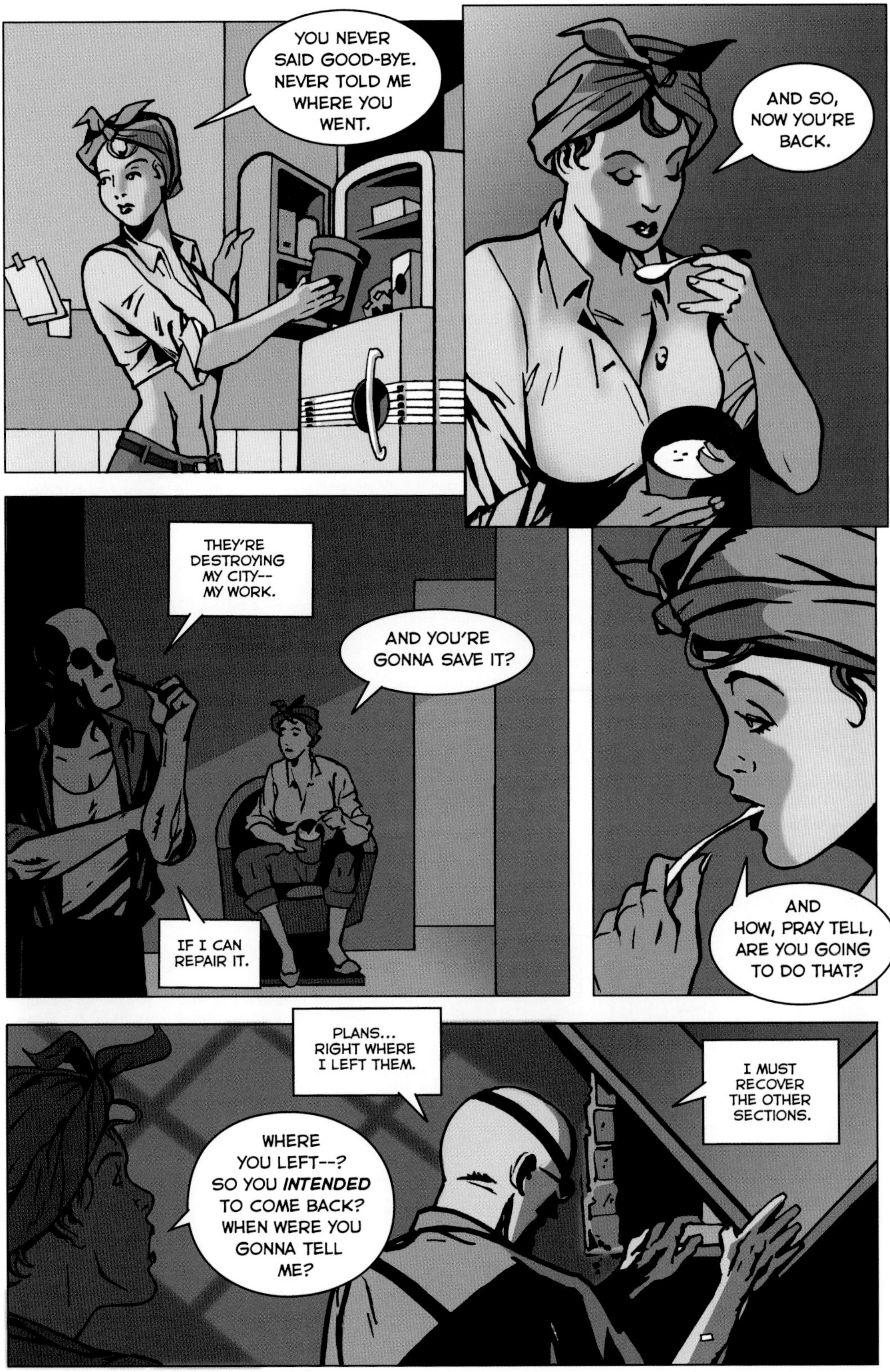
YOU NEVER SAID GOOD-BYE. NEVER TOLD ME WHERE YOU WENT.
AND SO, NOW YOU'RE BACK.
THEY'RE DESTROYING MY CITY-- MY WORK.
AND YOU'RE GONNA SAVE IT?
IF I CAN REPAIR IT.
AND HOW, PRAY TELL, ARE YOU GOING TO DO THAT?
PLANS... RIGHT WHERE I LEFT THEM.
I MUST RECOVER THE OTHER SECTIONS.
WHERE YOU LEFT--? SO YOU *INTENDED* TO COME BACK? WHEN WERE YOU GONNA TELL ME?

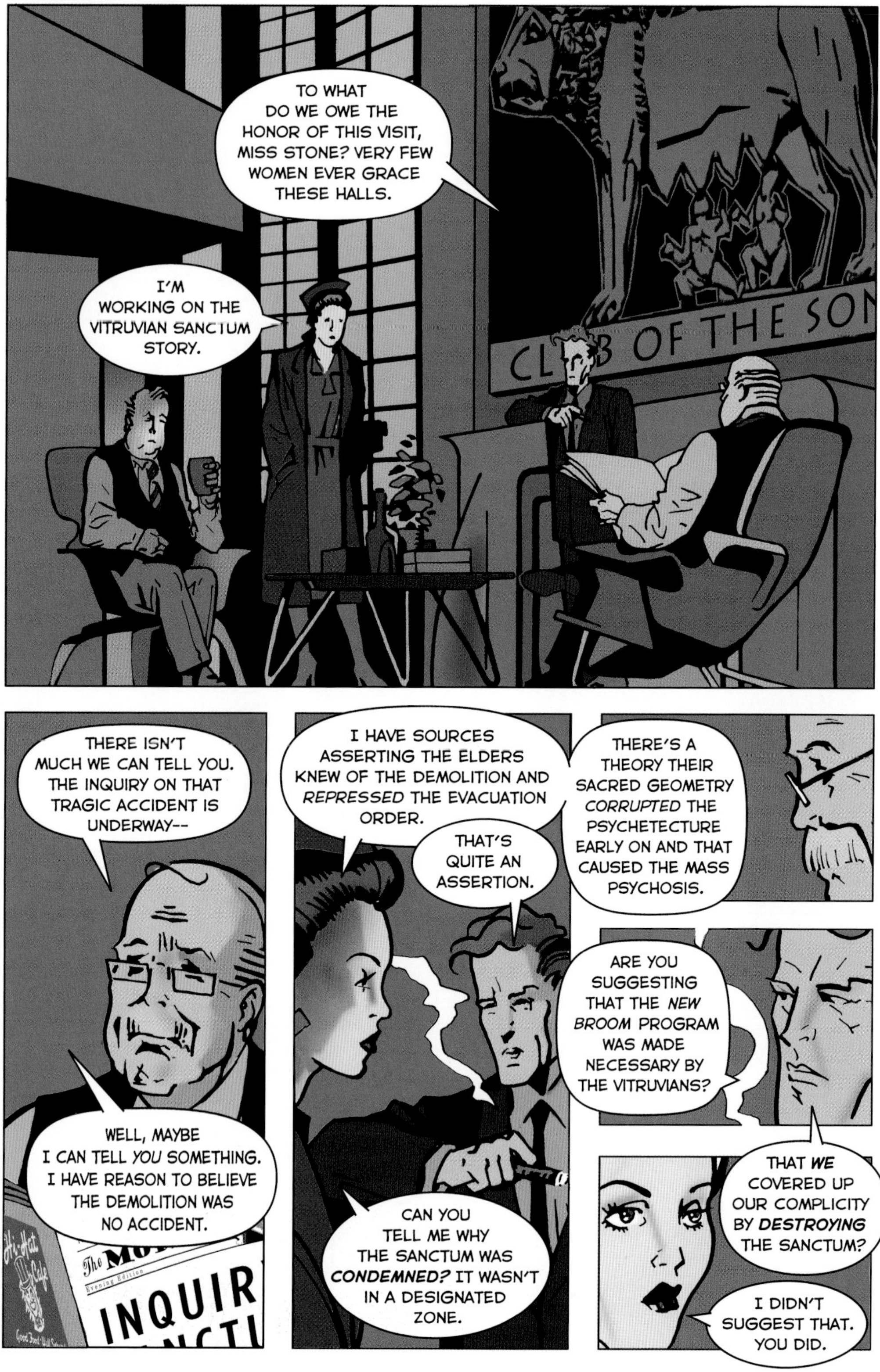
TO WHAT DO WE OWE THE HONOR OF THIS VISIT, MISS STONE? VERY FEW WOMEN EVER GRACE THESE HALLS.
I'M WORKING ON THE VITRUVIAN SANCTUM STORY.
CLUB OF THE SON
THERE ISN'T MUCH WE CAN TELL YOU. THE INQUIRY ON THAT TRAGIC ACCIDENT IS UNDERWAY--
WELL, MAYBE I CAN TELL *YOU* SOMETHING. I HAVE REASON TO BELIEVE THE DEMOLITION WAS NO ACCIDENT.
The MO
Evening Edition
INQUIR
NCTU
I HAVE SOURCES ASSERTING THE ELDERS KNEW OF THE DEMOLITION AND *REPRESSED* THE EVACUATION ORDER.
THAT'S QUITE AN ASSERTION.
CAN YOU TELL ME WHY THE SANCTUM WAS ***CONDEMNED?*** IT WASN'T IN A DESIGNATED ZONE.
THERE'S A THEORY THEIR SACRED GEOMETRY *CORRUPTED* THE PSYCHETECTURE EARLY ON AND THAT CAUSED THE MASS PSYCHOSIS.
ARE YOU SUGGESTING THAT THE *NEW BROOM* PROGRAM WAS MADE NECESSARY BY THE VITRUVIANS?
THAT ***WE*** COVERED UP OUR COMPLICITY BY ***DESTROYING*** THE SANCTUM?
I DIDN'T SUGGEST THAT. YOU DID.

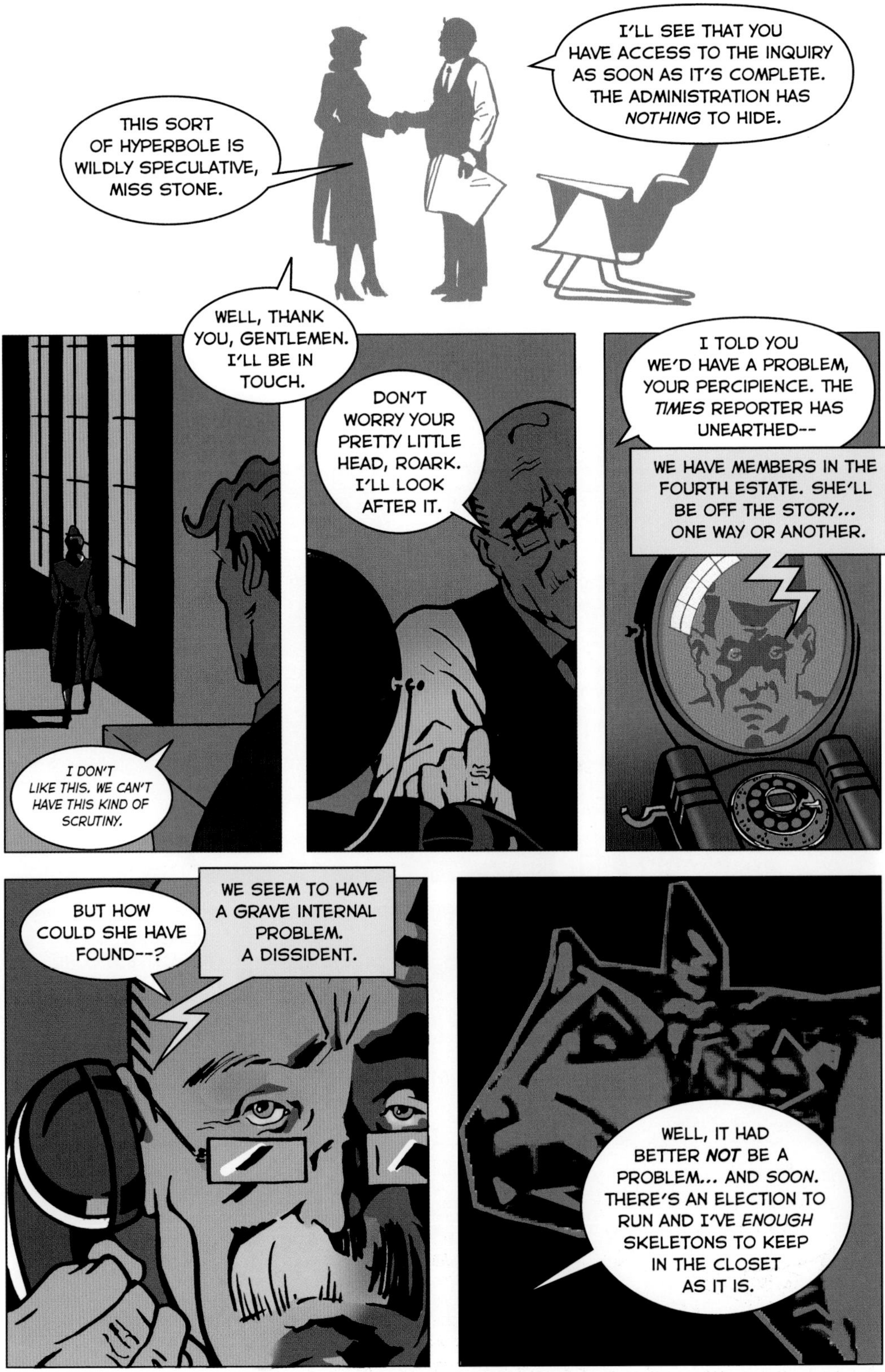
THIS SORT OF HYPERBOLE IS WILDLY SPECULATIVE, MISS STONE.
I'LL SEE THAT YOU HAVE ACCESS TO THE INQUIRY AS SOON AS IT'S COMPLETE. THE ADMINISTRATION HAS *NOTHING* TO HIDE.
WELL, THANK YOU, GENTLEMEN. I'LL BE IN TOUCH.
I DON'T LIKE THIS. WE CAN'T HAVE THIS KIND OF SCRUTINY.
DON'T WORRY YOUR PRETTY LITTLE HEAD, ROARK. I'LL LOOK AFTER IT.
I TOLD YOU WE'D HAVE A PROBLEM, YOUR PERCIPIENCE. THE *TIMES* REPORTER HAS UNEARTHED--
WE HAVE MEMBERS IN THE FOURTH ESTATE. SHE'LL BE OFF THE STORY... ONE WAY OR ANOTHER.
BUT HOW COULD SHE HAVE FOUND--?
WE SEEM TO HAVE A GRAVE INTERNAL PROBLEM. A DISSIDENT.
WELL, IT HAD BETTER ***NOT*** BE A PROBLEM... AND *SOON*. THERE'S AN ELECTION TO RUN AND I'VE *ENOUGH* SKELETONS TO KEEP IN THE CLOSET AS IT IS.

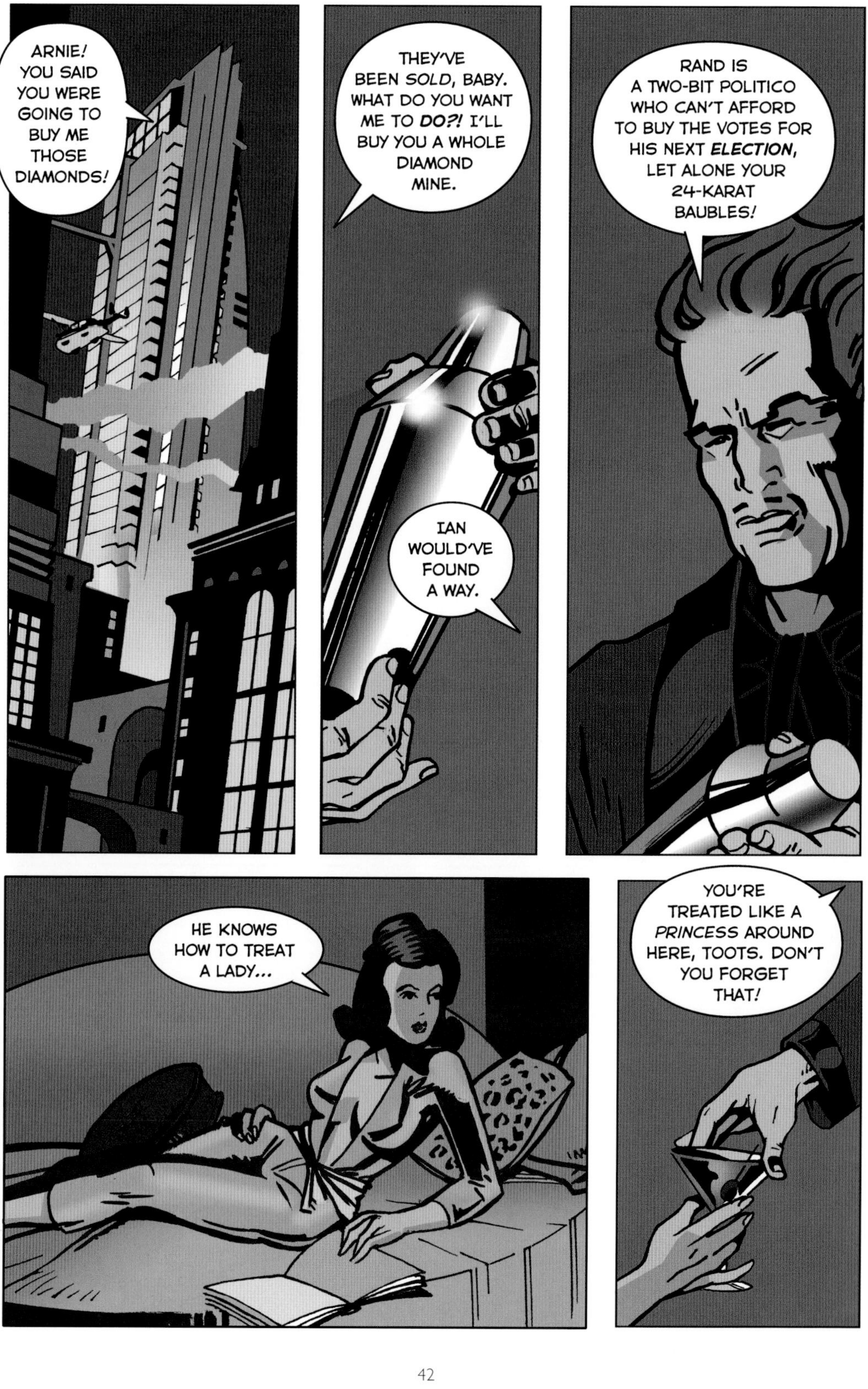
ARNIE! YOU SAID YOU WERE GOING TO BUY ME THOSE DIAMONDS!
THEY'VE BEEN SOLD, BABY. WHAT DO YOU WANT ME TO DO?! I'LL BUY YOU A WHOLE DIAMOND MINE.
IAN WOULD'VE FOUND A WAY.
RAND IS A TWO-BIT POLITICO WHO CAN'T AFFORD TO BUY THE VOTES FOR HIS NEXT ELECTION, LET ALONE YOUR 24-KARAT BAUBLES!
HE KNOWS HOW TO TREAT A LADY...
YOU'RE TREATED LIKE A PRINCESS AROUND HERE, TOOTS. DON'T YOU FORGET THAT!

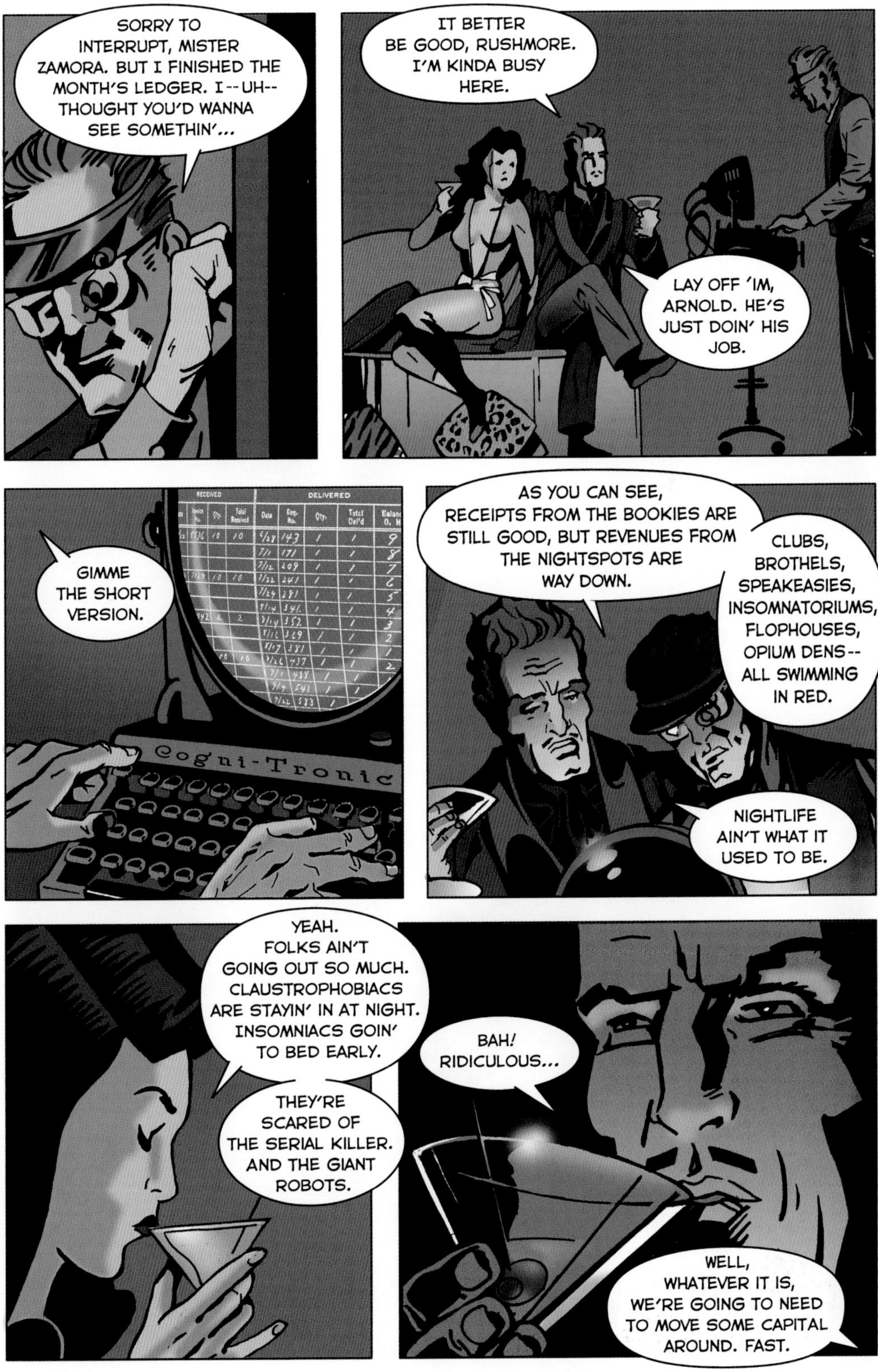
SORRY TO INTERRUPT, MISTER ZAMORA. BUT I FINISHED THE MONTH'S LEDGER. I--UH--THOUGHT YOU'D WANNA SEE SOMETHIN'...
IT BETTER BE GOOD, RUSHMORE. I'M KINDA BUSY HERE.
LAY OFF 'IM, ARNOLD. HE'S JUST DOIN' HIS JOB.
RECEIVED
DELIVERED
Cogni-Tronic
GIMME THE SHORT VERSION.
AS YOU CAN SEE, RECEIPTS FROM THE BOOKIES ARE STILL GOOD, BUT REVENUES FROM THE NIGHTSPOTS ARE WAY DOWN.
CLUBS, BROTHELS, SPEAKEASIES, INSOMNATORIUMS, FLOPHOUSES, OPIUM DENS--ALL SWIMMING IN RED.
NIGHTLIFE AIN'T WHAT IT USED TO BE.
YEAH. FOLKS AIN'T GOING OUT SO MUCH. CLAUSTROPHOBIACS ARE STAYIN' IN AT NIGHT. INSOMNIACS GOIN' TO BED EARLY.
THEY'RE SCARED OF THE SERIAL KILLER. AND THE GIANT ROBOTS.
BAH! RIDICULOUS...
WELL, WHATEVER IT IS, WE'RE GOING TO NEED TO MOVE SOME CAPITAL AROUND. FAST.

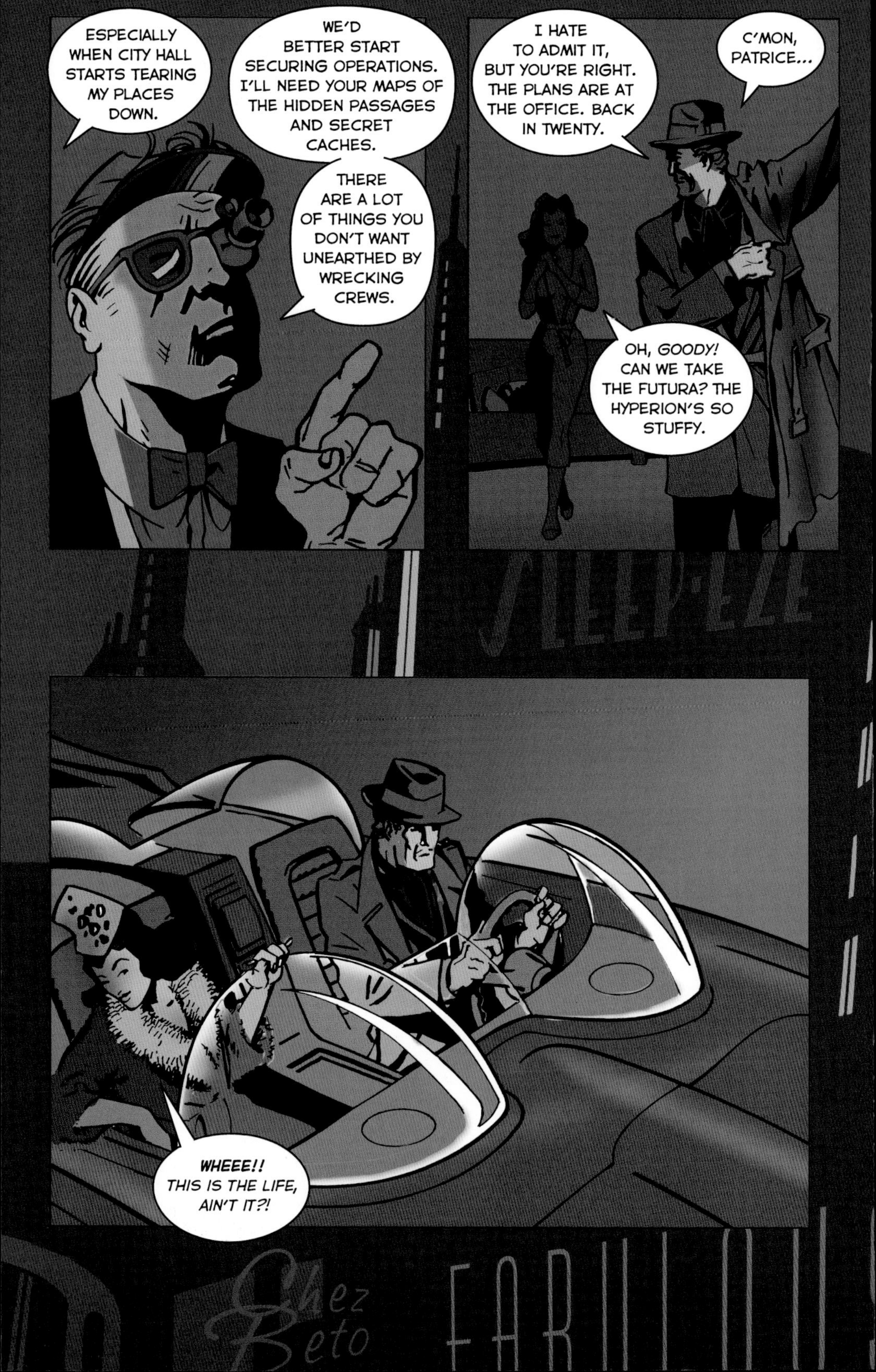
ESPECIALLY WHEN CITY HALL STARTS TEARING MY PLACES DOWN.
WE'D BETTER START SECURING OPERATIONS. I'LL NEED YOUR MAPS OF THE HIDDEN PASSAGES AND SECRET CACHES.
THERE ARE A LOT OF THINGS YOU DON'T WANT UNEARTHED BY WRECKING CREWS.
I HATE TO ADMIT IT, BUT YOU'RE RIGHT. THE PLANS ARE AT THE OFFICE. BACK IN TWENTY.
C'MON, PATRICE...
OH, *GOODY!* CAN WE TAKE THE FUTURA? THE HYPERION'S SO STUFFY.
WHEEE!! *THIS IS THE LIFE, AIN'T IT?!*
Chez Beto

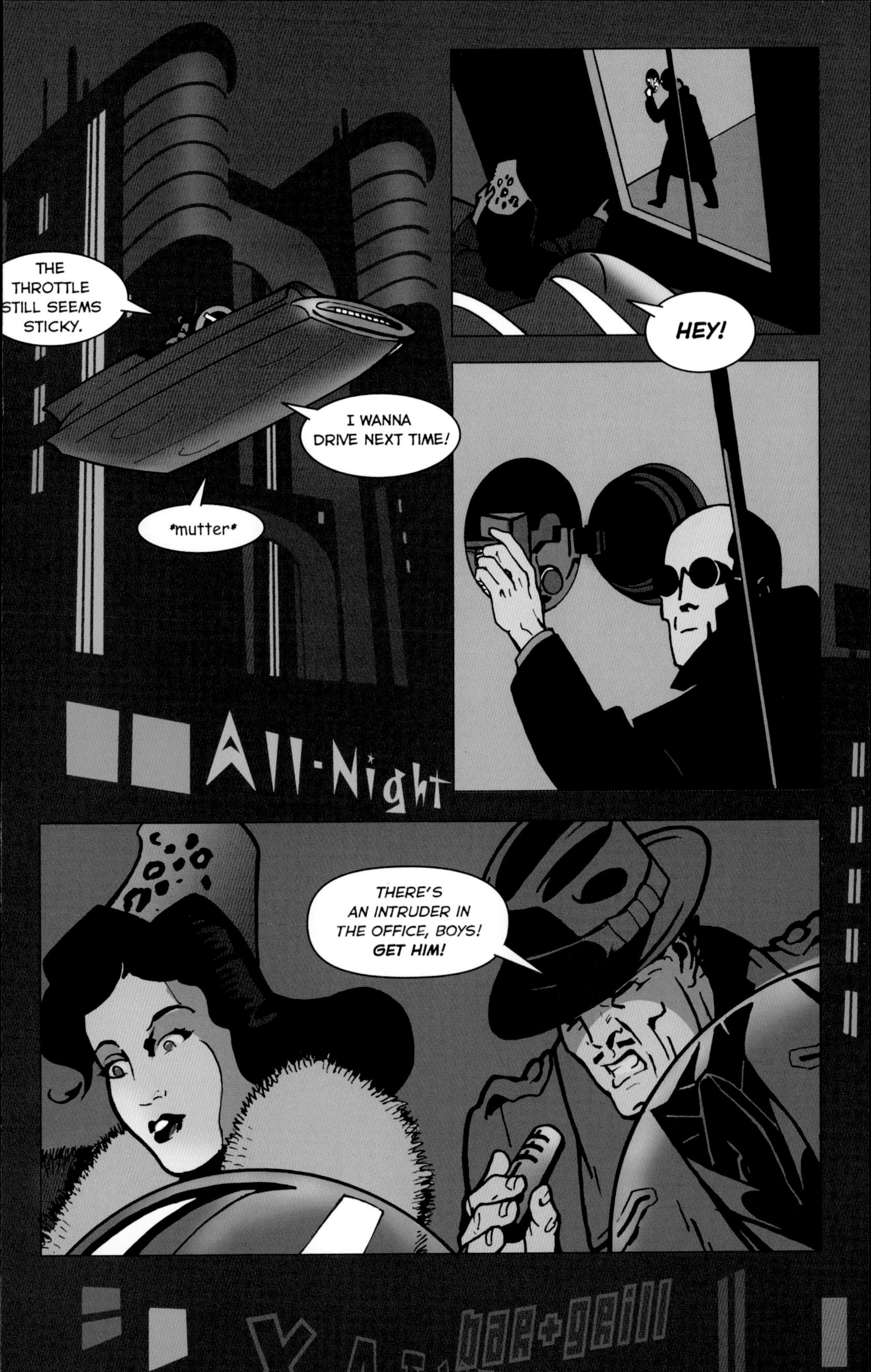
THE THROTTLE STILL SEEMS STICKY.
I WANNA DRIVE NEXT TIME!
mutter
All-Night
HEY!
THERE'S AN INTRUDER IN THE OFFICE, BOYS! GET HIM!
bar+grill

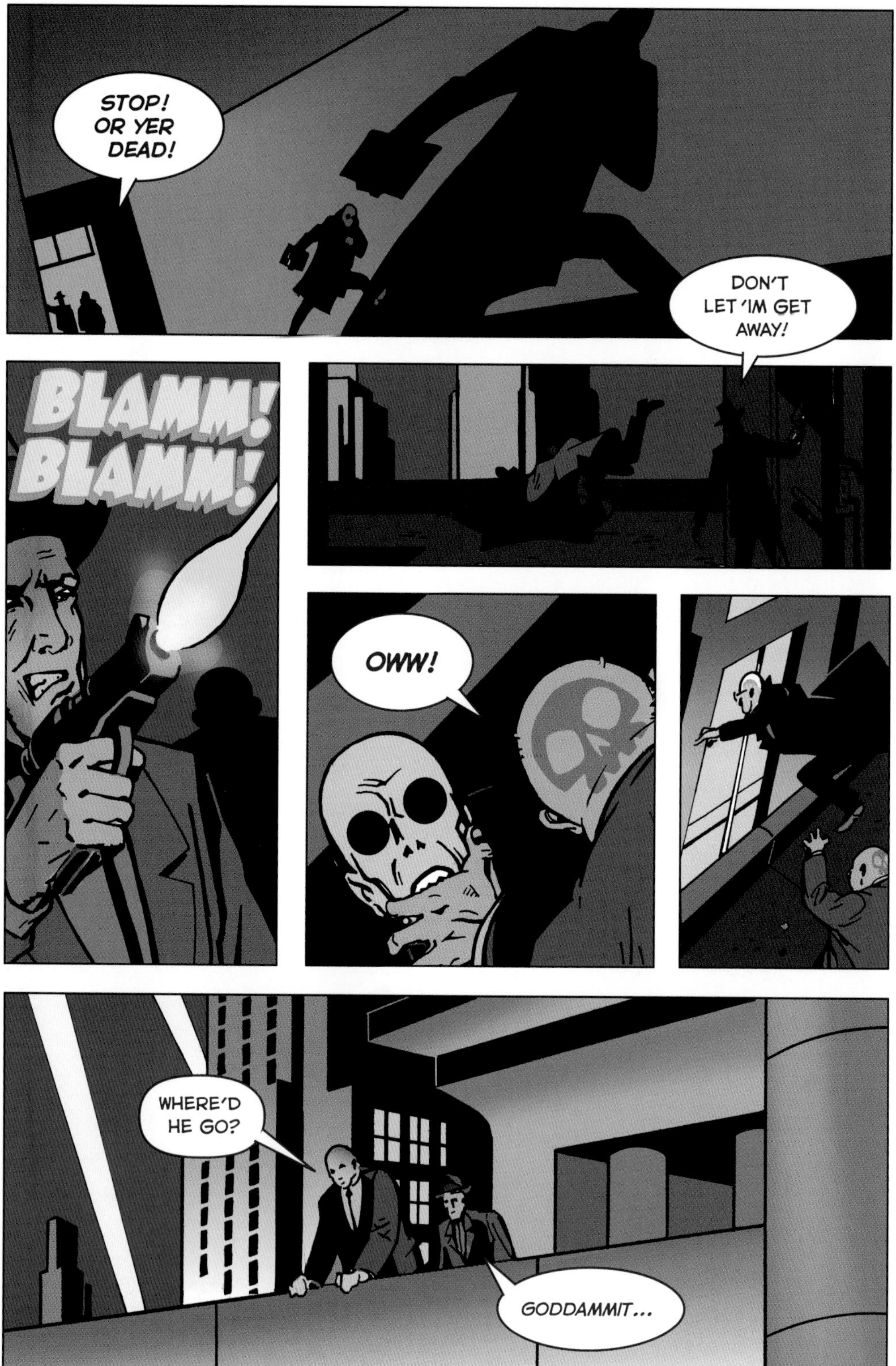
STOP! OR YER DEAD!
DON'T LET 'IM GET AWAY!
BLAMM! BLAMM!
OWW!
WHERE'D HE GO?
GODDAMMIT...

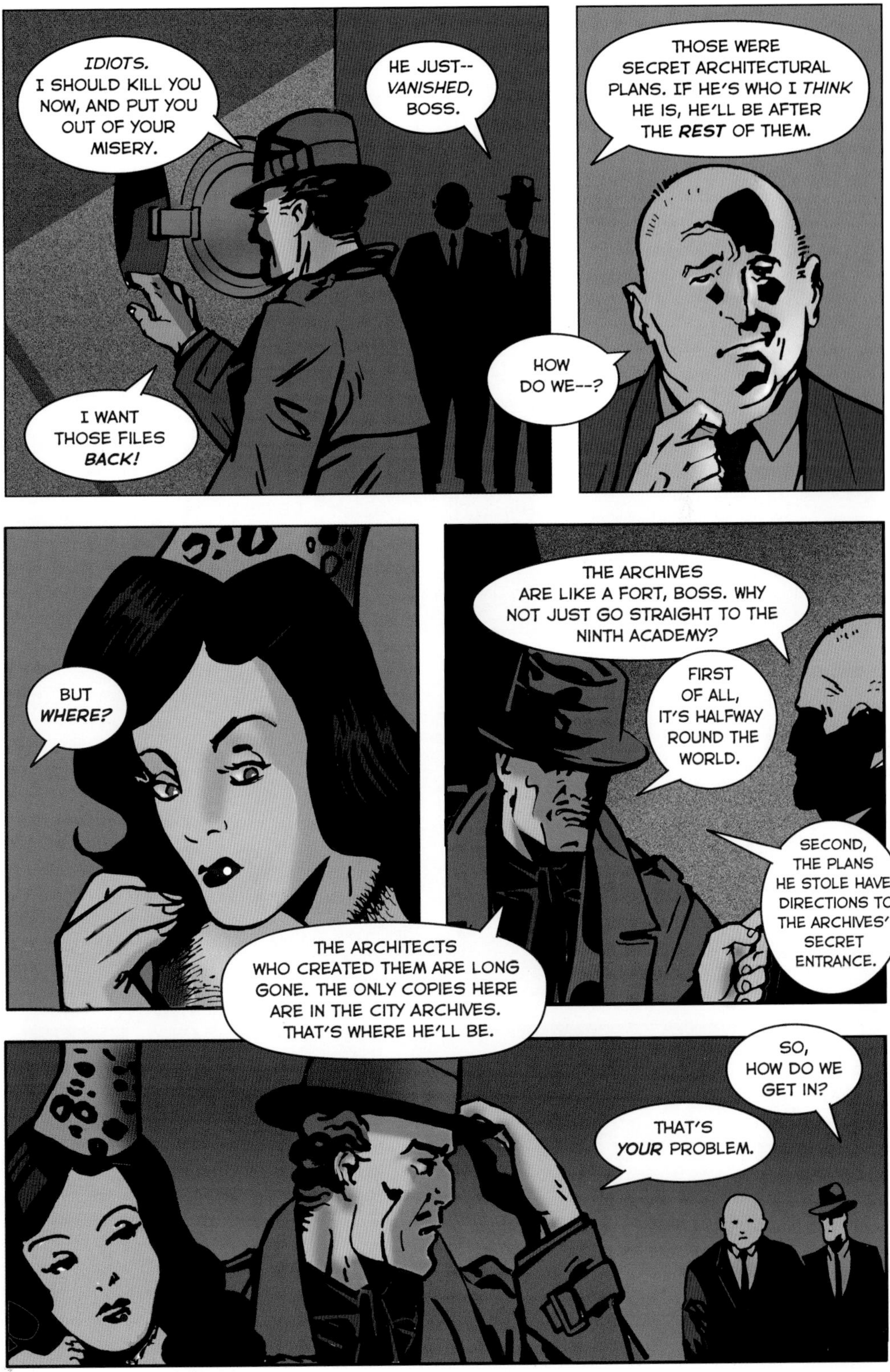
IDIOTS. I SHOULD KILL YOU NOW, AND PUT YOU OUT OF YOUR MISERY.
HE JUST--VANISHED, BOSS.
I WANT THOSE FILES BACK!
THOSE WERE SECRET ARCHITECTURAL PLANS. IF HE'S WHO I THINK HE IS, HE'LL BE AFTER THE REST OF THEM.
HOW DO WE--?
BUT WHERE?
THE ARCHITECTS WHO CREATED THEM ARE LONG GONE. THE ONLY COPIES HERE ARE IN THE CITY ARCHIVES. THAT'S WHERE HE'LL BE.
THE ARCHIVES ARE LIKE A FORT, BOSS. WHY NOT JUST GO STRAIGHT TO THE NINTH ACADEMY?
FIRST OF ALL, IT'S HALFWAY ROUND THE WORLD.
SECOND, THE PLANS HE STOLE HAVE DIRECTIONS TO THE ARCHIVES' SECRET ENTRANCE.
SO, HOW DO WE GET IN?
THAT'S YOUR PROBLEM.

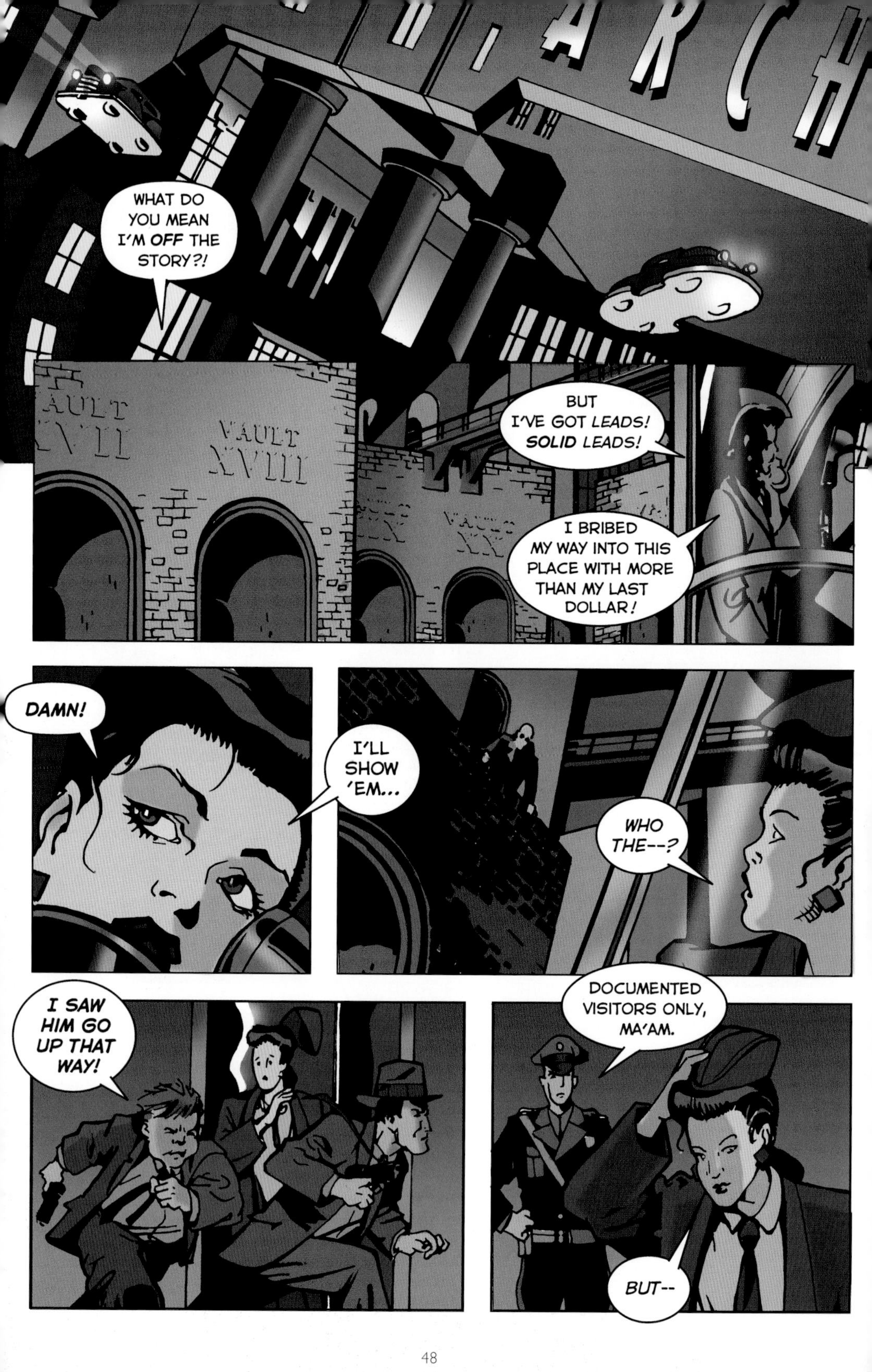
ARCH
WHAT DO YOU MEAN I'M *OFF* THE STORY?!
VAULT XVII
VAULT XVIII
BUT I'VE GOT *LEADS!* ***SOLID*** *LEADS!*
I BRIBED MY WAY INTO THIS PLACE WITH MORE THAN MY LAST DOLLAR*!*
DAMN!
I'LL SHOW 'EM...
WHO THE--?
I SAW HIM GO UP THAT WAY!
DOCUMENTED VISITORS ONLY, MA'AM.
BUT--

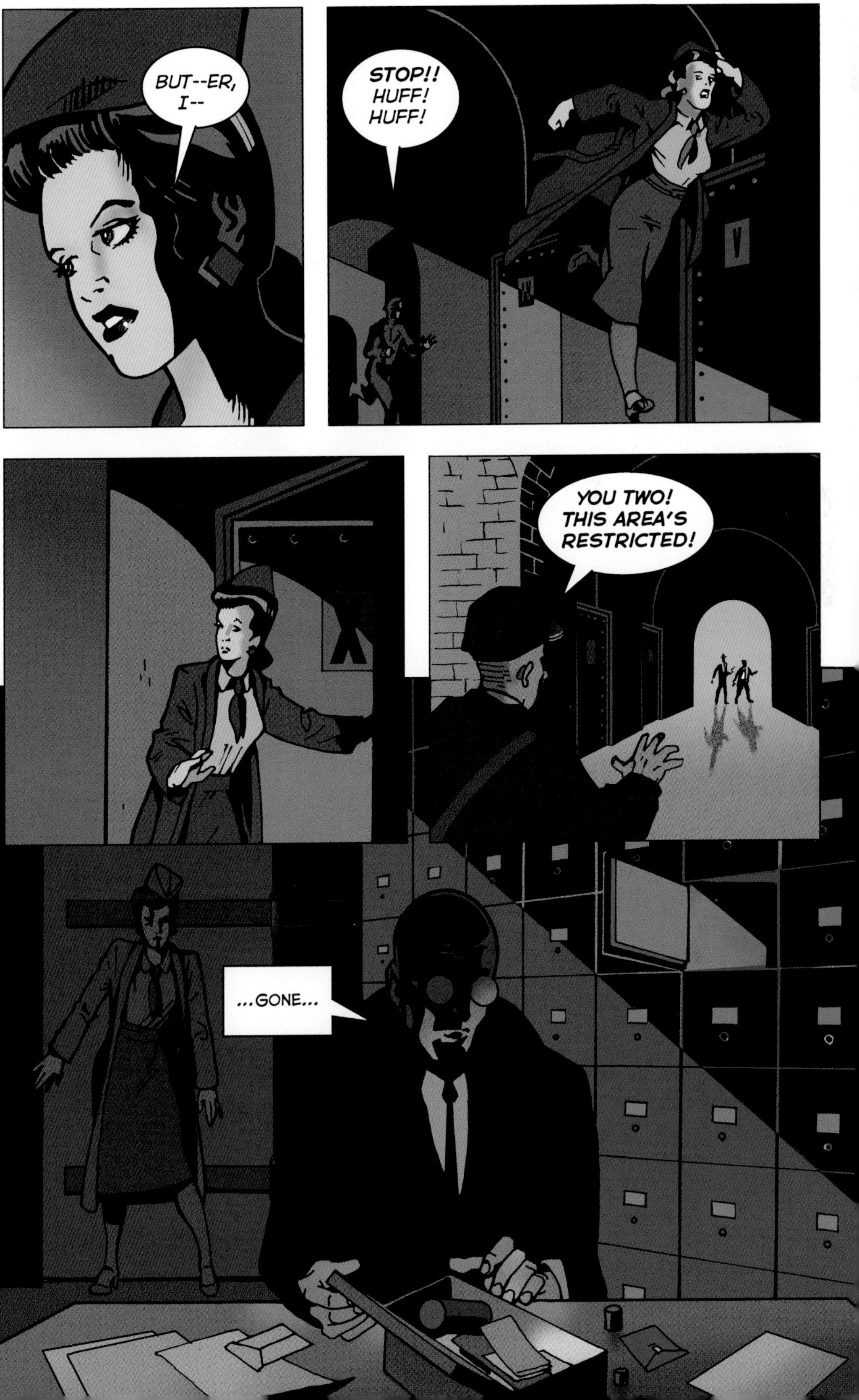
BUT--ER, I--
STOP!! HUFF! HUFF!
YOU TWO! THIS AREA'S RESTRICTED!
...GONE...

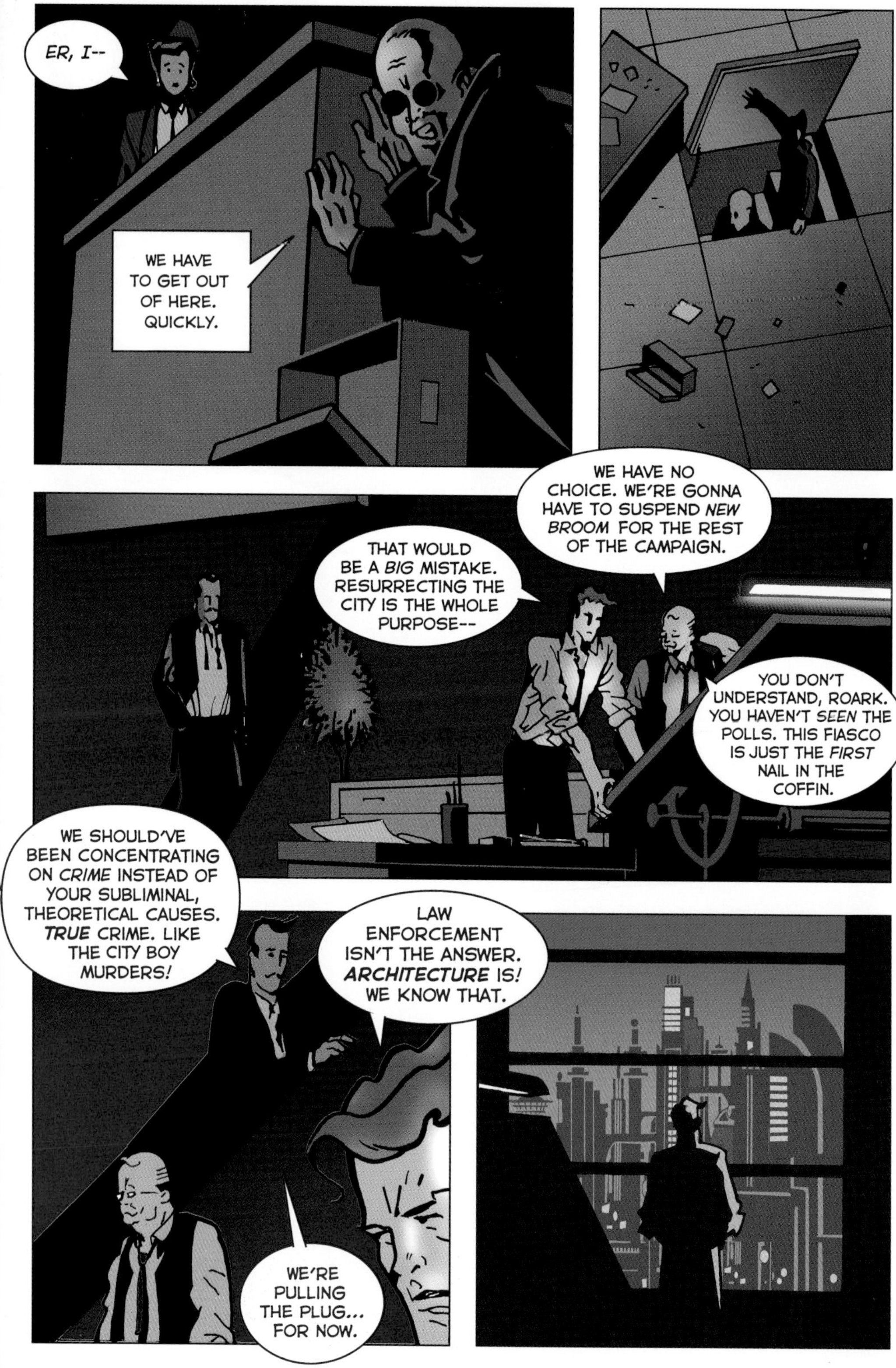

ER, I--
WE HAVE TO GET OUT OF HERE. QUICKLY.
WE HAVE NO CHOICE. WE'RE GONNA HAVE TO SUSPEND *NEW BROOM* FOR THE REST OF THE CAMPAIGN.
THAT WOULD BE A *BIG* MISTAKE. RESURRECTING THE CITY IS THE WHOLE PURPOSE--
YOU DON'T UNDERSTAND, ROARK. YOU HAVEN'T *SEEN* THE POLLS. THIS FIASCO IS JUST THE *FIRST* NAIL IN THE COFFIN.
WE SHOULD'VE BEEN CONCENTRATING ON *CRIME* INSTEAD OF YOUR SUBLIMINAL, THEORETICAL CAUSES. ***TRUE*** CRIME. LIKE THE CITY BOY MURDERS!
LAW ENFORCEMENT ISN'T THE ANSWER. ***ARCHITECTURE*** IS! WE KNOW THAT.
WE'RE PULLING THE PLUG... FOR NOW.

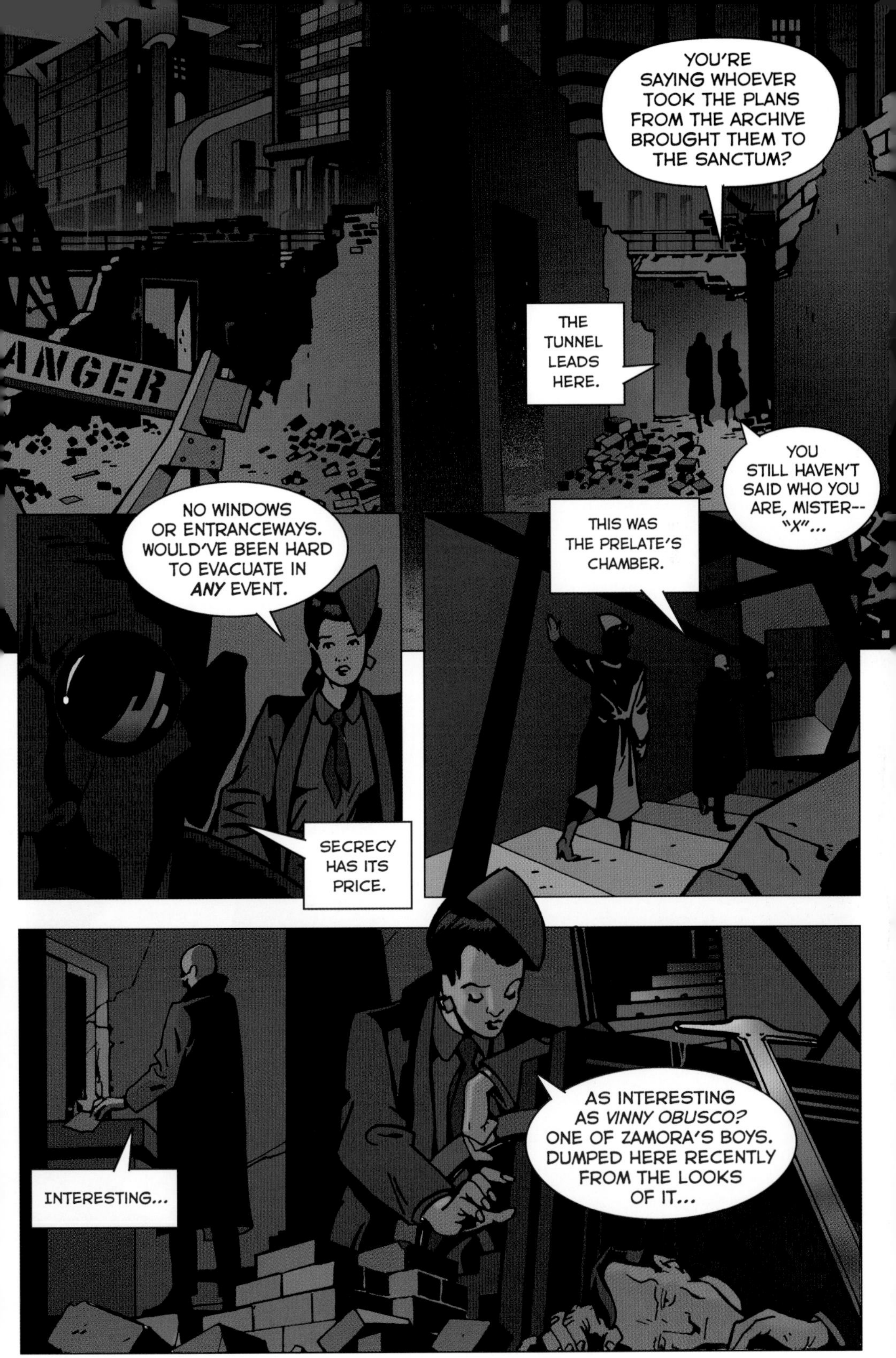
ANGER
YOU'RE SAYING WHOEVER TOOK THE PLANS FROM THE ARCHIVE BROUGHT THEM TO THE SANCTUM?
THE TUNNEL LEADS HERE.
YOU STILL HAVEN'T SAID WHO YOU ARE, MISTER-- "X"...
NO WINDOWS OR ENTRANCEWAYS. WOULD'VE BEEN HARD TO EVACUATE IN *ANY* EVENT.
SECRECY HAS ITS PRICE.
THIS WAS THE PRELATE'S CHAMBER.
INTERESTING...
AS INTERESTING AS *VINNY OBUSCO?* ONE OF ZAMORA'S BOYS. DUMPED HERE RECENTLY FROM THE LOOKS OF IT...

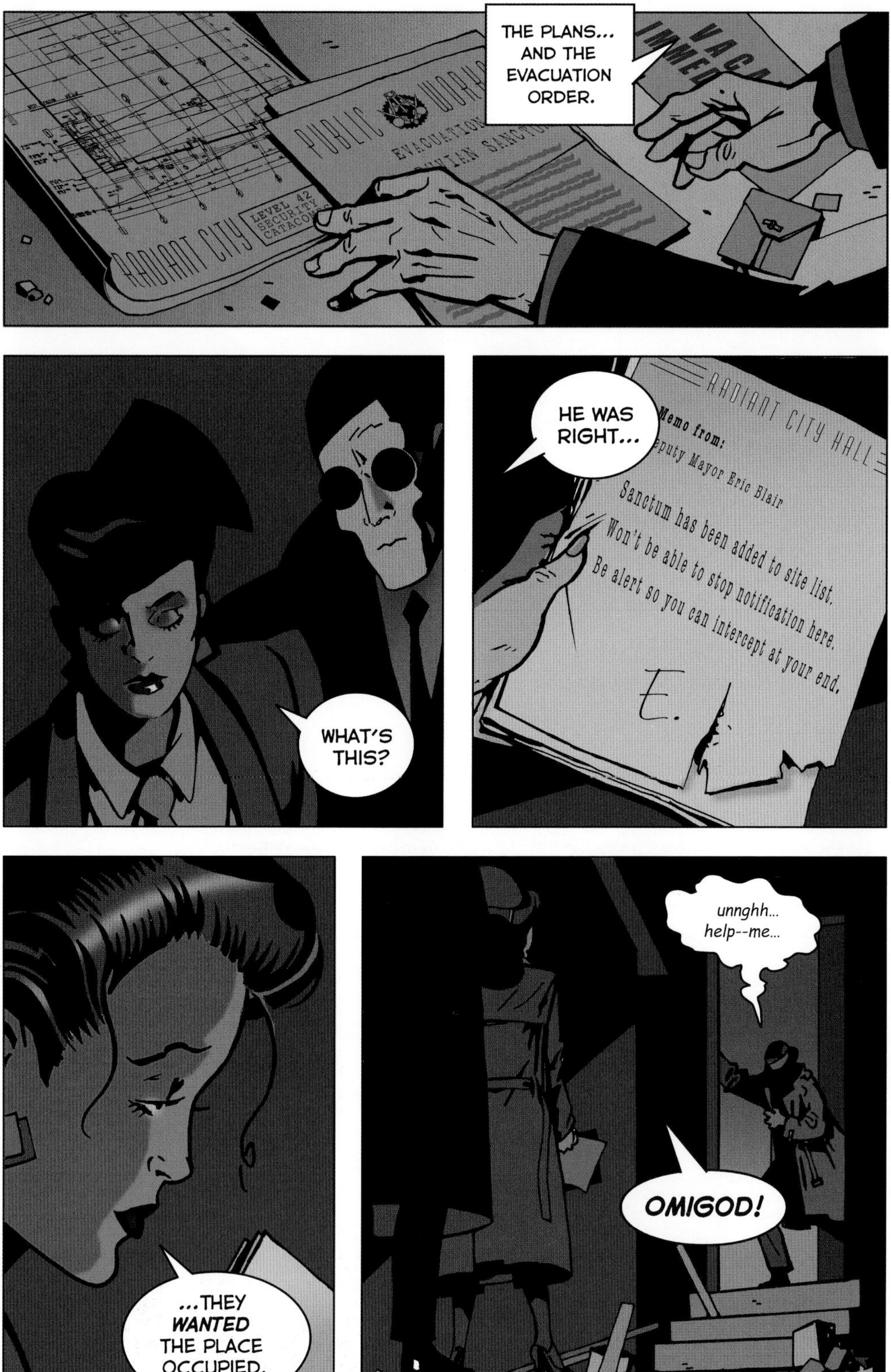
THE PLANS... AND THE EVACUATION ORDER.
RADIANT CITY
LEVEL 42
SECURITY
WHAT'S THIS?
HE WAS RIGHT...
RADIANT CITY HALL
Memo from:
Sanctum has been added to site list.
Won't be able to stop notification here.
Be alert so you can intercept at your end.
E.
...THEY *WANTED* THE PLACE OCCUPIED.
unnghh... help--me...
OMIGOD!

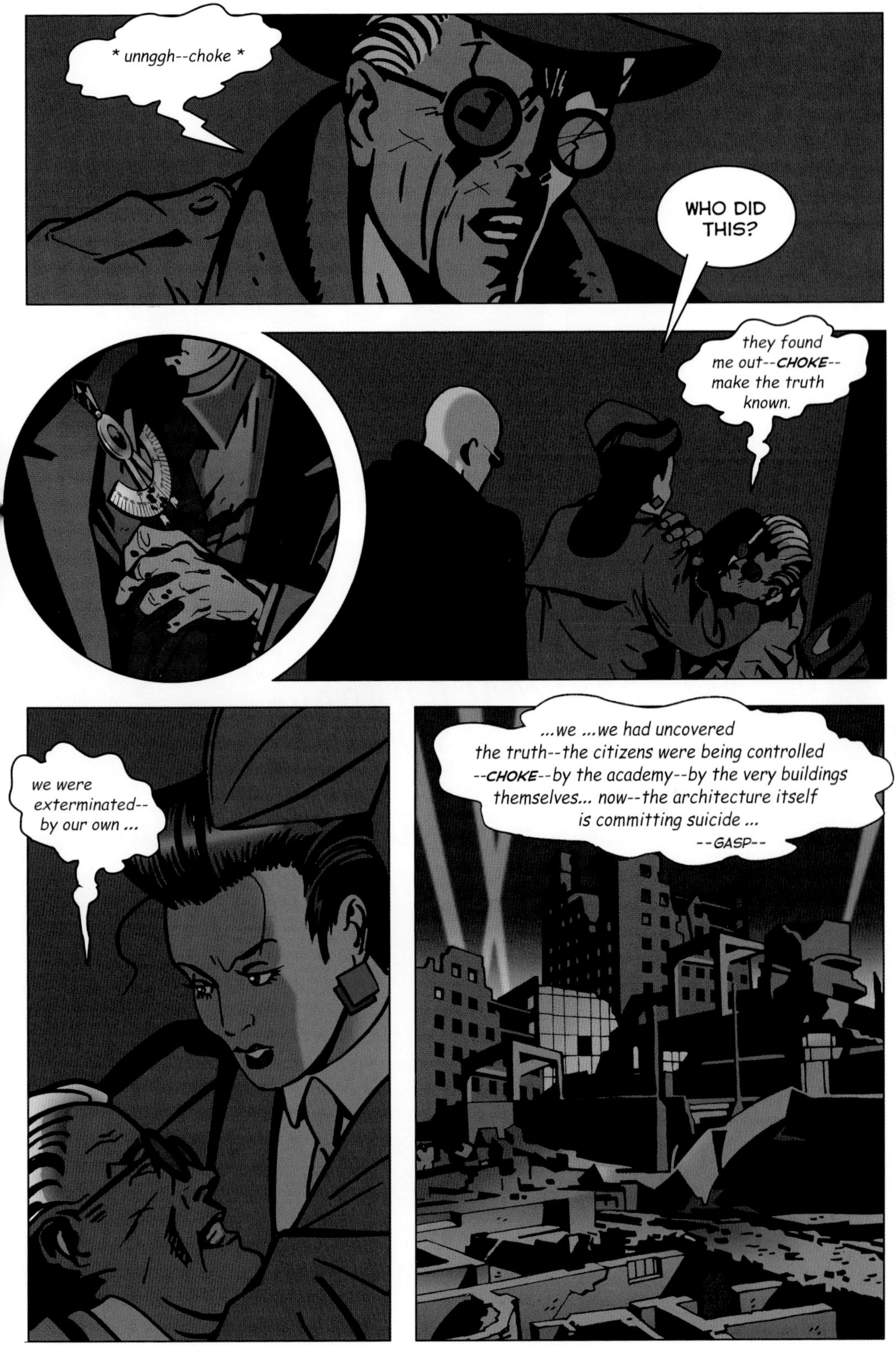
* unnggh--choke *
WHO DID THIS?
they found me out--CHOKE--make the truth known.
we were exterminated--by our own ...
...we ...we had uncovered the truth--the citizens were being controlled --CHOKE--by the academy--by the very buildings themselves... now--the architecture itself is committing suicide ...
--GASP--

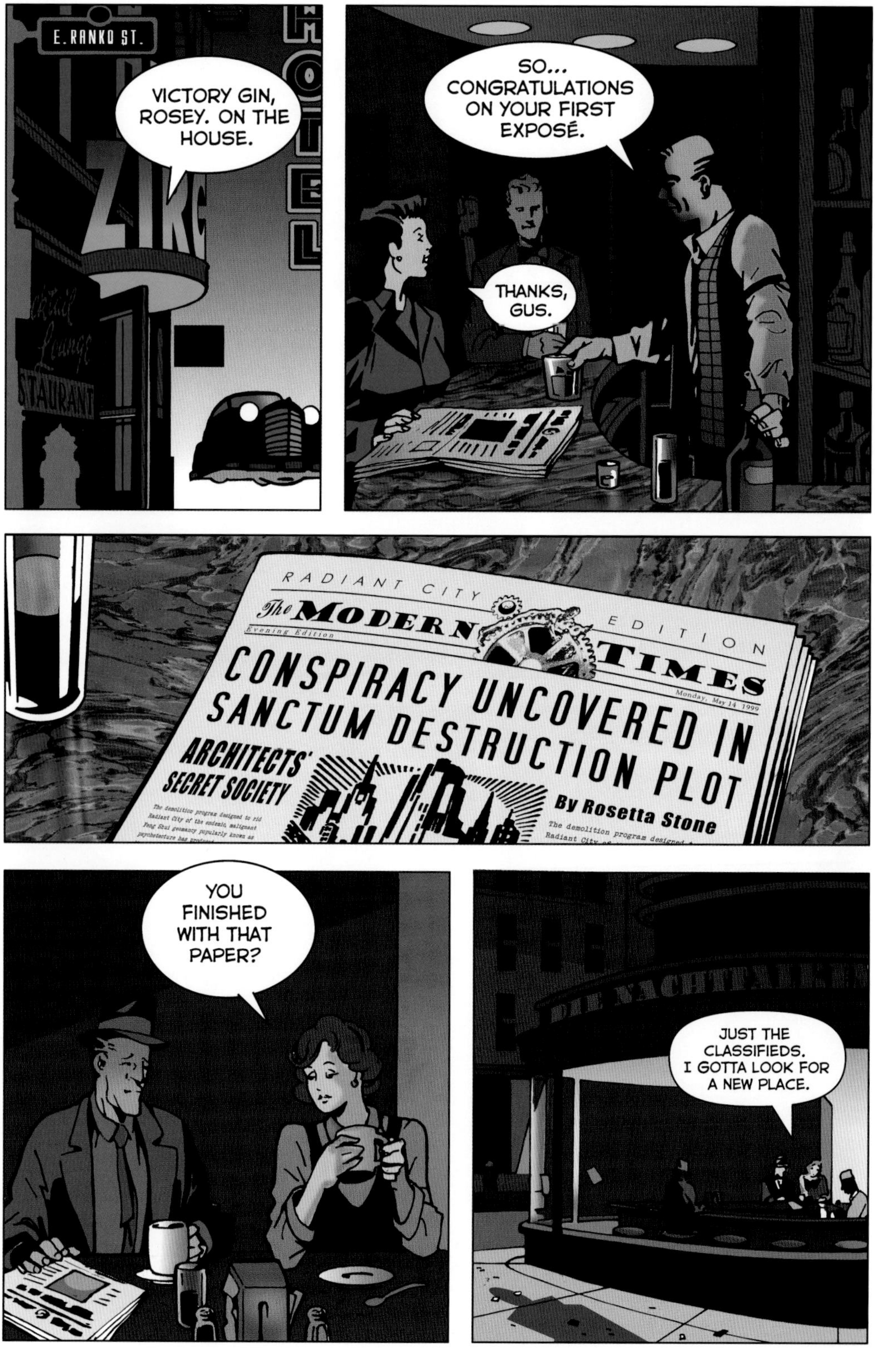
E. RANKO ST.
VICTORY GIN, ROSEY. ON THE HOUSE.
SO... CONGRATULATIONS ON YOUR FIRST EXPOSÉ.
THANKS, GUS.
RADIANT CITY EDITION
The MODERN TIMES
Evening Edition
Monday, May 14 1999
CONSPIRACY UNCOVERED IN SANCTUM DESTRUCTION PLOT
ARCHITECTS' SECRET SOCIETY
By Rosetta Stone
YOU FINISHED WITH THAT PAPER?
JUST THE CLASSIFIEDS. I GOTTA LOOK FOR A NEW PLACE.

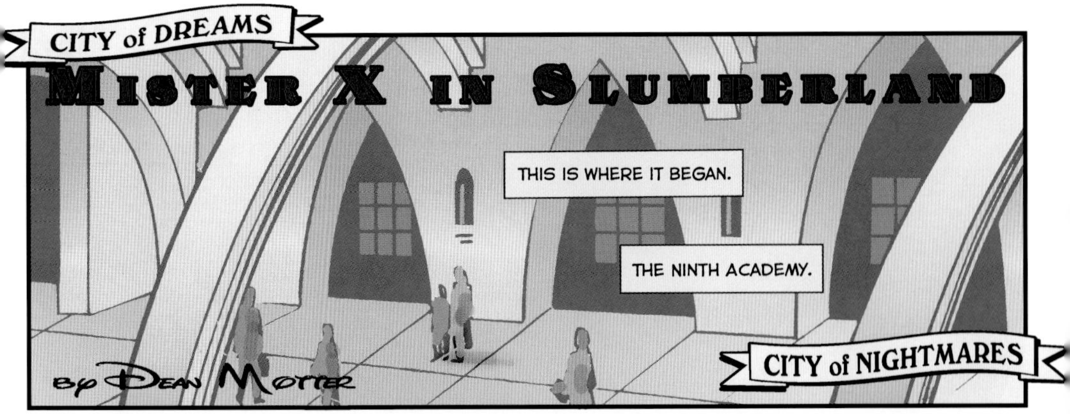
CITY of DREAMS
MISTER X IN SLUMBERLAND
THIS IS WHERE IT BEGAN.
THE NINTH ACADEMY.
CITY of NIGHTMARES
BY DEAN MOTTER

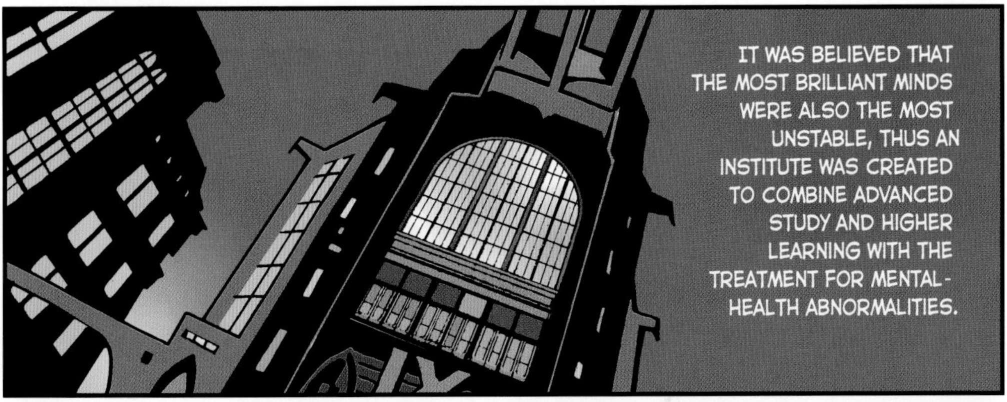
IT WAS BELIEVED THAT THE MOST BRILLIANT MINDS WERE ALSO THE MOST UNSTABLE, THUS AN INSTITUTE WAS CREATED TO COMBINE ADVANCED STUDY AND HIGHER LEARNING WITH THE TREATMENT FOR MENTAL-HEALTH ABNORMALITIES.

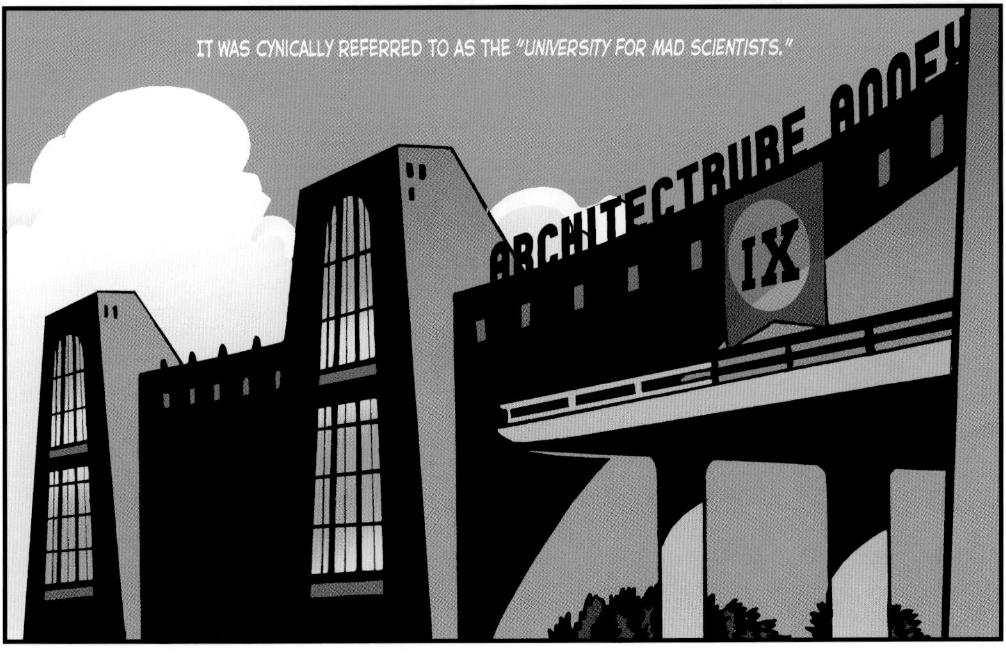
IT WAS CYNICALLY REFERRED TO AS THE "UNIVERSITY FOR MAD SCIENTISTS."
ARCHITECTRURE ANNE
IX

THIS IS WHERE THE MEN DESIGNED THE CITY OF DREAMS.

THIS IS WHERE THE MEN DREAMT OF THEIR CITY OF DREAMS.

ONE DREAMT OF THE CITY OF TOMORROW: WHERE FUTURISTIC TECHNOLOGY WOULD ENRICH OUR EVERYDAY LIVES.

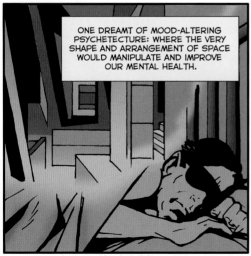

ONE DREAMT OF MOOD-ALTERING PSYCHETECTURE: WHERE THE VERY SHAPE AND ARRANGEMENT OF SPACE WOULD MANIPULATE AND IMPROVE OUR MENTAL HEALTH.

ONE DREAMT OF ADAPTIVE KINETECTURE: WHERE STRUCTURES WOULD TRANSFORM ACCORDING TO THE SEASON, TIME OF DAY, OR PURPOSE.

THERE WERE OTHERS. ENGINEERS, ECONOMISTS, ELECTRICIANS, CHEMISTS... ALL HAD VISIONS OF THE CITY OF DREAMS.

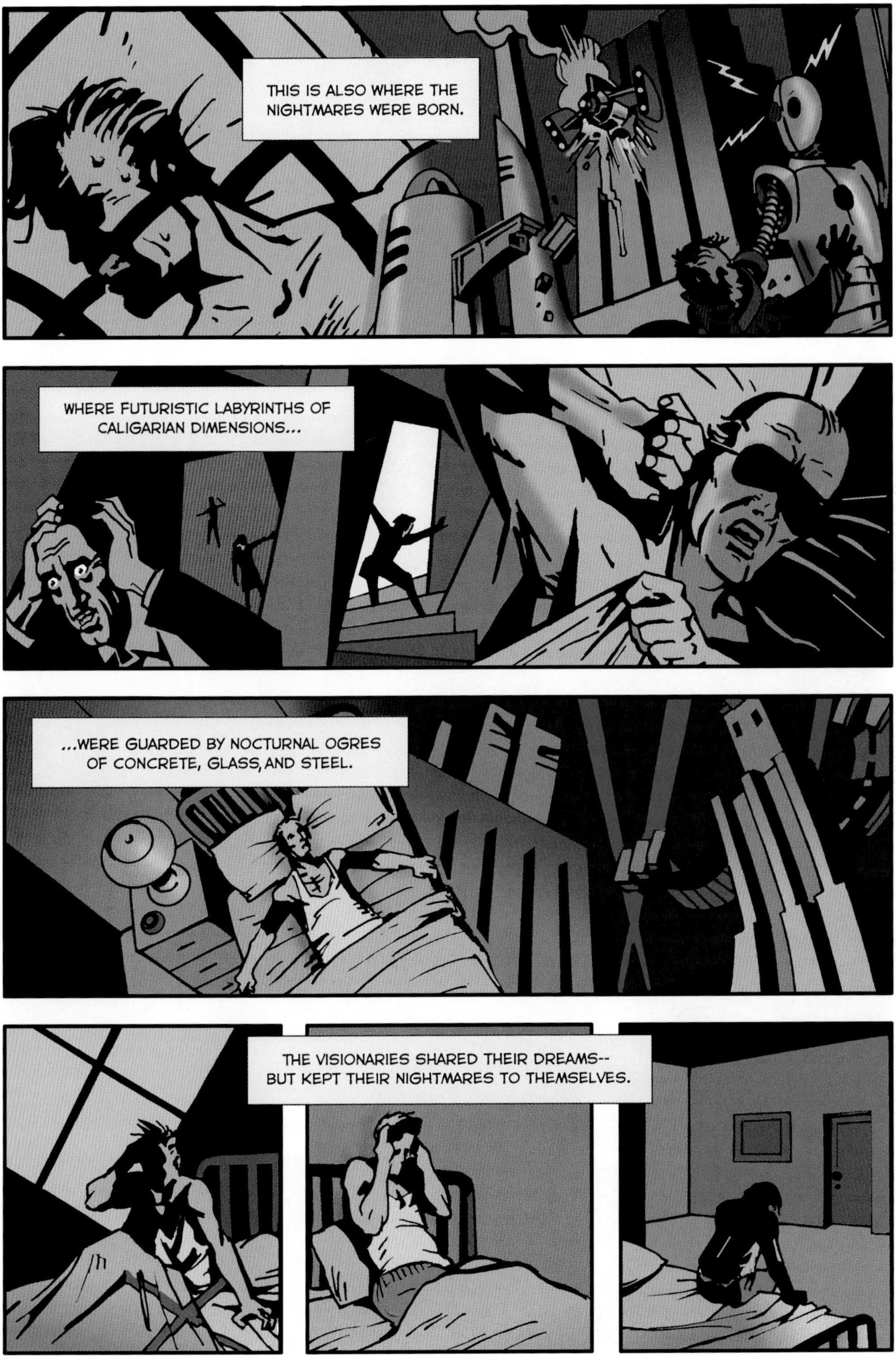
THIS IS ALSO WHERE THE NIGHTMARES WERE BORN.
WHERE FUTURISTIC LABYRINTHS OF CALIGARIAN DIMENSIONS...
...WERE GUARDED BY NOCTURNAL OGRES OF CONCRETE, GLASS, AND STEEL.
THE VISIONARIES SHARED THEIR DREAMS-- BUT KEPT THEIR NIGHTMARES TO THEMSELVES.

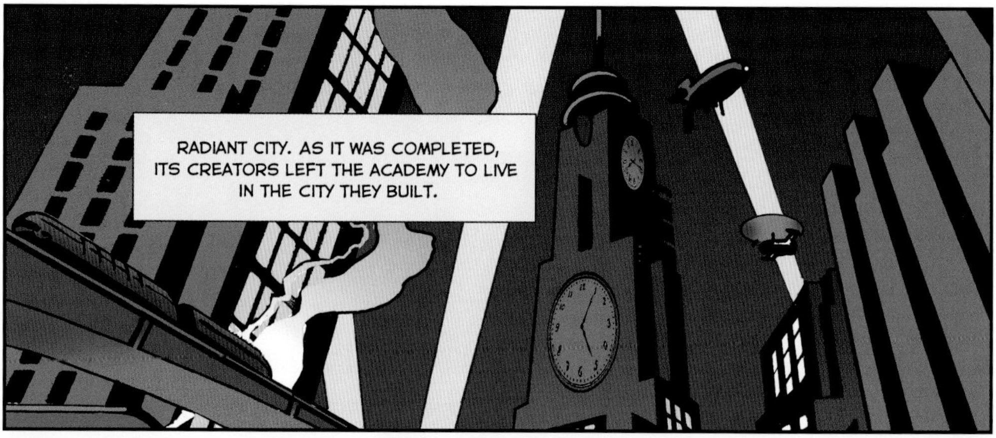
RADIANT CITY. AS IT WAS COMPLETED, ITS CREATORS LEFT THE ACADEMY TO LIVE IN THE CITY THEY BUILT.

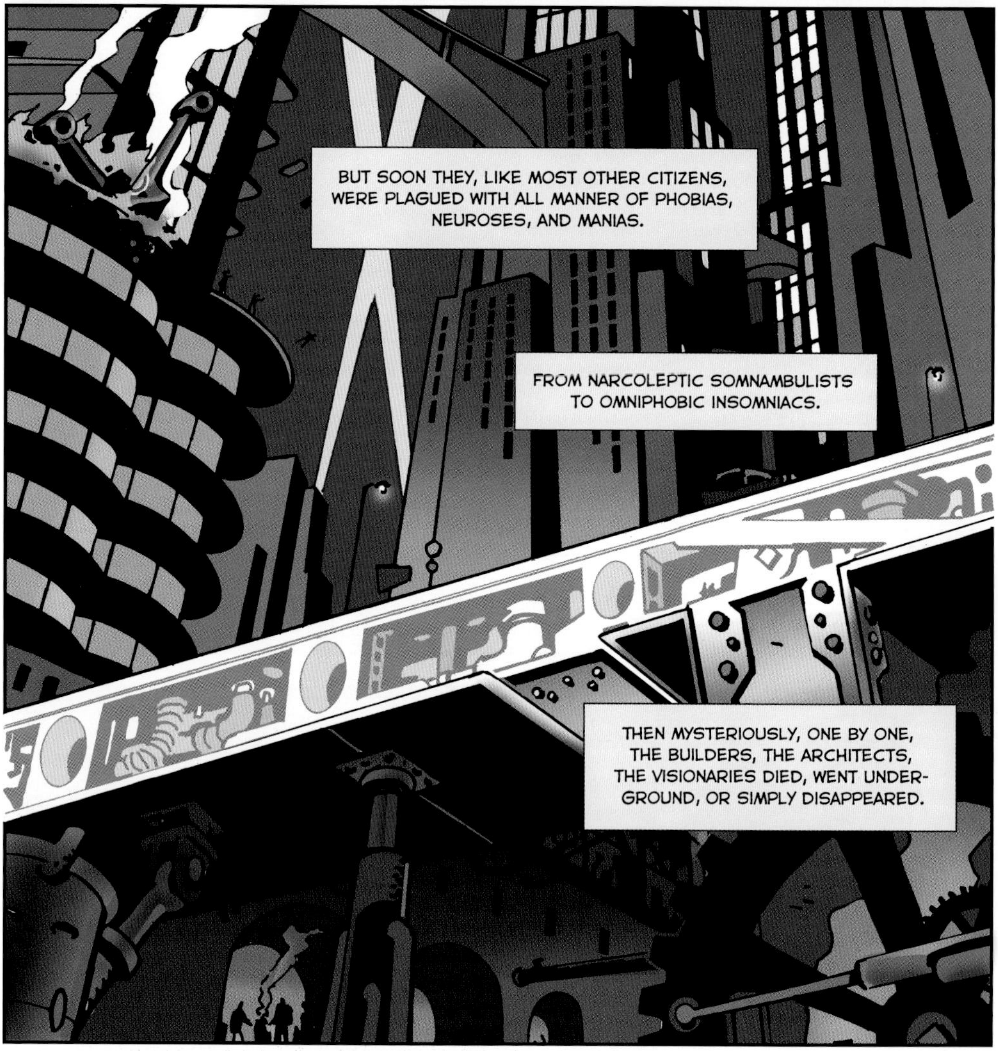
BUT SOON THEY, LIKE MOST OTHER CITIZENS, WERE PLAGUED WITH ALL MANNER OF PHOBIAS, NEUROSES, AND MANIAS.
FROM NARCOLEPTIC SOMNAMBULISTS TO OMNIPHOBIC INSOMNIACS.
THEN MYSTERIOUSLY, ONE BY ONE, THE BUILDERS, THE ARCHITECTS, THE VISIONARIES DIED, WENT UNDER-GROUND, OR SIMPLY DISAPPEARED.

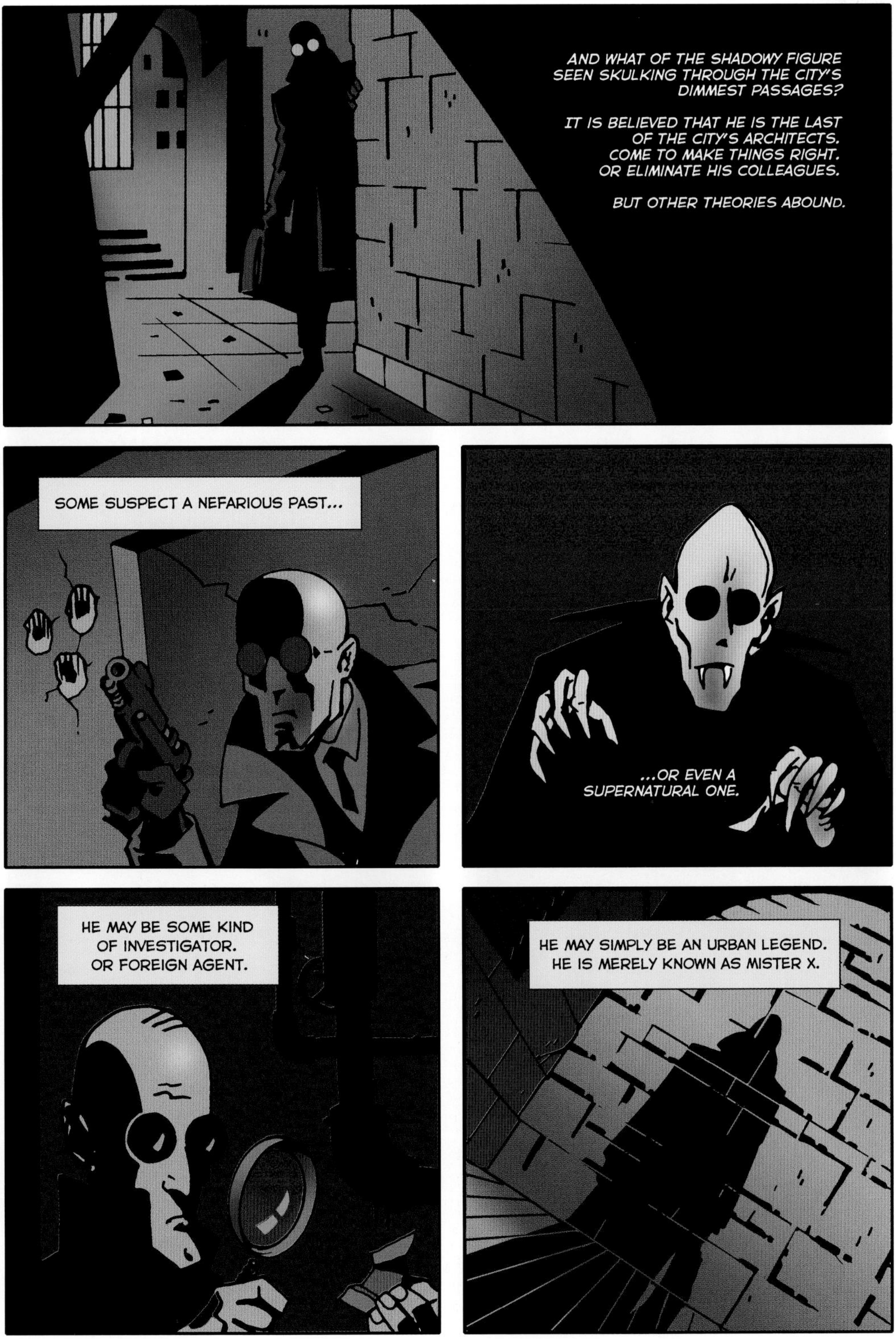
AND WHAT OF THE SHADOWY FIGURE SEEN SKULKING THROUGH THE CITY'S DIMMEST PASSAGES?
IT IS BELIEVED THAT HE IS THE LAST OF THE CITY'S ARCHITECTS. COME TO MAKE THINGS RIGHT. OR ELIMINATE HIS COLLEAGUES.
BUT OTHER THEORIES ABOUND.
SOME SUSPECT A NEFARIOUS PAST...
...OR EVEN A SUPERNATURAL ONE.
HE MAY BE SOME KIND OF INVESTIGATOR. OR FOREIGN AGENT.
HE MAY SIMPLY BE AN URBAN LEGEND. HE IS MERELY KNOWN AS MISTER X.

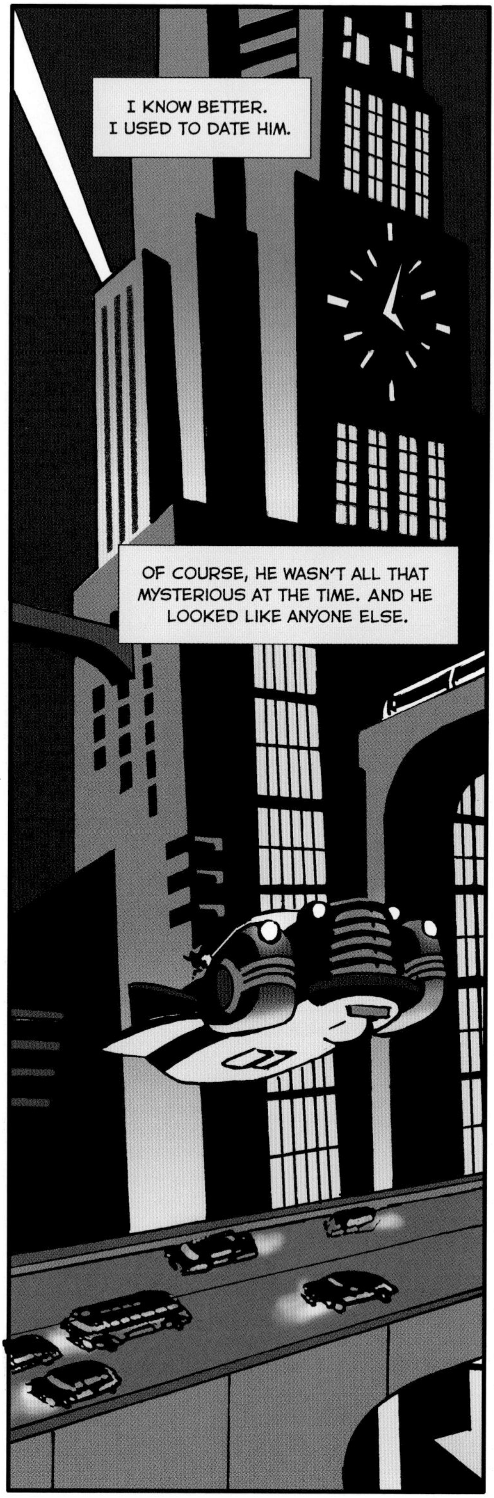
I KNOW BETTER.
I USED TO DATE HIM.
OF COURSE, HE WASN'T ALL THAT MYSTERIOUS AT THE TIME. AND HE LOOKED LIKE ANYONE ELSE.

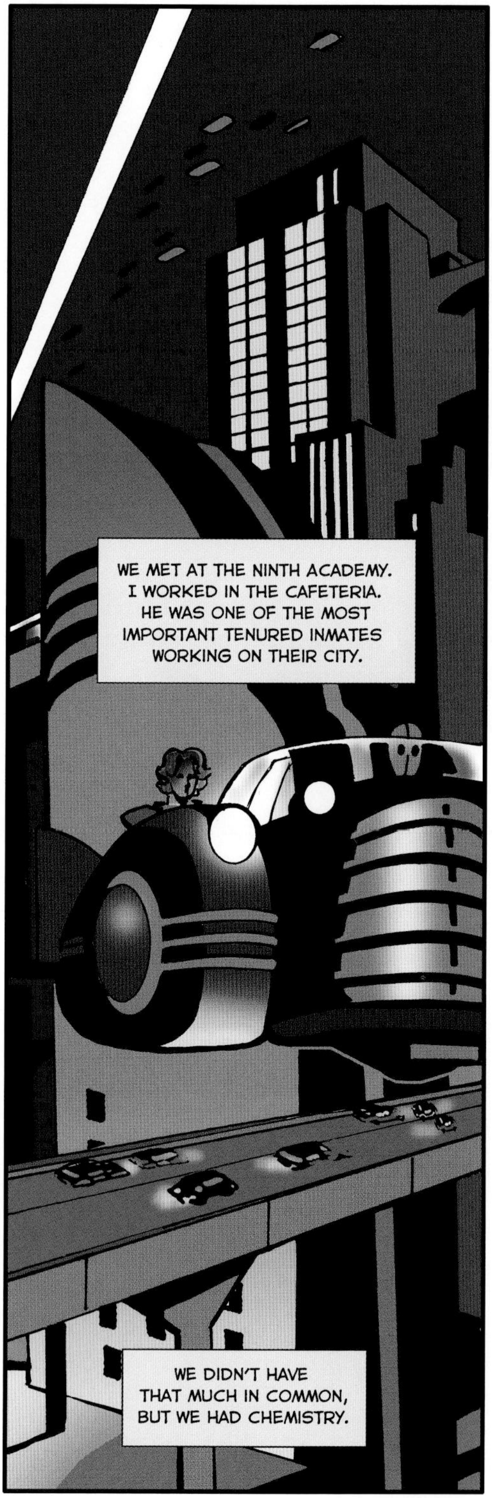
WE MET AT THE NINTH ACADEMY. I WORKED IN THE CAFETERIA. HE WAS ONE OF THE MOST IMPORTANT TENURED INMATES WORKING ON THEIR CITY.
WE DIDN'T HAVE THAT MUCH IN COMMON, BUT WE HAD CHEMISTRY.

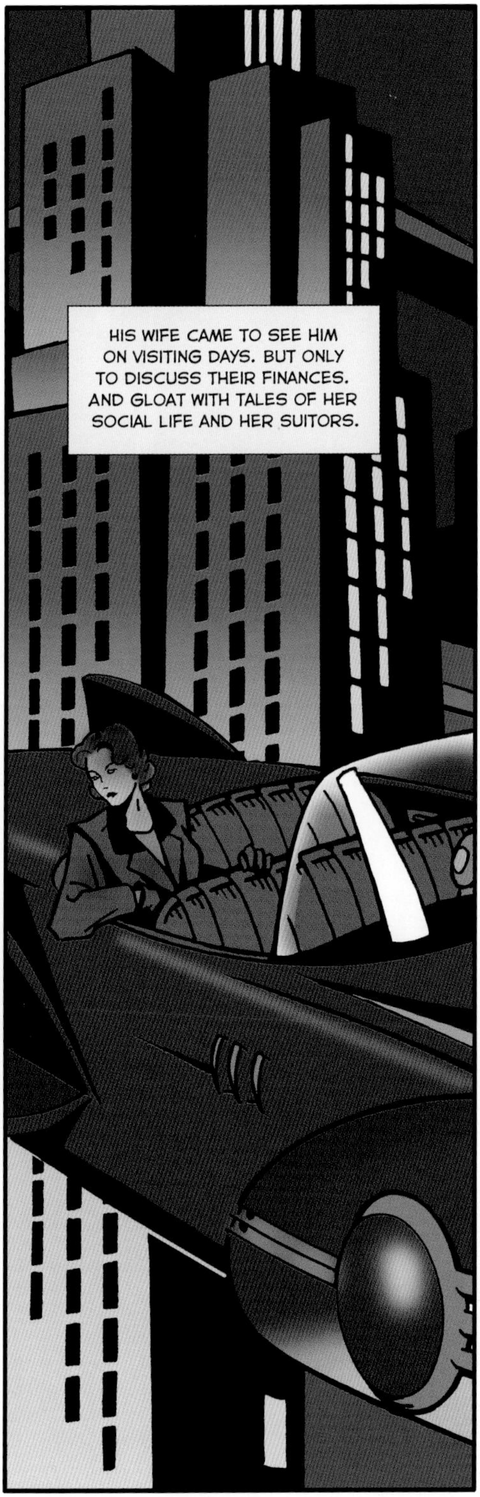
HIS WIFE CAME TO SEE HIM ON VISITING DAYS. BUT ONLY TO DISCUSS THEIR FINANCES. AND GLOAT WITH TALES OF HER SOCIAL LIFE AND HER SUITORS.

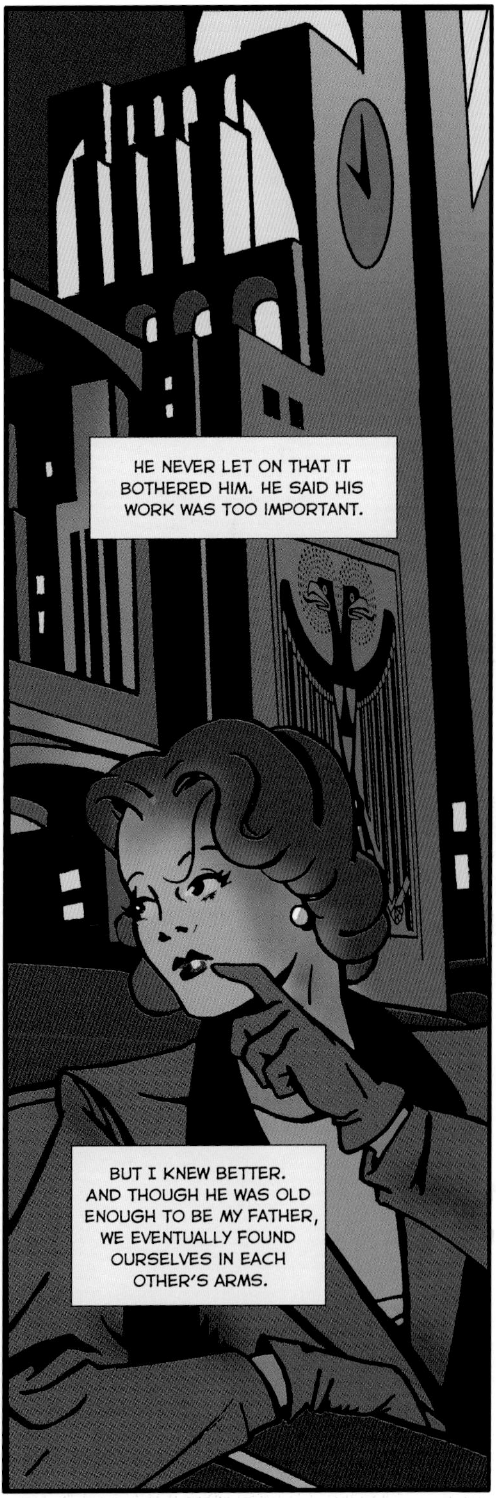
HE NEVER LET ON THAT IT BOTHERED HIM. HE SAID HIS WORK WAS TOO IMPORTANT.
BUT I KNEW BETTER. AND THOUGH HE WAS OLD ENOUGH TO BE MY FATHER, WE EVENTUALLY FOUND OURSELVES IN EACH OTHER'S ARMS.

HE SUGGESTED THAT WE SHARE AN ADDRESS... I AGREED.

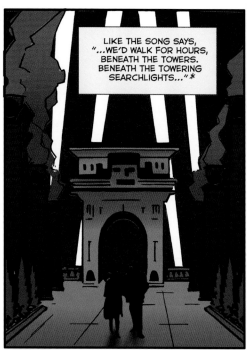

LIKE THE SONG SAYS, "...WE'D WALK FOR HOURS, BENEATH THE TOWERS. BENEATH THE TOWERING SEARCHLIGHTS..." *

BUT LIKE SO MANY OTHER PEOPLE, THE CITY SEEMED TO DRIVE HIM INSANE. AND BEING ITS CREATOR, HE BECAME MADDEST OF ALL.

AND FINALLY ONE NIGHT-- YEARS AGO--HE JUST VANISHED.

NOW THEY SAY HE'S RETURNED TO THE RADIANT CITY. I'D LIKE TO THINK IT'S FOR ME BUT--

OOG! I GOTTA' STOP EATING THAT CHEESE AND SUSHI BEFORE BED.

* "OLYMPIAD", FROM THE ALBUM
THRILLING WOMEN BY
THE AIR PIRATES, 1977

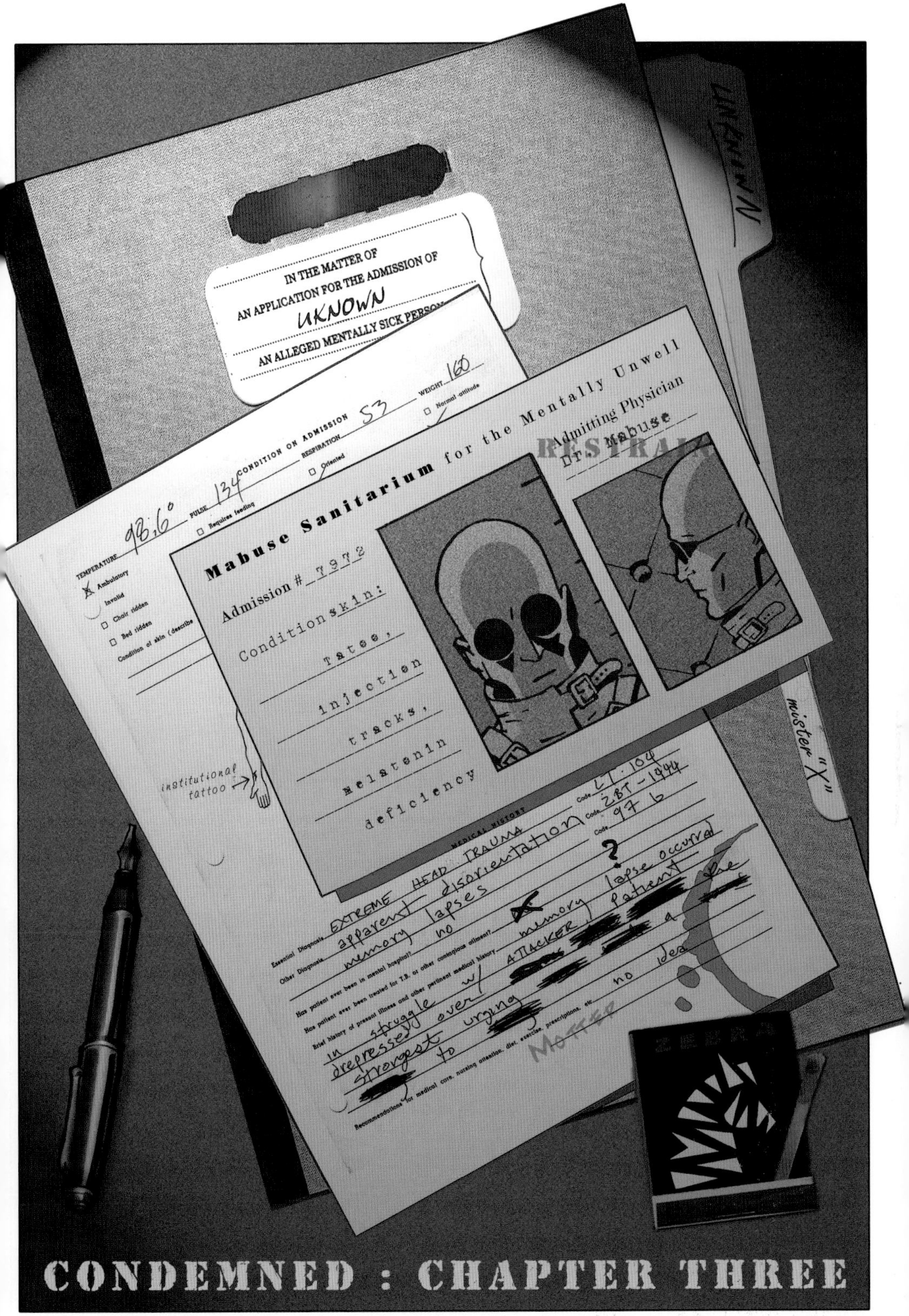
UNKNOWN
IN THE MATTER OF
AN APPLICATION FOR THE ADMISSION OF
UKNOWN
AN ALLEGED MENTALLY SICK PERSON
TEMPERATURE 98.6° PULSE 134 CONDITION ON ADMISSION RESPIRATION 53 WEIGHT 160
Ambulatory
Invalid
Chair ridden
Bed ridden
Condition of skin (describe
Requires feeding
Oriented
Normal attitude
Mabuse Sanitarium for the Mentally Unwell
Admitting Physician
Dr. Mabuse
Admission # 7972
Condition skin: Tatoo, injection tracks, melatonin deficiency
institutional tattoo
mister "X"
MEDICAL HISTORY
Code 27-104
Code 2BT-1444
Code 97 b
Essential Diagnosis EXTREME HEAD TRAUMA
Other Diagnosis apparent disorientation
memory lapses
no [redacted] memory lapse occurred
?
ATTACKER [redacted] patient [redacted]
in struggle w/ [redacted] a
depressed over [redacted] no idea
strongest urging [redacted] to
[redacted]
Recommendations for medical care, nursing attention, diet, exercise, prescriptions, etc.
CONDEMNED : CHAPTER THREE

SO, INSPECTOR? WHO'S MY NEW PATIENT?

NO IDEA. RIGHT NOW HE'S A JOHN DOE... A "MISTER X."

WHAT REMAINS OF AN IDENTITY TATTOO SUGGESTS HE MIGHT BE AN ACADEMICIAN, BUT HIS FINGERPRINTS HAVE BEEN OBLITERATED, AS WELL AS THE NUMBER.

JUST A NIGHTCLUB MATCHBOOK IN HIS POCKET.

LOCKED HIMSELF IN THE JOHN OF AN AFTER-HOURS JOINT. FILLED THE WALLS WITH SOME KIND OF ALGEBRAIC GRAFFITI.

THE FLYING SQUAD FINALLY DRAGGED HIM OUT.

GASSED HIM, BUT HE WOULDN'T PASS OUT.

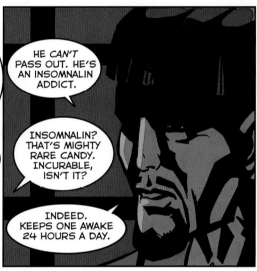

HE CAN'T PASS OUT. HE'S AN INSOMNALIN ADDICT.

INSOMNALIN? THAT'S MIGHTY RARE CANDY. INCURABLE, ISN'T IT?

INDEED. KEEPS ONE AWAKE 24 HOURS A DAY.

WITHOUT A FIX, WITHDRAWAL INDUCES A PERMANENT STATE OF SLEEP.

HE WAS MANIC WHEN YOUR BOYS BROUGHT HIM IN, INSPECTOR LOHMANN. RIGHT NOW HE'S ON SEDATIVES.

THAT WORKS AGAINST THE INSOMNALIN?

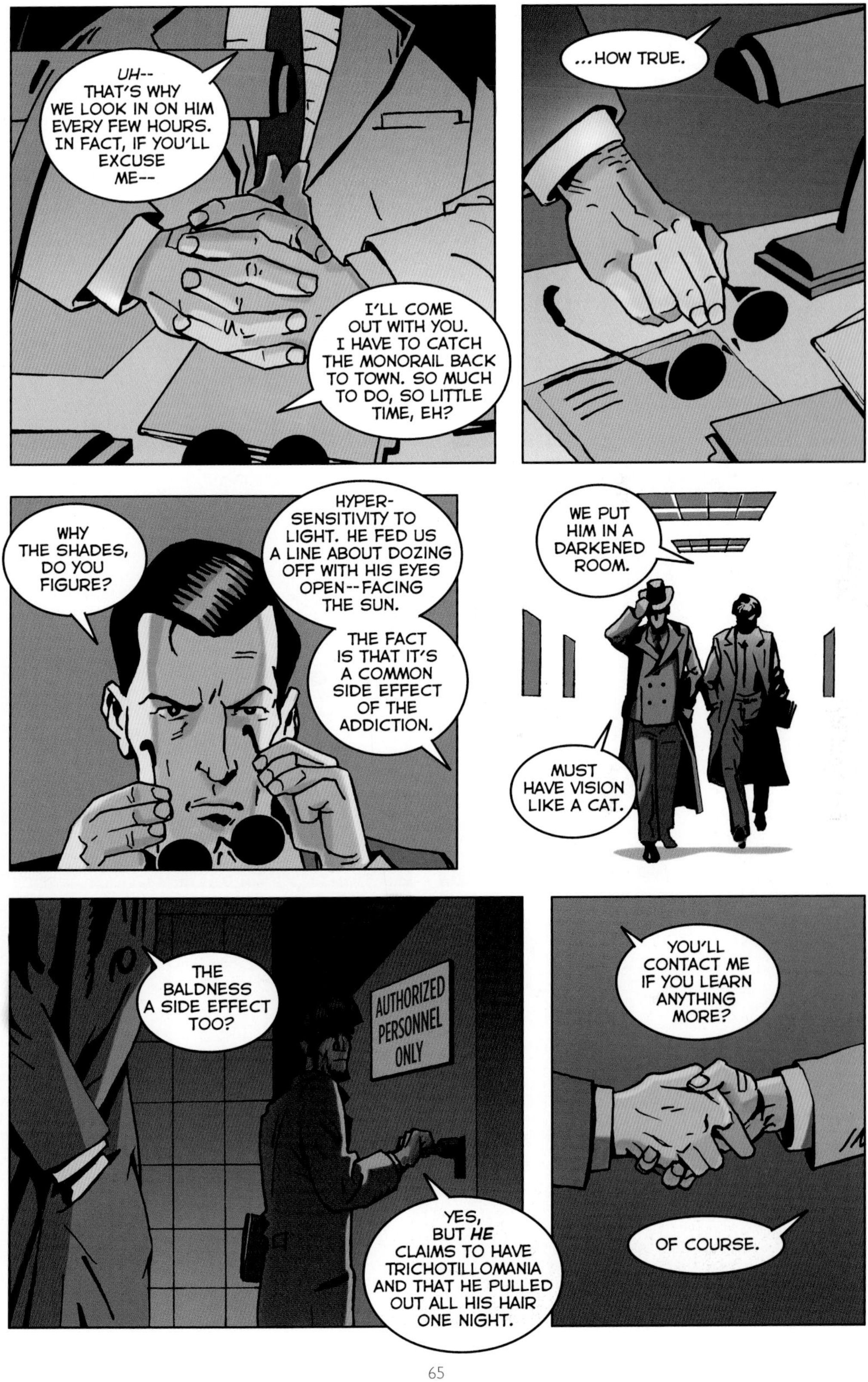
UH-- THAT'S WHY WE LOOK IN ON HIM EVERY FEW HOURS. IN FACT, IF YOU'LL EXCUSE ME--
I'LL COME OUT WITH YOU. I HAVE TO CATCH THE MONORAIL BACK TO TOWN. SO MUCH TO DO, SO LITTLE TIME, EH?
...HOW TRUE.
WHY THE SHADES, DO YOU FIGURE?
HYPER-SENSITIVITY TO LIGHT. HE FED US A LINE ABOUT DOZING OFF WITH HIS EYES OPEN--FACING THE SUN.
THE FACT IS THAT IT'S A COMMON SIDE EFFECT OF THE ADDICTION.
WE PUT HIM IN A DARKENED ROOM.
MUST HAVE VISION LIKE A CAT.
THE BALDNESS A SIDE EFFECT TOO?
AUTHORIZED PERSONNEL ONLY
YES, BUT *HE* CLAIMS TO HAVE TRICHOTILLOMANIA AND THAT HE PULLED OUT ALL HIS HAIR ONE NIGHT.
YOU'LL CONTACT ME IF YOU LEARN ANYTHING MORE?
OF COURSE.

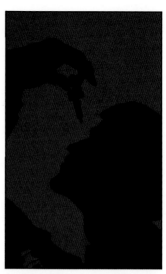

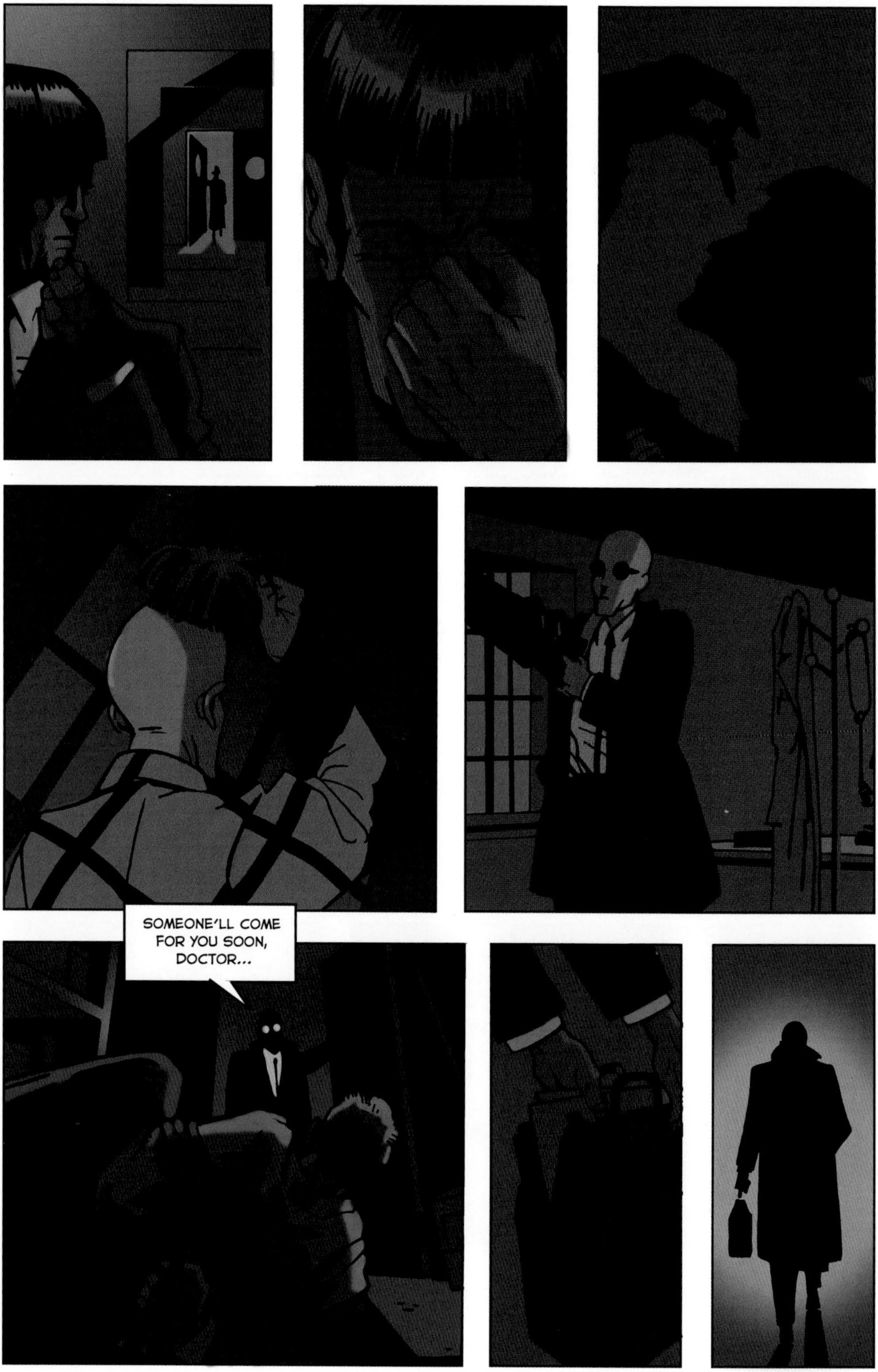
SOMEONE'LL COME
FOR YOU SOON,
DOCTOR...

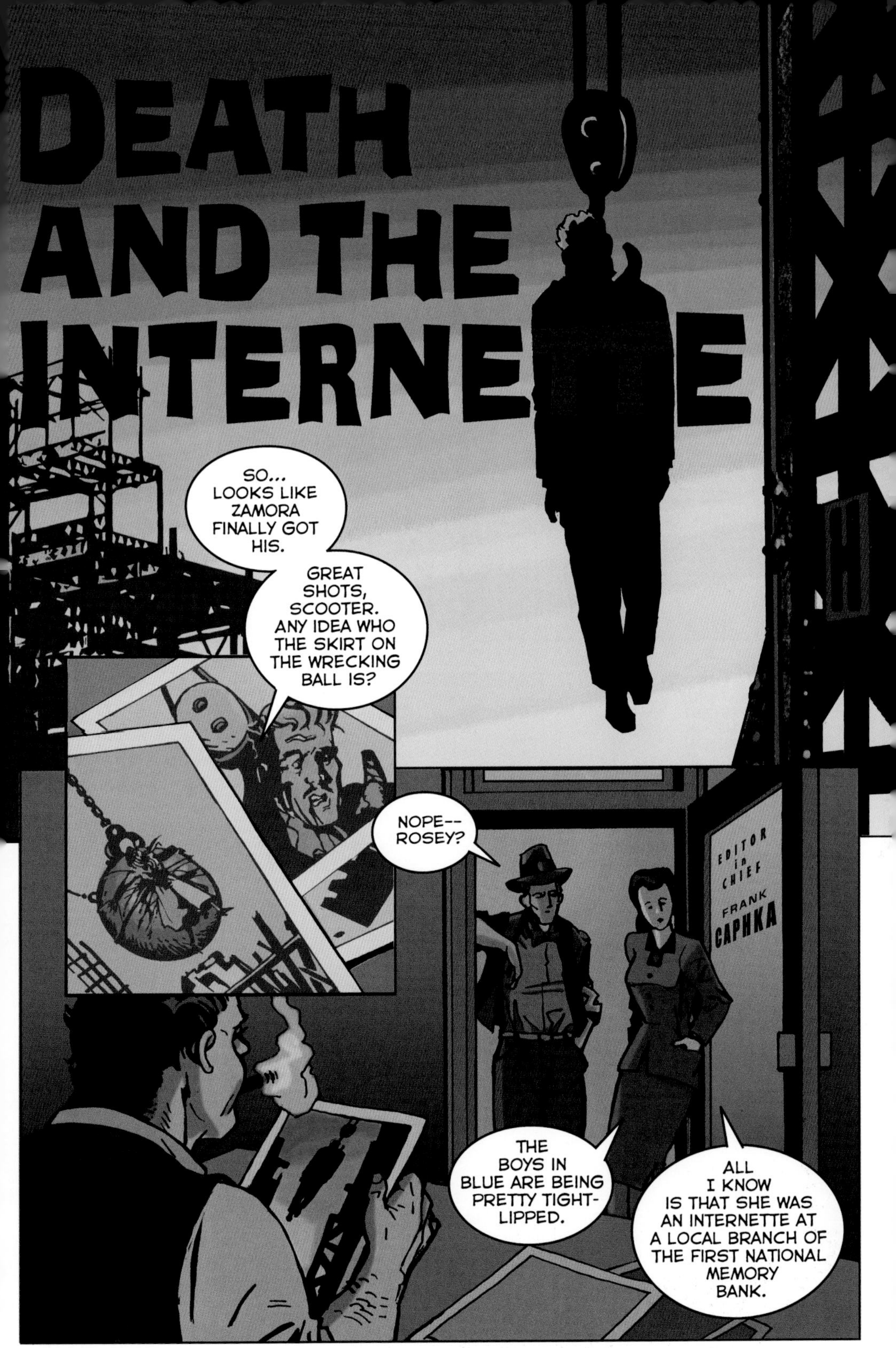
DEATH AND THE INTERNETTE
SO... LOOKS LIKE ZAMORA FINALLY GOT HIS.
GREAT SHOTS, SCOOTER. ANY IDEA WHO THE SKIRT ON THE WRECKING BALL IS?
NOPE-- ROSEY?
EDITOR in CHIEF FRANK CAPHKA
THE BOYS IN BLUE ARE BEING PRETTY TIGHT-LIPPED.
ALL I KNOW IS THAT SHE WAS AN INTERNETTE AT A LOCAL BRANCH OF THE FIRST NATIONAL MEMORY BANK.

HOW IS IT YOU WERE THERE AT JUST THE RIGHT TIME?

WE'VE BEEN HANGING AROUND THE DEMO SITES SINCE THE VITRUVIAN INCIDENT, BOSS.

PASSES THE TIME.

WELL-- WE'VE RECEIVED ANOTHER *CITY BOY* LETTER. TAKING *CREDIT* FOR ZAMORA.

THAT'S A BIT OUT OF CHARACTER, ISN'T IT? HIS GRIPES HAVE BEEN WITH THE *HAUTE MONDE*, NOT UNDERWORLD TYPES.

ACCORDING TO HIM, ZAMORA WAS JUST ANOTHER *NEW BROOM* PROFITEER. HIS PROTECTION SERVICES HAVE BEEN LUCRATIVE LATELY.

BUT NOT VERY EFFECTIVE. THEY'VE TAKEN OUT A LOT OF HIS TURF.

SAY YOU RAN A BUSINESS AND ARNOLD PUT THE TOUCH ON YOU...

WHO WOULD YOU COMPLAIN TO IF HE DIDN'T DELIVER?

NO MENTION OF THE GIRL, HUH?

NOTHING. *HOWEVER*-- THIS IS THE FIRST TIME HE'S USED STATIONERY.

NO PRINTS, BUT ARCHIVES IS WORKING ON THE WATERMARK.

THE BULLS ARE GONNA WANT IT...

THEY'RE WELCOME TO IT-- WHEN WE'RE FINISHED.

From the City Boy
To the babylonians
There will be no more
The Gollaths have
temple. Be Warned
Zamora has met the sun.

Modern Times
Editor

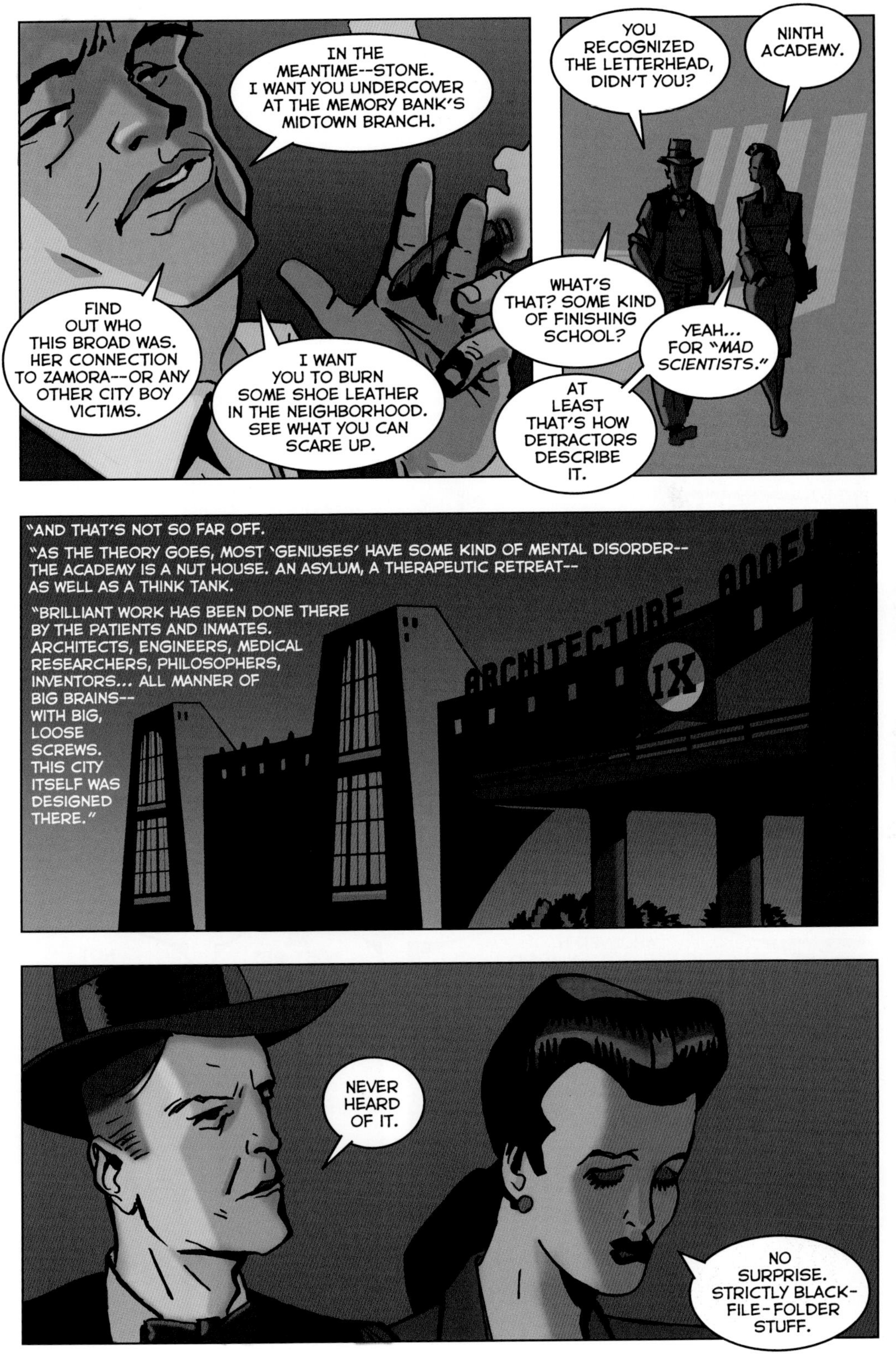
IN THE MEANTIME--STONE. I WANT YOU UNDERCOVER AT THE MEMORY BANK'S MIDTOWN BRANCH.
FIND OUT WHO THIS BROAD WAS. HER CONNECTION TO ZAMORA--OR ANY OTHER CITY BOY VICTIMS.
I WANT YOU TO BURN SOME SHOE LEATHER IN THE NEIGHBORHOOD. SEE WHAT YOU CAN SCARE UP.
YOU RECOGNIZED THE LETTERHEAD, DIDN'T YOU?
NINTH ACADEMY.
WHAT'S THAT? SOME KIND OF FINISHING SCHOOL?
YEAH... FOR "*MAD SCIENTISTS.*"
AT LEAST THAT'S HOW DETRACTORS DESCRIBE IT.
"AND THAT'S NOT SO FAR OFF.
"AS THE THEORY GOES, MOST 'GENIUSES' HAVE SOME KIND OF MENTAL DISORDER-- THE ACADEMY IS A NUT HOUSE. AN ASYLUM, A THERAPEUTIC RETREAT-- AS WELL AS A THINK TANK.
"BRILLIANT WORK HAS BEEN DONE THERE BY THE PATIENTS AND INMATES. ARCHITECTS, ENGINEERS, MEDICAL RESEARCHERS, PHILOSOPHERS, INVENTORS... ALL MANNER OF BIG BRAINS-- WITH BIG, LOOSE SCREWS. THIS CITY ITSELF WAS DESIGNED THERE."
ARCHITECTURE
IX
NEVER HEARD OF IT.
NO SURPRISE. STRICTLY BLACK-FILE-FOLDER STUFF.

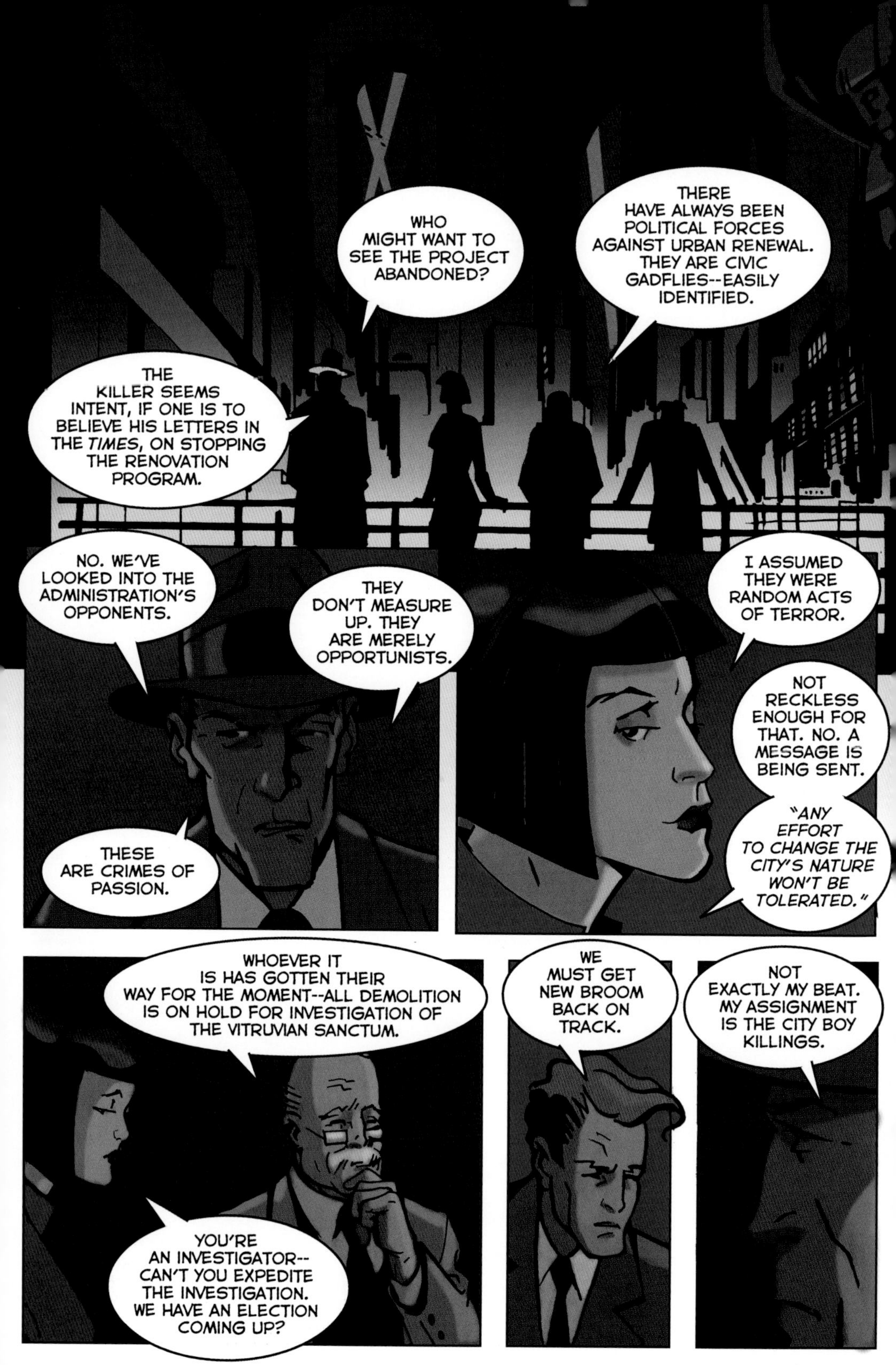
THE KILLER SEEMS INTENT, IF ONE IS TO BELIEVE HIS LETTERS IN THE *TIMES*, ON STOPPING THE RENOVATION PROGRAM.
WHO MIGHT WANT TO SEE THE PROJECT ABANDONED?
THERE HAVE ALWAYS BEEN POLITICAL FORCES AGAINST URBAN RENEWAL. THEY ARE CIVIC GADFLIES--EASILY IDENTIFIED.
NO. WE'VE LOOKED INTO THE ADMINISTRATION'S OPPONENTS.
THEY DON'T MEASURE UP. THEY ARE MERELY OPPORTUNISTS.
THESE ARE CRIMES OF PASSION.
I ASSUMED THEY WERE RANDOM ACTS OF TERROR.
NOT RECKLESS ENOUGH FOR THAT. NO. A MESSAGE IS BEING SENT.
"ANY EFFORT TO CHANGE THE CITY'S NATURE WON'T BE TOLERATED."
WHOEVER IT IS HAS GOTTEN THEIR WAY FOR THE MOMENT--ALL DEMOLITION IS ON HOLD FOR INVESTIGATION OF THE VITRUVIAN SANCTUM.
YOU'RE AN INVESTIGATOR--CAN'T YOU EXPEDITE THE INVESTIGATION. WE HAVE AN ELECTION COMING UP?
WE MUST GET NEW BROOM BACK ON TRACK.
NOT EXACTLY MY BEAT. MY ASSIGNMENT IS THE CITY BOY KILLINGS.

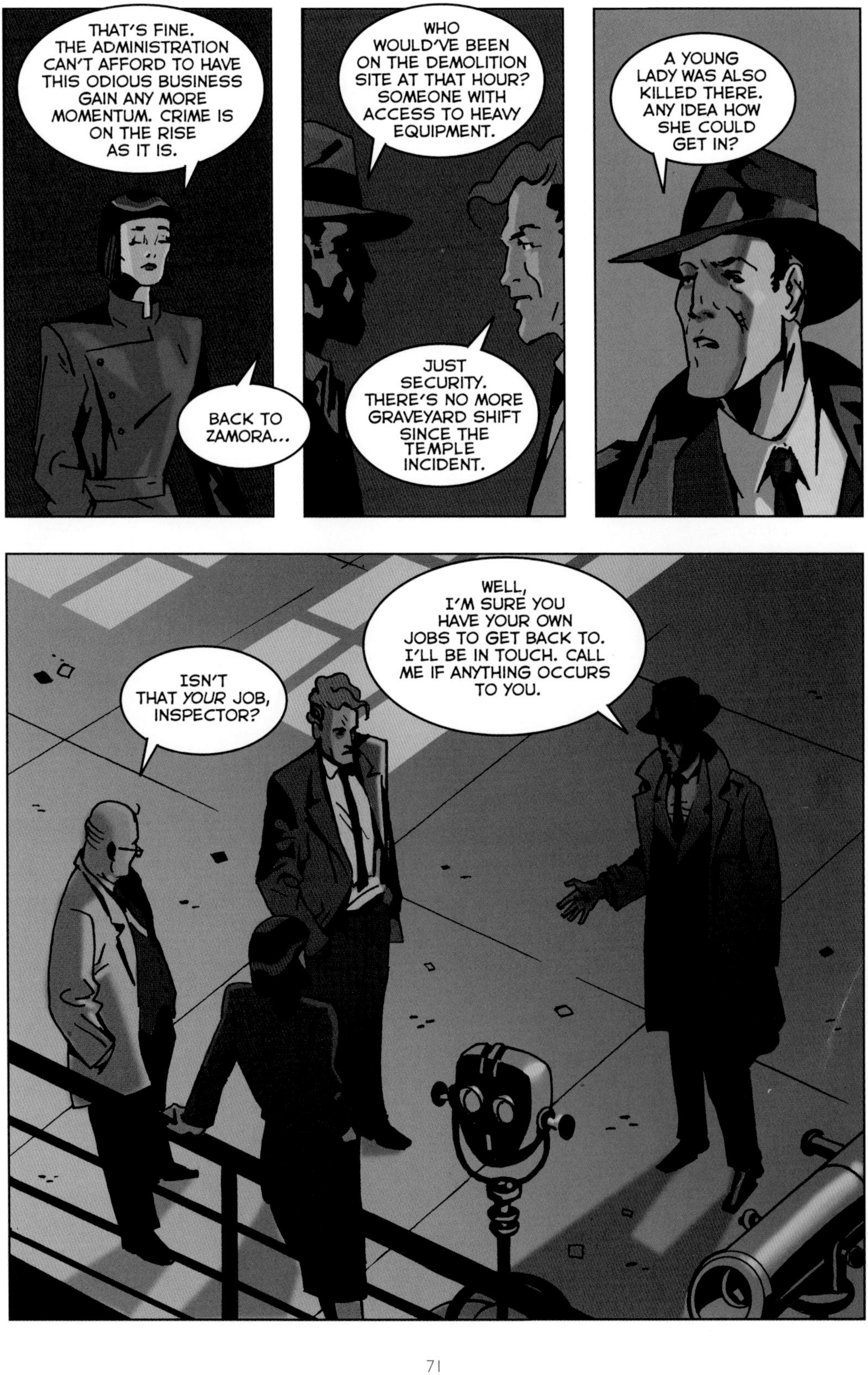
THAT'S FINE. THE ADMINISTRATION CAN'T AFFORD TO HAVE THIS ODIOUS BUSINESS GAIN ANY MORE MOMENTUM. CRIME IS ON THE RISE AS IT IS.
BACK TO ZAMORA...
WHO WOULD'VE BEEN ON THE DEMOLITION SITE AT THAT HOUR? SOMEONE WITH ACCESS TO HEAVY EQUIPMENT.
JUST SECURITY. THERE'S NO MORE GRAVEYARD SHIFT SINCE THE TEMPLE INCIDENT.
A YOUNG LADY WAS ALSO KILLED THERE. ANY IDEA HOW SHE COULD GET IN?
WELL, I'M SURE YOU HAVE YOUR OWN JOBS TO GET BACK TO. I'LL BE IN TOUCH. CALL ME IF ANYTHING OCCURS TO YOU.
ISN'T THAT *YOUR* JOB, INSPECTOR?

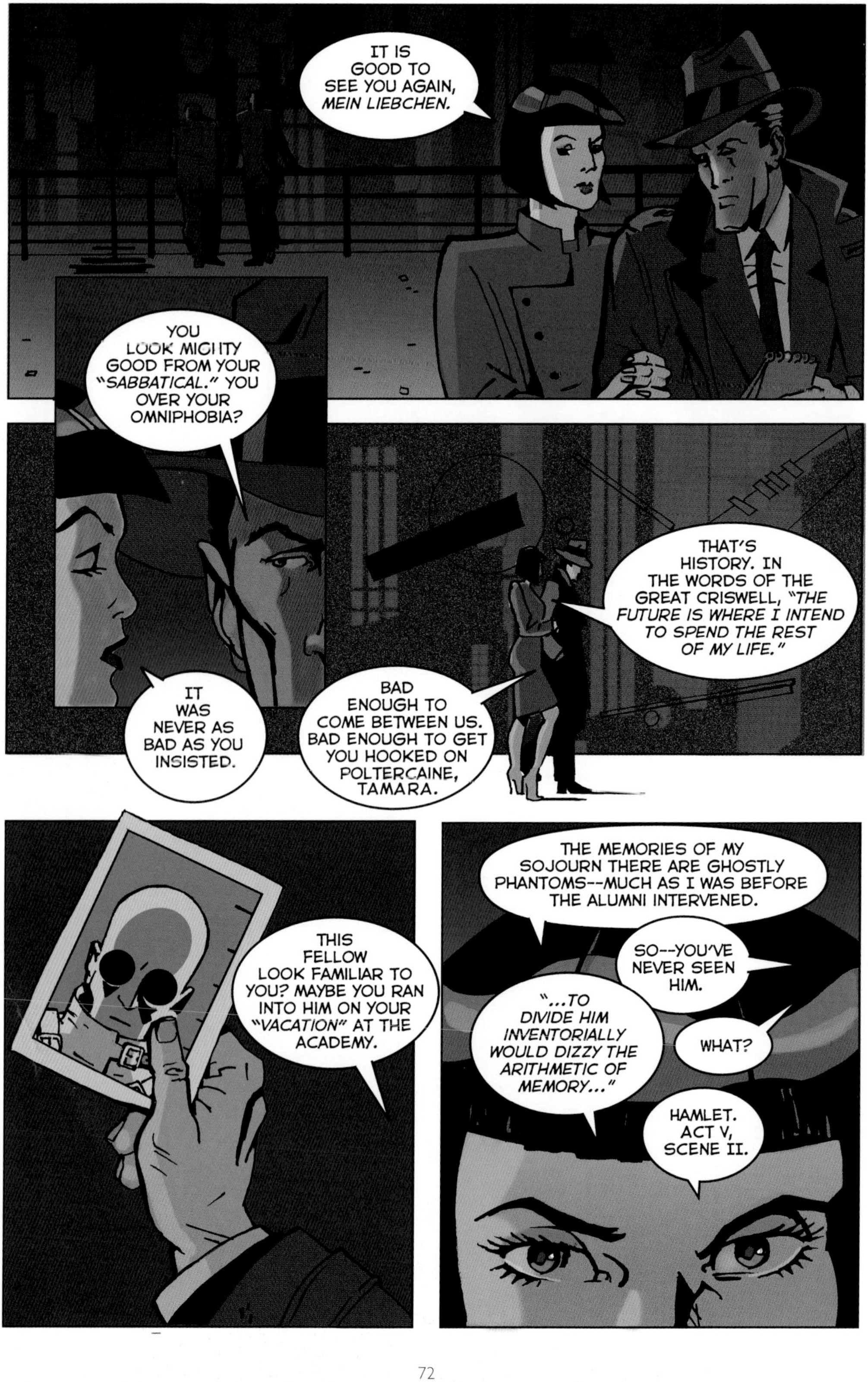
IT IS GOOD TO SEE YOU AGAIN, *MEIN LIEBCHEN.*
YOU LOOK MIGHTY GOOD FROM YOUR "*SABBATICAL.*" YOU OVER YOUR OMNIPHOBIA?
IT WAS NEVER AS BAD AS YOU INSISTED.
BAD ENOUGH TO COME BETWEEN US. BAD ENOUGH TO GET YOU HOOKED ON POLTERCAINE, TAMARA.
THAT'S HISTORY. IN THE WORDS OF THE GREAT CRISWELL, "*THE FUTURE IS WHERE I INTEND TO SPEND THE REST OF MY LIFE.*"
THIS FELLOW LOOK FAMILIAR TO YOU? MAYBE YOU RAN INTO HIM ON YOUR "*VACATION*" AT THE ACADEMY.
THE MEMORIES OF MY SOJOURN THERE ARE GHOSTLY PHANTOMS--MUCH AS I WAS BEFORE THE ALUMNI INTERVENED.
SO--YOU'VE NEVER SEEN HIM.
"*...TO DIVIDE HIM INVENTORIALLY WOULD DIZZY THE ARITHMETIC OF MEMORY...*"
WHAT?
HAMLET. ACT V, SCENE II.

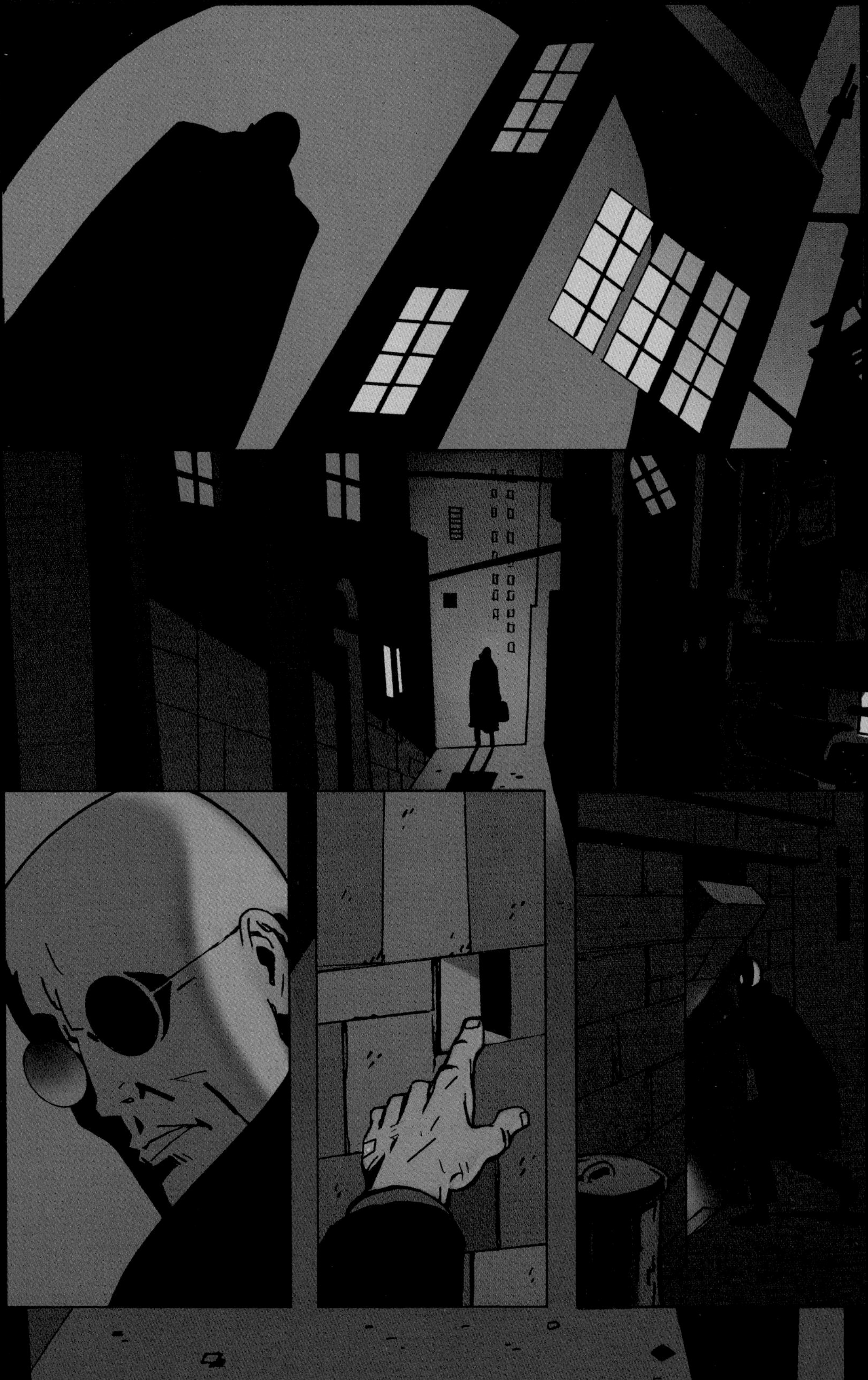

"YOU HAVE TO UNDERSTAND, MY DEAR INSPECTOR, THE ACADEMY WAS A STRANGE PLACE. WITH STRANGE OCCUPANTS.

"THE WORK WAS CLANDESTINE BY NATURE, AND OFTEN THE SHADOWS WE LABORED IN PRODUCED ALL NATURE OF PHANTOMS.

"BENEATH THE SPECTACULAR RESEARCH AND FEATS OF ENGINEERING CONSPIRACIES WERE HATCHED, UNAUTHORIZED EXPERIMENTS WERE CONDUCTED, PSYCHES WERE WARPED.

"MANY OF OUR MORE UNSTABLE MEMBERS DEVELOPED EXTREME PERSONALITY ABERRATIONS.

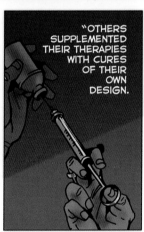

"OTHERS SUPPLEMENTED THEIR THERAPIES WITH CURES OF THEIR OWN DESIGN.

"THERE WERE THOSE OF US WHO SIMPLY REINVENTED OURSELVES AND ERASED OUR OLD IDENTITIES.

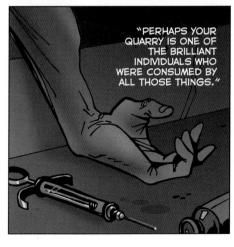

"PERHAPS YOUR QUARRY IS ONE OF THE BRILLIANT INDIVIDUALS WHO WERE CONSUMED BY ALL THOSE THINGS."

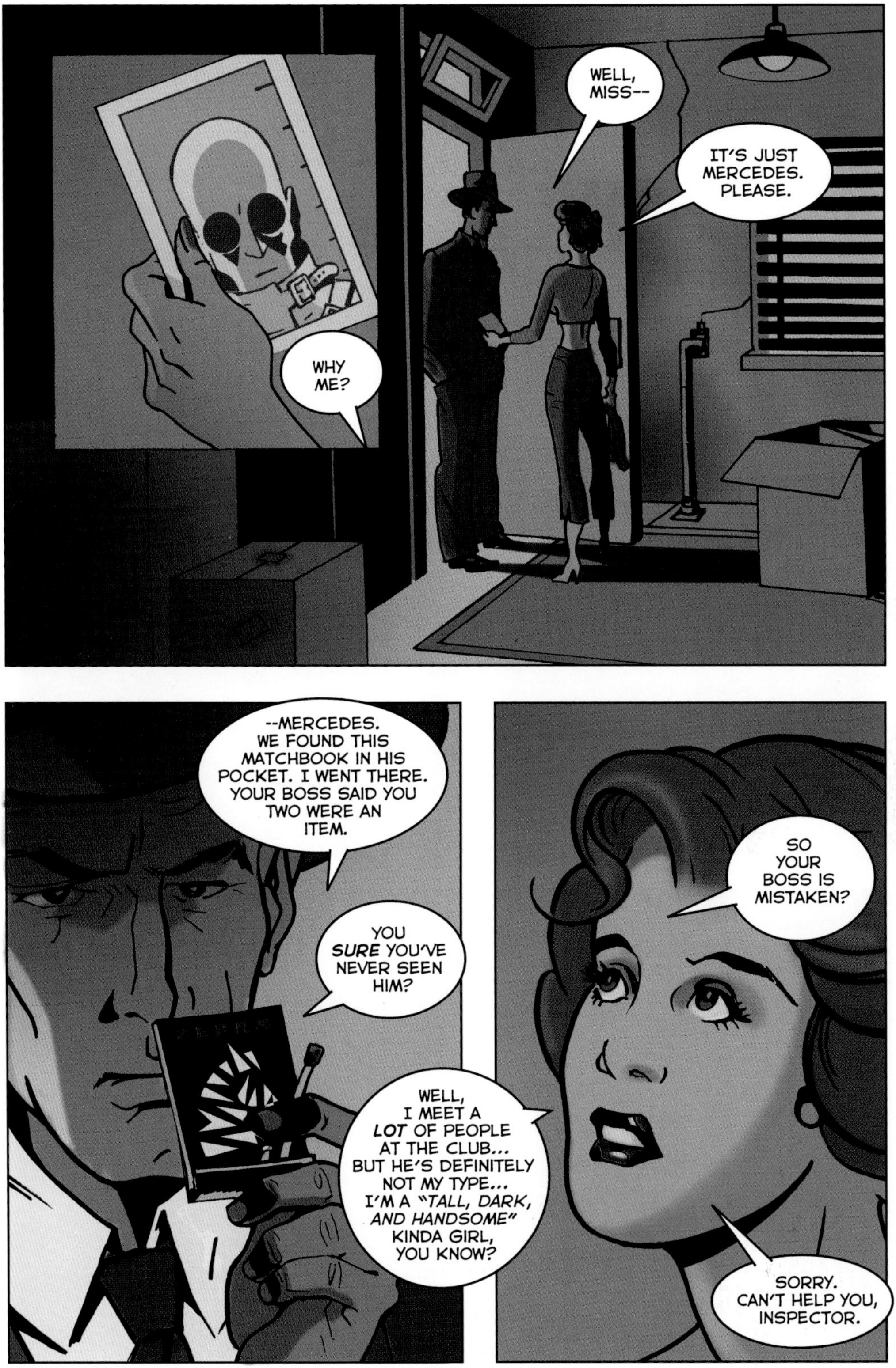

WHY ME?
WELL, MISS--
IT'S JUST MERCEDES. PLEASE.
--MERCEDES. WE FOUND THIS MATCHBOOK IN HIS POCKET. I WENT THERE. YOUR BOSS SAID YOU TWO WERE AN ITEM.
YOU SURE YOU'VE NEVER SEEN HIM?
SO YOUR BOSS IS MISTAKEN?
WELL, I MEET A LOT OF PEOPLE AT THE CLUB... BUT HE'S DEFINITELY NOT MY TYPE... I'M A "TALL, DARK, AND HANDSOME" KINDA GIRL, YOU KNOW?
SORRY. CAN'T HELP YOU, INSPECTOR.

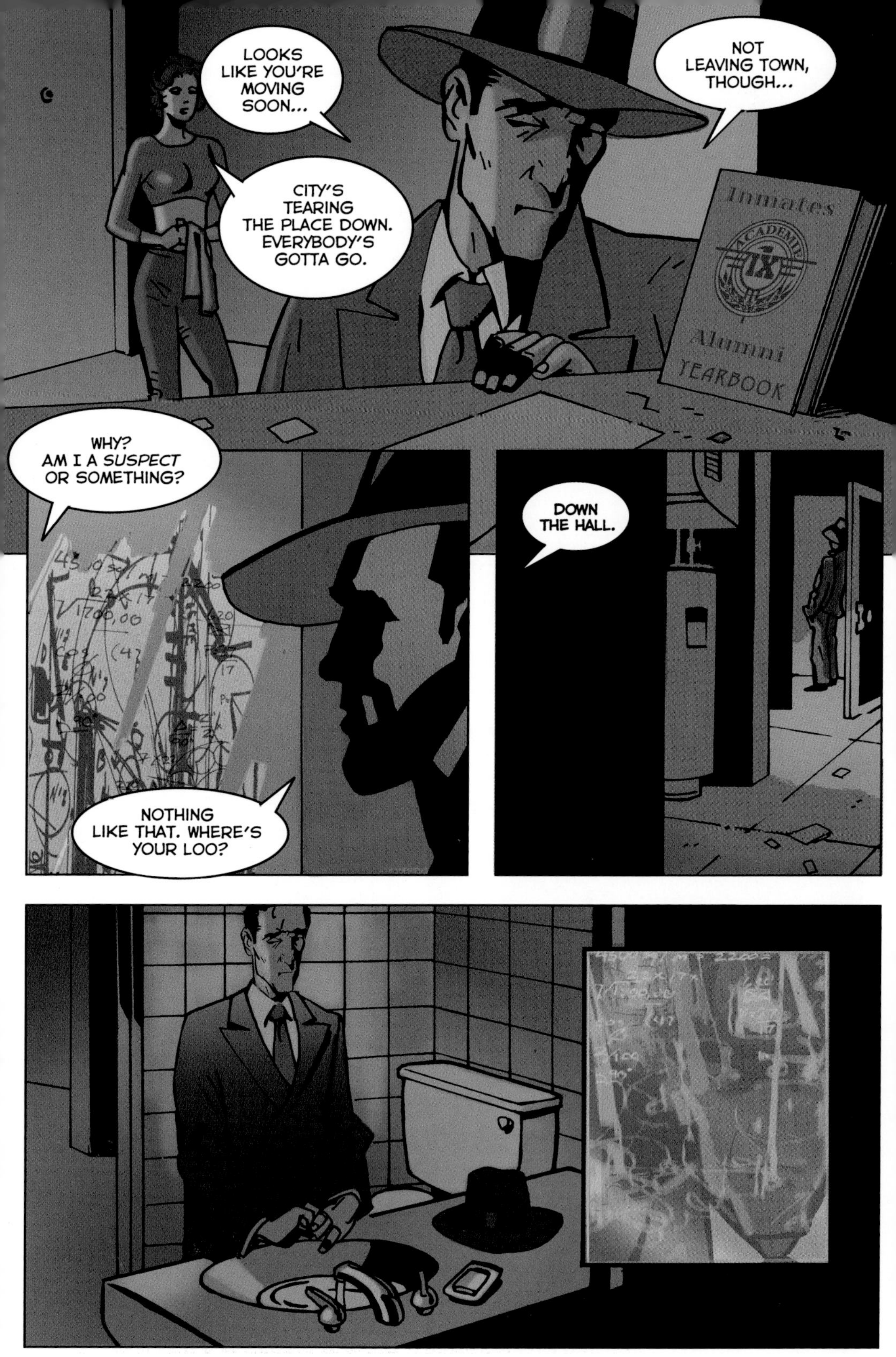
LOOKS LIKE YOU'RE MOVING SOON...
CITY'S TEARING THE PLACE DOWN. EVERYBODY'S GOTTA GO.
NOT LEAVING TOWN, THOUGH...
Inmates
ACADEMIE
IX
Alumni
YEARBOOK
WHY? AM I A *SUSPECT* OR SOMETHING?
NOTHING LIKE THAT. WHERE'S YOUR LOO?
DOWN THE HALL.

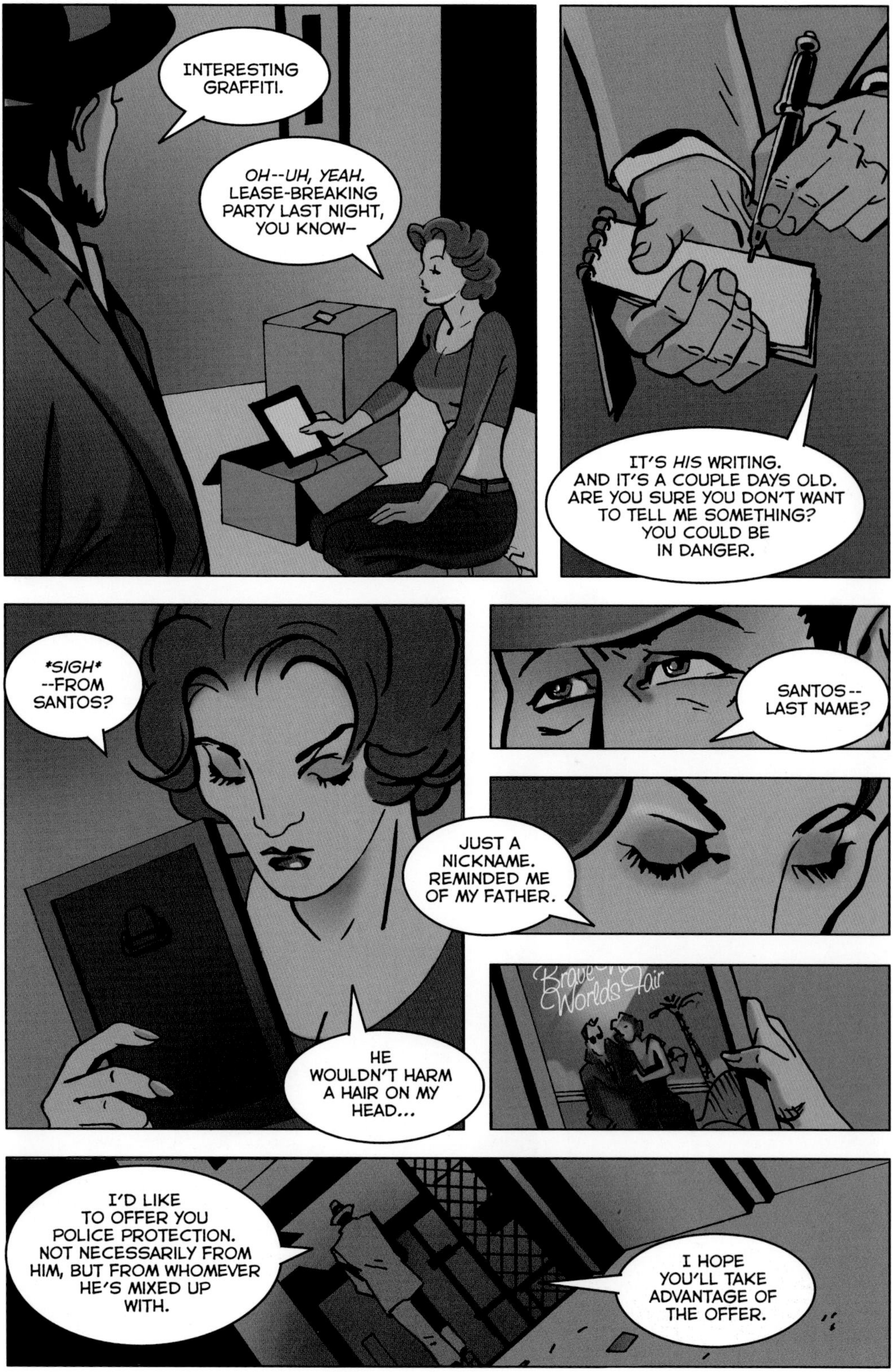
INTERESTING GRAFFITI.
OH--UH, YEAH. LEASE-BREAKING PARTY LAST NIGHT, YOU KNOW–
IT'S HIS WRITING. AND IT'S A COUPLE DAYS OLD. ARE YOU SURE YOU DON'T WANT TO TELL ME SOMETHING? YOU COULD BE IN DANGER.
SIGH --FROM SANTOS?
SANTOS-- LAST NAME?
JUST A NICKNAME. REMINDED ME OF MY FATHER.
HE WOULDN'T HARM A HAIR ON MY HEAD...
I'D LIKE TO OFFER YOU POLICE PROTECTION. NOT NECESSARILY FROM HIM, BUT FROM WHOMEVER HE'S MIXED UP WITH.
I HOPE YOU'LL TAKE ADVANTAGE OF THE OFFER.

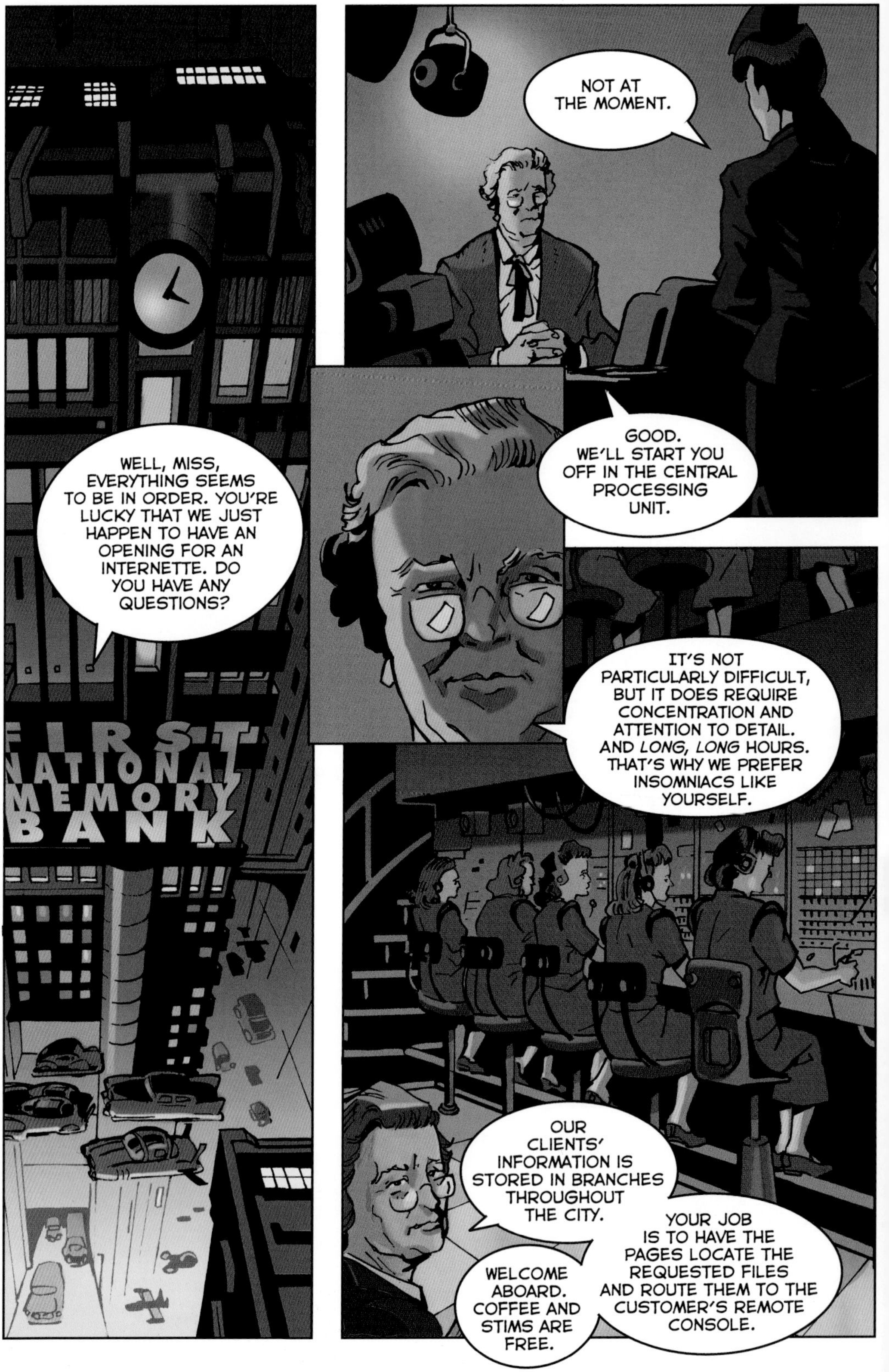
FIRST NATIONAL MEMORY BANK
WELL, MISS, EVERYTHING SEEMS TO BE IN ORDER. YOU'RE LUCKY THAT WE JUST HAPPEN TO HAVE AN OPENING FOR AN INTERNETTE. DO YOU HAVE ANY QUESTIONS?
NOT AT THE MOMENT.
GOOD. WE'LL START YOU OFF IN THE CENTRAL PROCESSING UNIT.
IT'S NOT PARTICULARLY DIFFICULT, BUT IT DOES REQUIRE CONCENTRATION AND ATTENTION TO DETAIL. AND *LONG, LONG* HOURS. THAT'S WHY WE PREFER INSOMNIACS LIKE YOURSELF.
OUR CLIENTS' INFORMATION IS STORED IN BRANCHES THROUGHOUT THE CITY.
YOUR JOB IS TO HAVE THE PAGES LOCATE THE REQUESTED FILES AND ROUTE THEM TO THE CUSTOMER'S REMOTE CONSOLE.
WELCOME ABOARD. COFFEE AND STIMS ARE FREE.

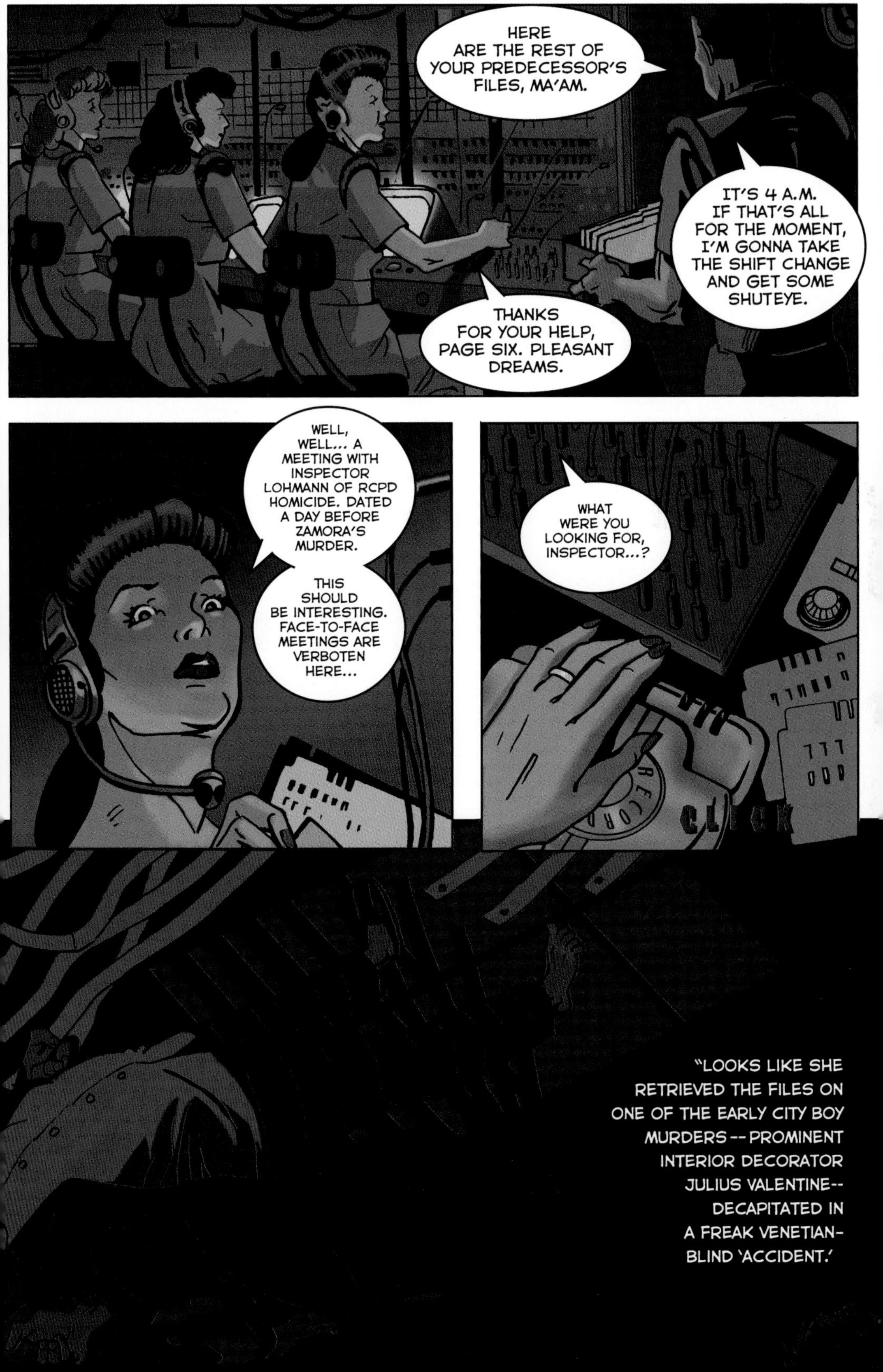
HERE ARE THE REST OF YOUR PREDECESSOR'S FILES, MA'AM.
IT'S 4 A.M. IF THAT'S ALL FOR THE MOMENT, I'M GONNA TAKE THE SHIFT CHANGE AND GET SOME SHUTEYE.
THANKS FOR YOUR HELP, PAGE SIX. PLEASANT DREAMS.
WELL, WELL... A MEETING WITH INSPECTOR LOHMANN OF RCPD HOMICIDE. DATED A DAY BEFORE ZAMORA'S MURDER.
THIS SHOULD BE INTERESTING. FACE-TO-FACE MEETINGS ARE VERBOTEN HERE...
WHAT WERE YOU LOOKING FOR, INSPECTOR...?
CLICK
"LOOKS LIKE SHE RETRIEVED THE FILES ON ONE OF THE EARLY CITY BOY MURDERS--PROMINENT INTERIOR DECORATOR JULIUS VALENTINE--DECAPITATED IN A FREAK VENETIAN-BLIND 'ACCIDENT.'

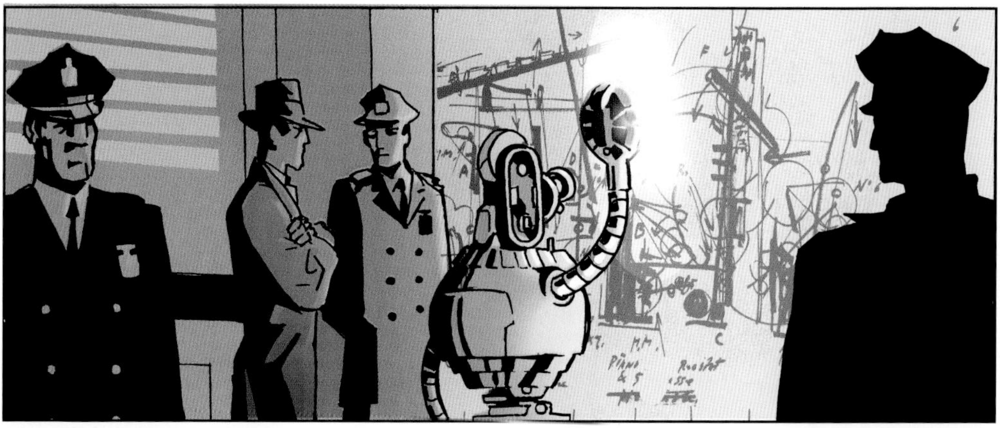

"THEY FOUND SOME ODD WRITING ON THE BOUDOIR WALL AT THE SCENE OF THE CRIME. NO ONE THOUGHT MUCH OF IT AT THE TIME. NO ONE EXCEPT INSPECTOR LOHMANN.

"IT APPEARED TO BE A POTPOURRI OF ARCHITECTURAL SKETCHES, FORMULAS, DIAGRAMS, NOTES--NEARLY INDECIPHERABLE BY ANYONE OTHER THAN THE ORIGINAL DESIGNERS OF RADIANT CITY.

"MOST OF THOSE DESIGNERS HAD WORKED WITH VALENTINE AT ONE TIME OR OTHER. THE QUESTION WAS WHICH HAD MADE THE NOCTURNAL VISIT.

"IT WAS DOUBTFUL THAT IT WAS VITRUVIAN ARCHITECT COLEMAN CROSS. THE VITRUVIANS WERE SLAVES TO SYMMETRY AND MATHEMATICAL ORDER. THE GOLDEN SECTION, THE FIBONACCI SEQUENCE, ETC.

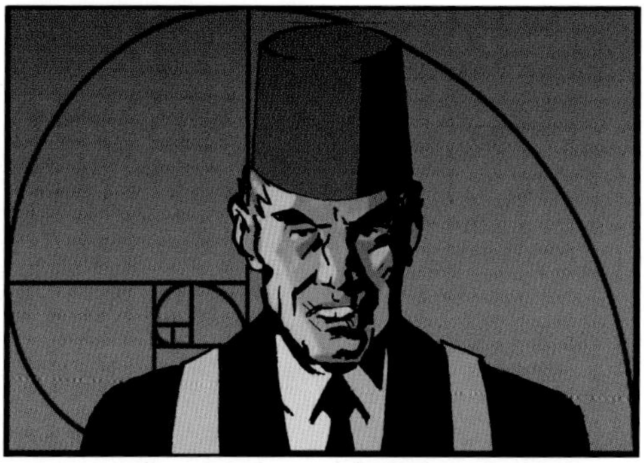

"THEY WERE PURISTS AND WOULD NEVER PERMIT THEIR ARITHMETIC TO BE MIXED WITH 'EXPERIMENTAL' GEOMETRY. BESIDES, CROSS HAD AN ALIBI. HE HAD BEEN ON THE VERGE OF A MATHEMATICAL BREAKTHROUGH, A UNIFIED EQUATION, WHEN THE ELUSIVE SOLUTION FINALLY DROVE HIM MAD. HE WAS COMMITTED TO THE ACADEMY.

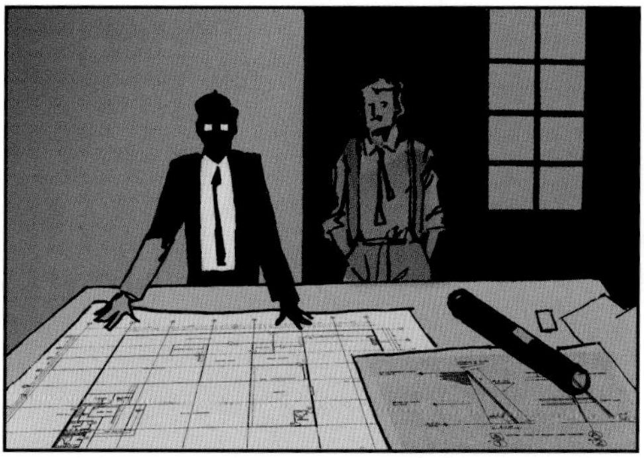

"THEN, OF COURSE THERE WERE EICHMANN AND REINHART-- THE CREATORS OF PSYCHETECTURE. THEY WERE OFTEN AT ODDS WITH ONE ANOTHER. EICHMANN'S DESIGNS RELIED ON ABSTRACT PRINCIPLES. ON SHAPE AND VOLUME, ON SUBTLE, ASYMMETRICAL, DISTORTED ELEMENTS. IT WAS A PASSIVE DESIGN IN DIRECT CONFLICT WITH THE VITRUVIANS.

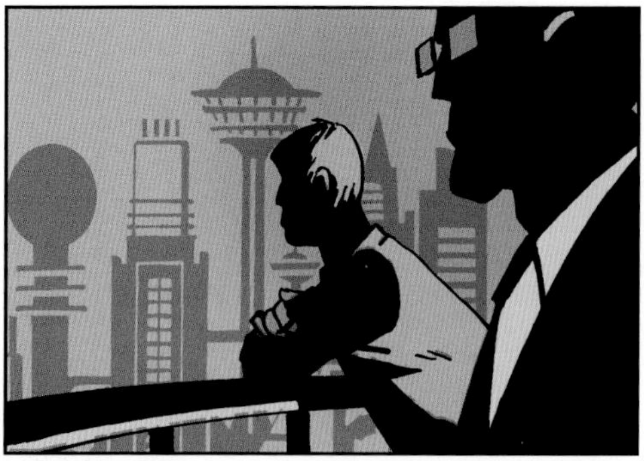

"REINHART, ON THE OTHER HAND, GOT HIS START BUILDING REVOLVING RESTAURANTS, RETRACTABLE ROOFS, AND SUCH. HE DEVELOPED A KINETIC THEORY AND DESIGNED BUILDINGS WHICH ROTATED, RAISED, AND LOWERED TO ALTER THE SKYLINE, AND MOVED ABOUT TO CHANGE THEIR FUNCTION AND EVEN THEIR MOOD-ALTERING CHARACTERISTICS.

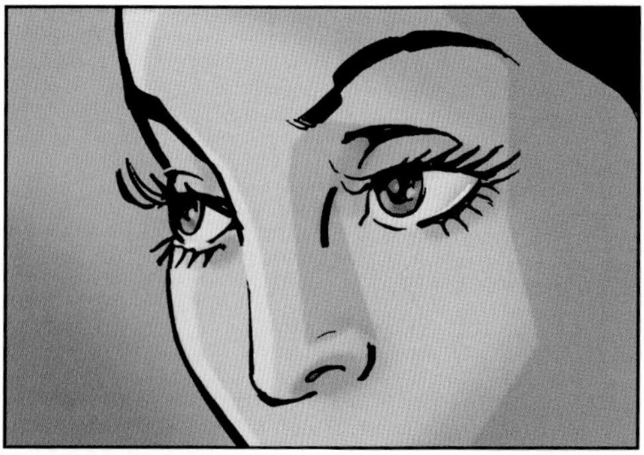

"NOSTRAND WAS THE ENGINEER BEHIND THE GIANT, SUBTERRANEAN ENGINES THAT FACILITATED REINHART'S DESIGNS. AND WHEN HE DISAPPEARED, THE ENGINES CEASED FUNCTIONING. ALL DIED OR DISAPPEARED IN THE PAST TWO DECADES. BUT WHAT IS THEIR CONNECTION TO CITY BOY AND ZAMORA? AND WAS OUR LITTLE INTERNETTE KILLED BECAUSE SHE HAD OPENED THIS PANDORA'S BOX--?"

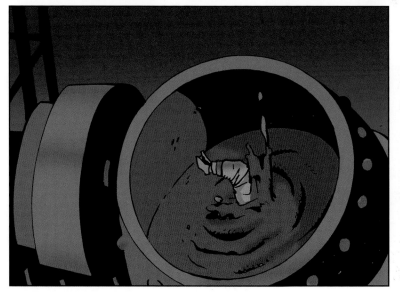

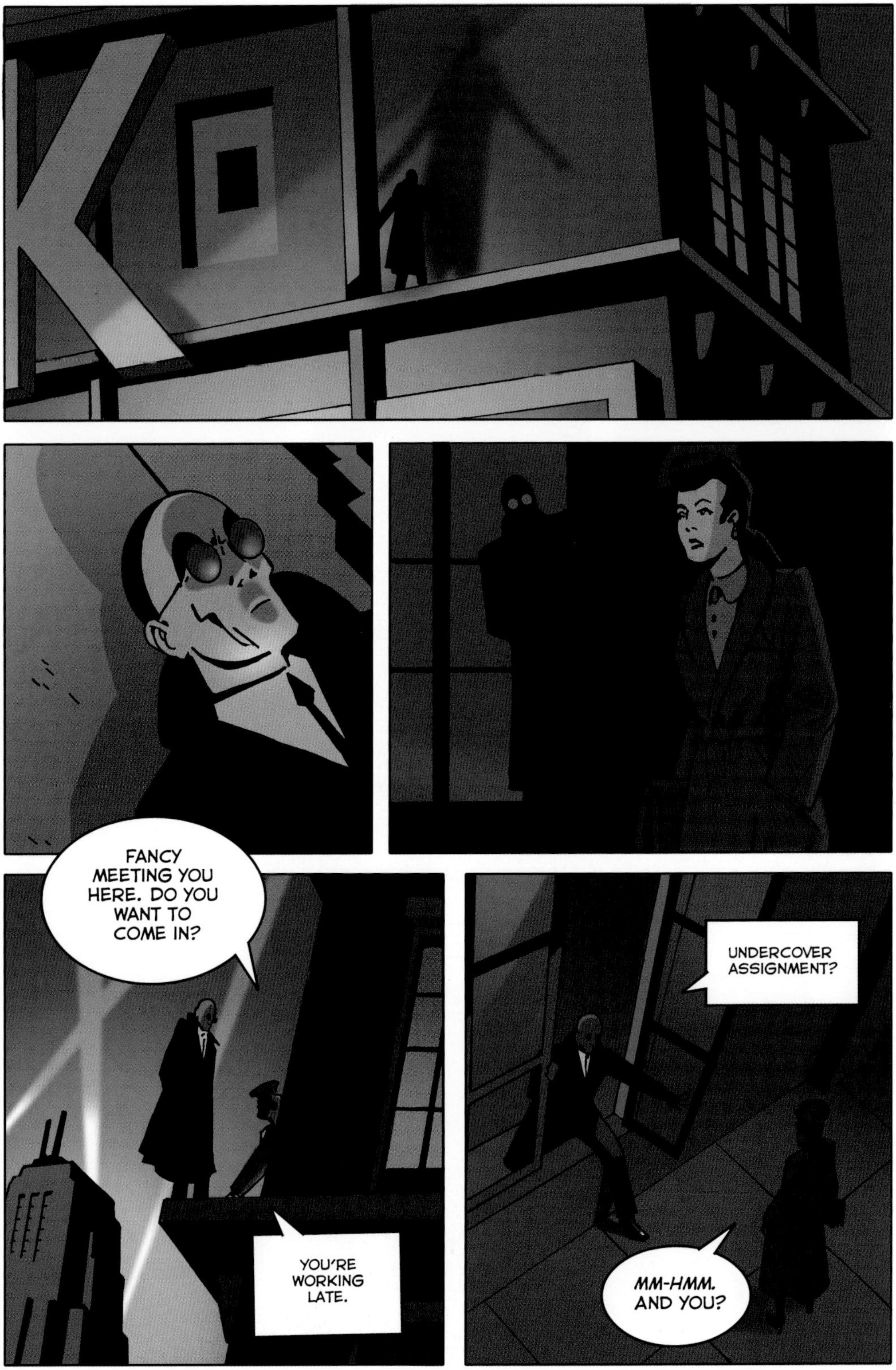
FANCY MEETING YOU HERE. DO YOU WANT TO COME IN?
YOU'RE WORKING LATE.
UNDERCOVER ASSIGNMENT?
MM-HMM. AND YOU?

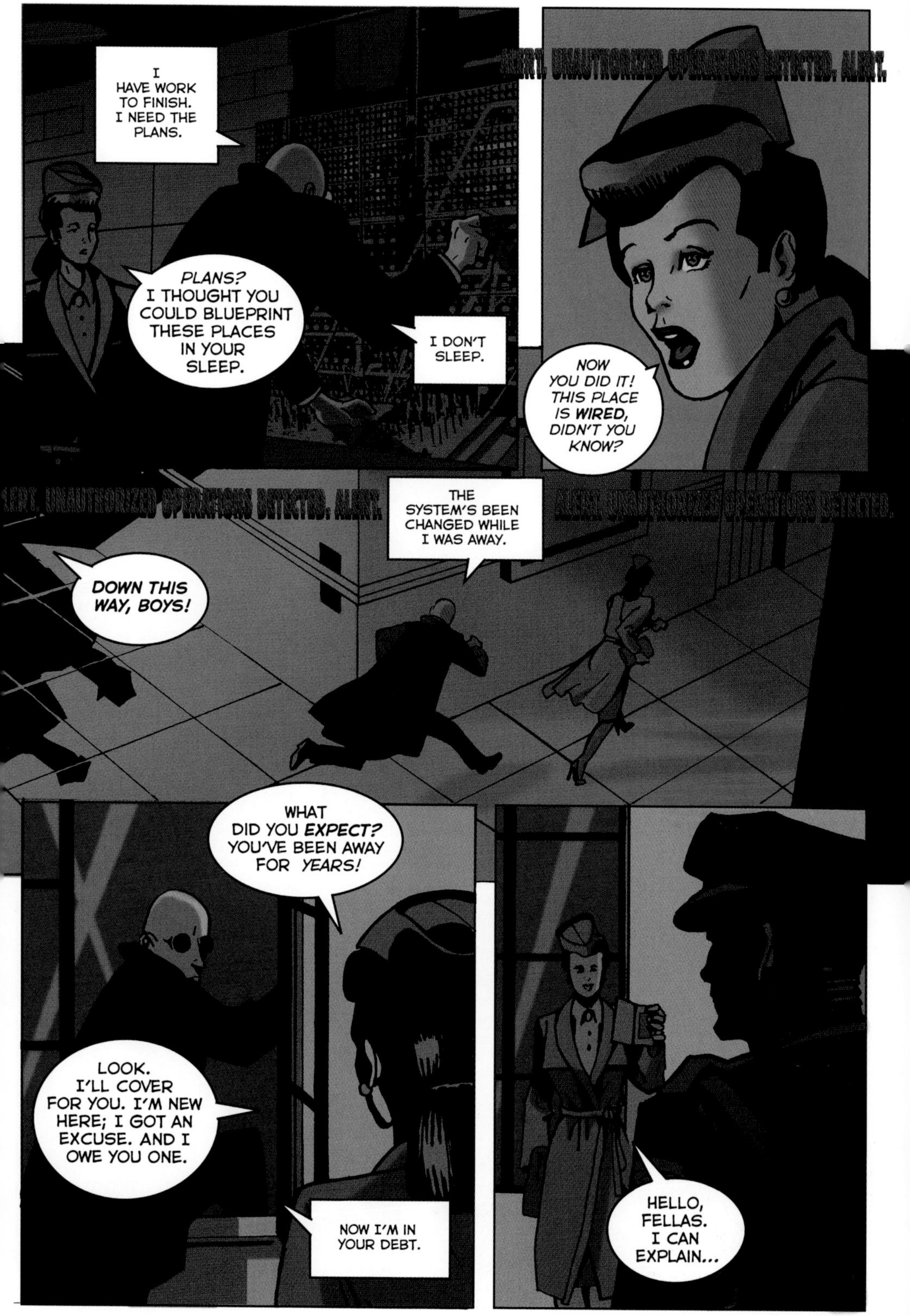
I HAVE WORK TO FINISH. I NEED THE PLANS.
PLANS? I THOUGHT YOU COULD BLUEPRINT THESE PLACES IN YOUR SLEEP.
I DON'T SLEEP.
ALERT. UNAUTHORIZED OPERATIONS DETECTED. ALERT.
NOW YOU DID IT! THIS PLACE IS WIRED, DIDN'T YOU KNOW?
LERT. UNAUTHORIZED OPERATIONS DETECTED. ALERT.
THE SYSTEM'S BEEN CHANGED WHILE I WAS AWAY.
ALERT. UNAUTHORIZED OPERATIONS DETECTED.
DOWN THIS WAY, BOYS!
WHAT DID YOU EXPECT? YOU'VE BEEN AWAY FOR YEARS!
LOOK. I'LL COVER FOR YOU. I'M NEW HERE; I GOT AN EXCUSE. AND I OWE YOU ONE.
NOW I'M IN YOUR DEBT.
HELLO, FELLAS. I CAN EXPLAIN...

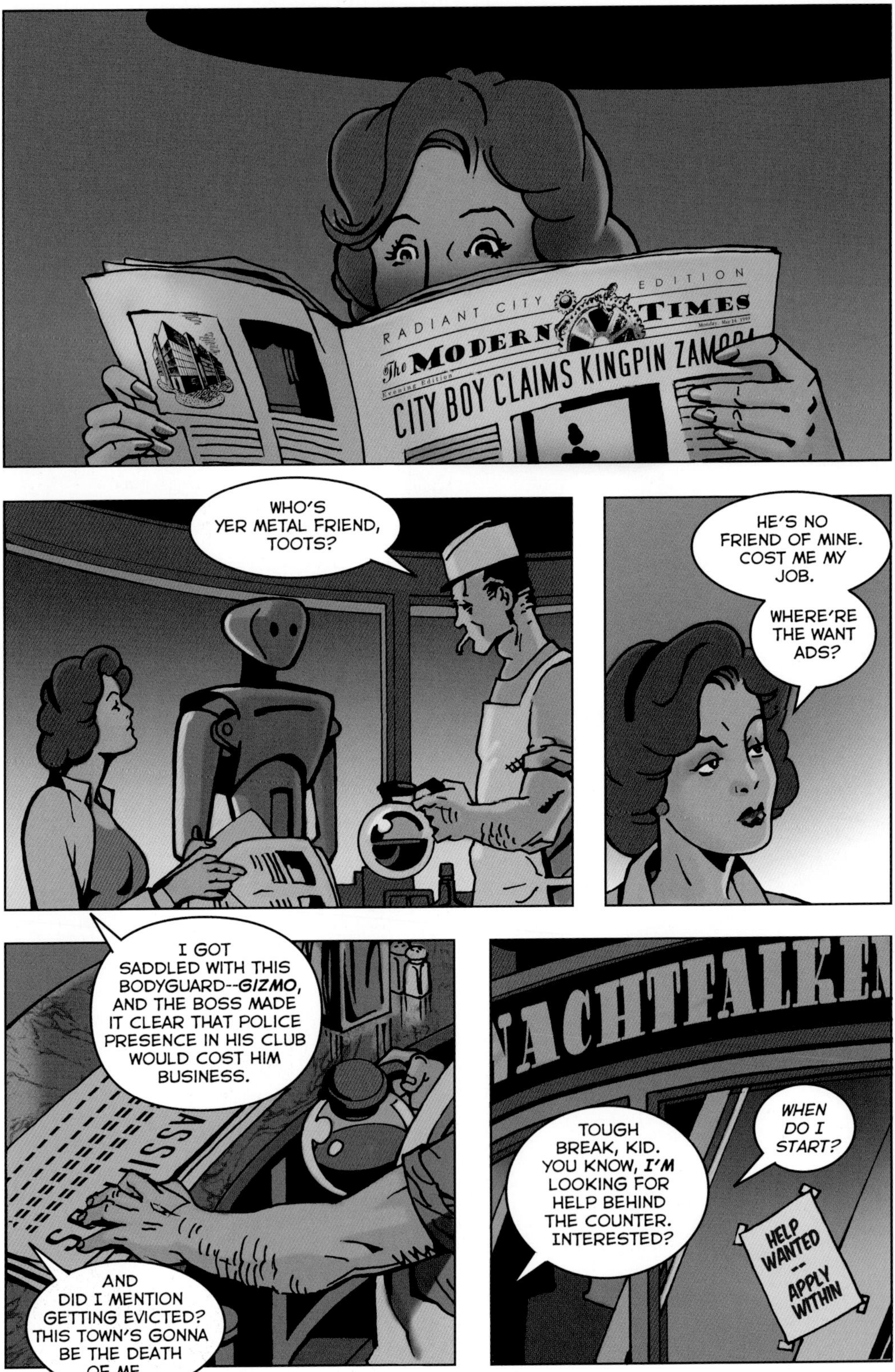
RADIANT CITY EDITION
The MODERN TIMES
Evening Edition
CITY BOY CLAIMS KINGPIN ZAM
WHO'S YER METAL FRIEND, TOOTS?
HE'S NO FRIEND OF MINE. COST ME MY JOB.
WHERE'RE THE WANT ADS?
I GOT SADDLED WITH THIS BODYGUARD--**GIZMO**, AND THE BOSS MADE IT CLEAR THAT POLICE PRESENCE IN HIS CLUB WOULD COST HIM BUSINESS.
AND DID I MENTION GETTING EVICTED? THIS TOWN'S GONNA BE THE DEATH OF ME...
NACHTFALKE
TOUGH BREAK, KID. YOU KNOW, ***I'M*** LOOKING FOR HELP BEHIND THE COUNTER. INTERESTED?
WHEN DO I START?
HELP WANTED -- APPLY WITHIN

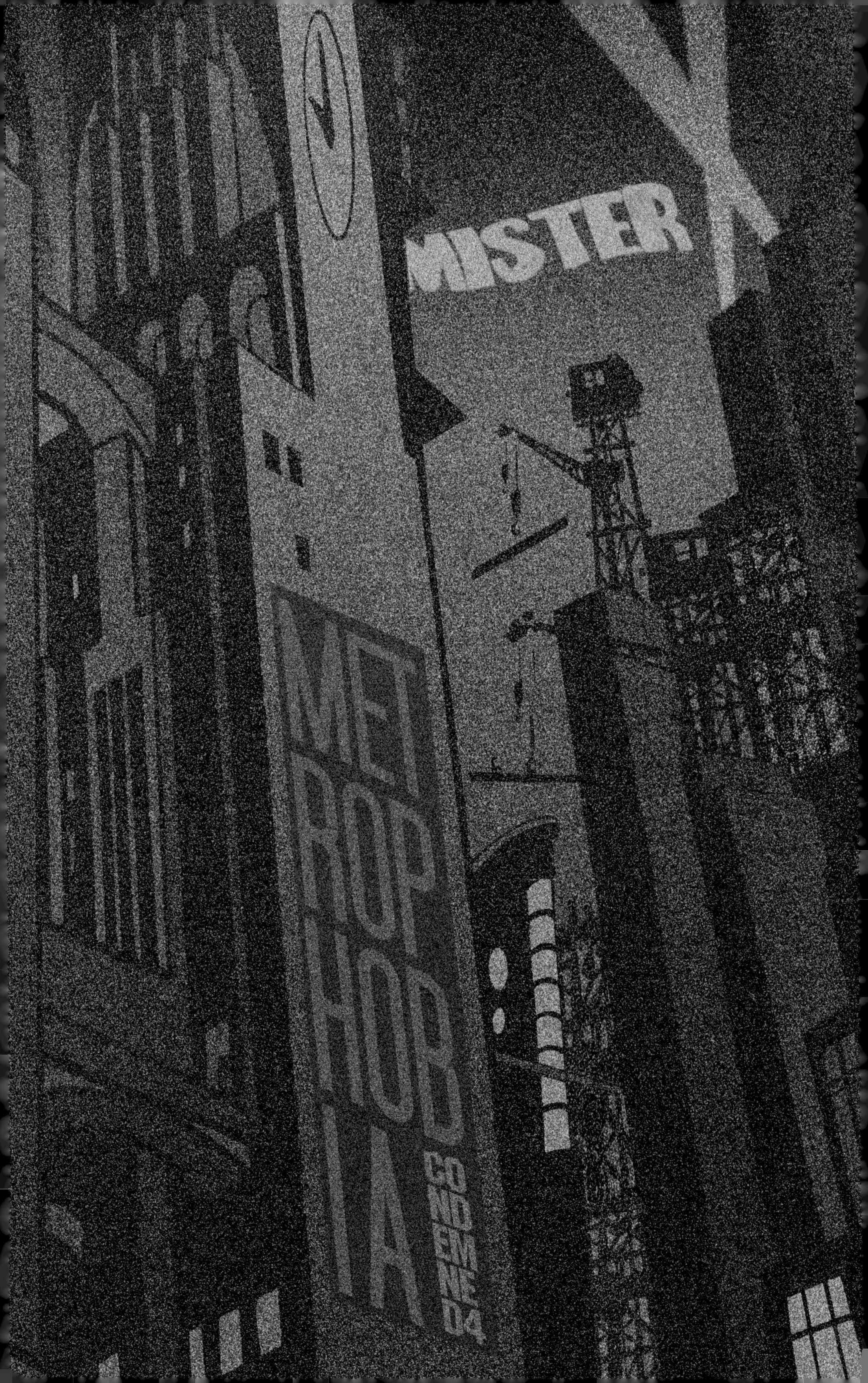
MISTER X
METROPHOBIA
CONDEMNED 04

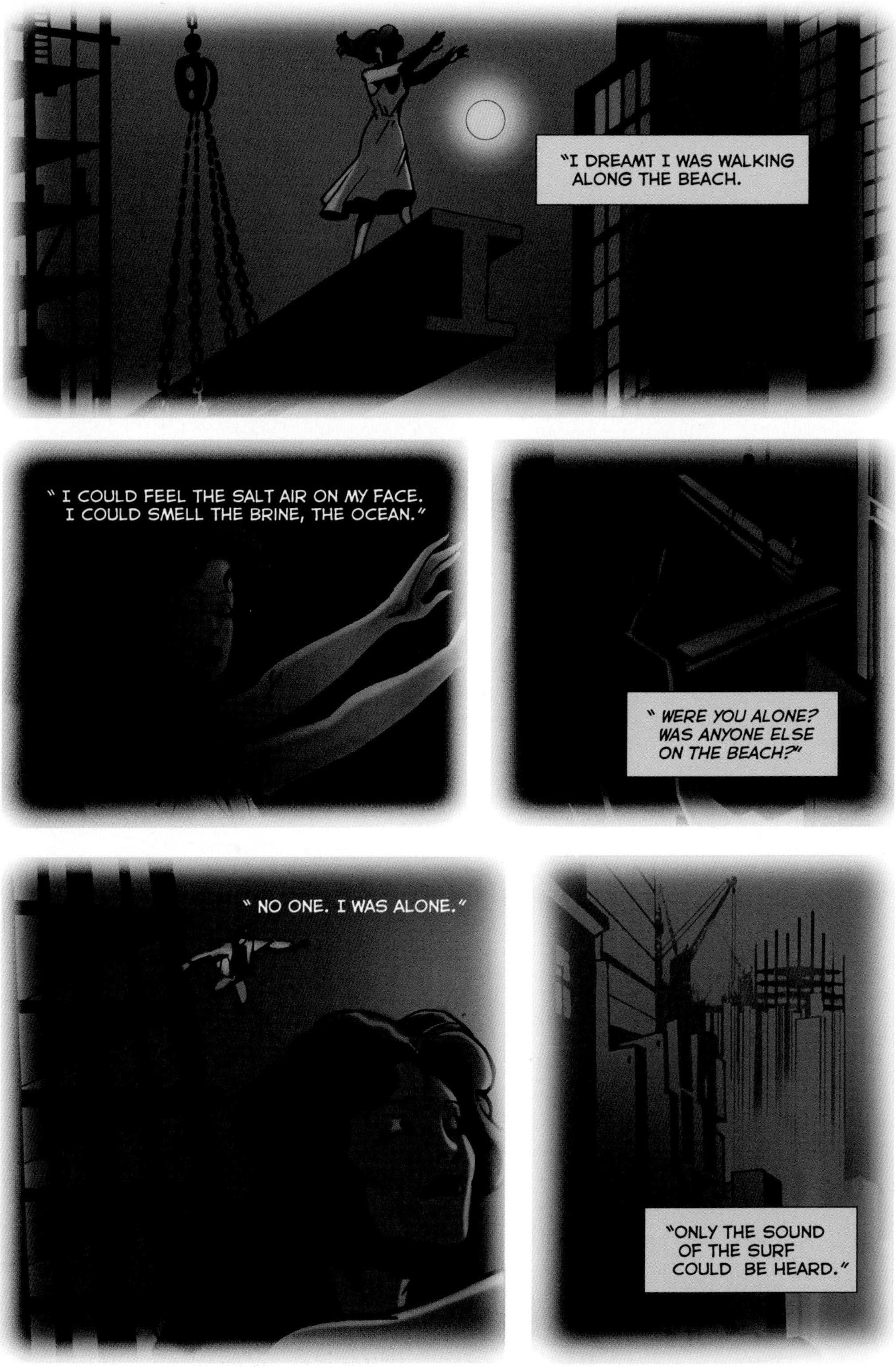
"I DREAMT I WAS WALKING ALONG THE BEACH.
" I COULD FEEL THE SALT AIR ON MY FACE. I COULD SMELL THE BRINE, THE OCEAN."
" WERE YOU ALONE? WAS ANYONE ELSE ON THE BEACH?"
" NO ONE. I WAS ALONE."
"ONLY THE SOUND OF THE SURF COULD BE HEARD."

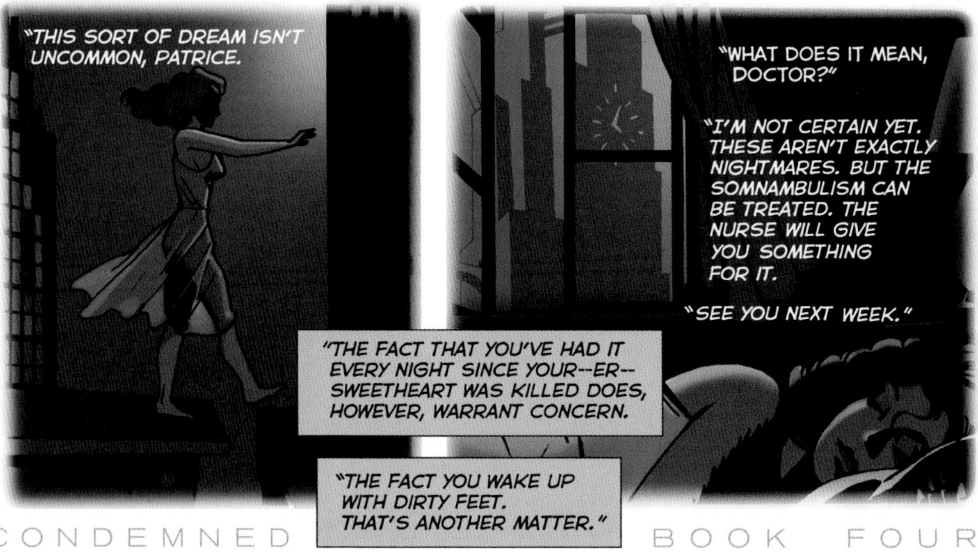
"THIS SORT OF DREAM ISN'T UNCOMMON, PATRICE.
"THE FACT THAT YOU'VE HAD IT EVERY NIGHT SINCE YOUR--ER--SWEETHEART WAS KILLED DOES, HOWEVER, WARRANT CONCERN.
"THE FACT YOU WAKE UP WITH DIRTY FEET. THAT'S ANOTHER MATTER."
"WHAT DOES IT MEAN, DOCTOR?"
"I'M NOT CERTAIN YET. THESE AREN'T EXACTLY NIGHTMARES. BUT THE SOMNAMBULISM CAN BE TREATED. THE NURSE WILL GIVE YOU SOMETHING FOR IT.
"SEE YOU NEXT WEEK."

CONDEMNED BOOK FOUR

metrophobia

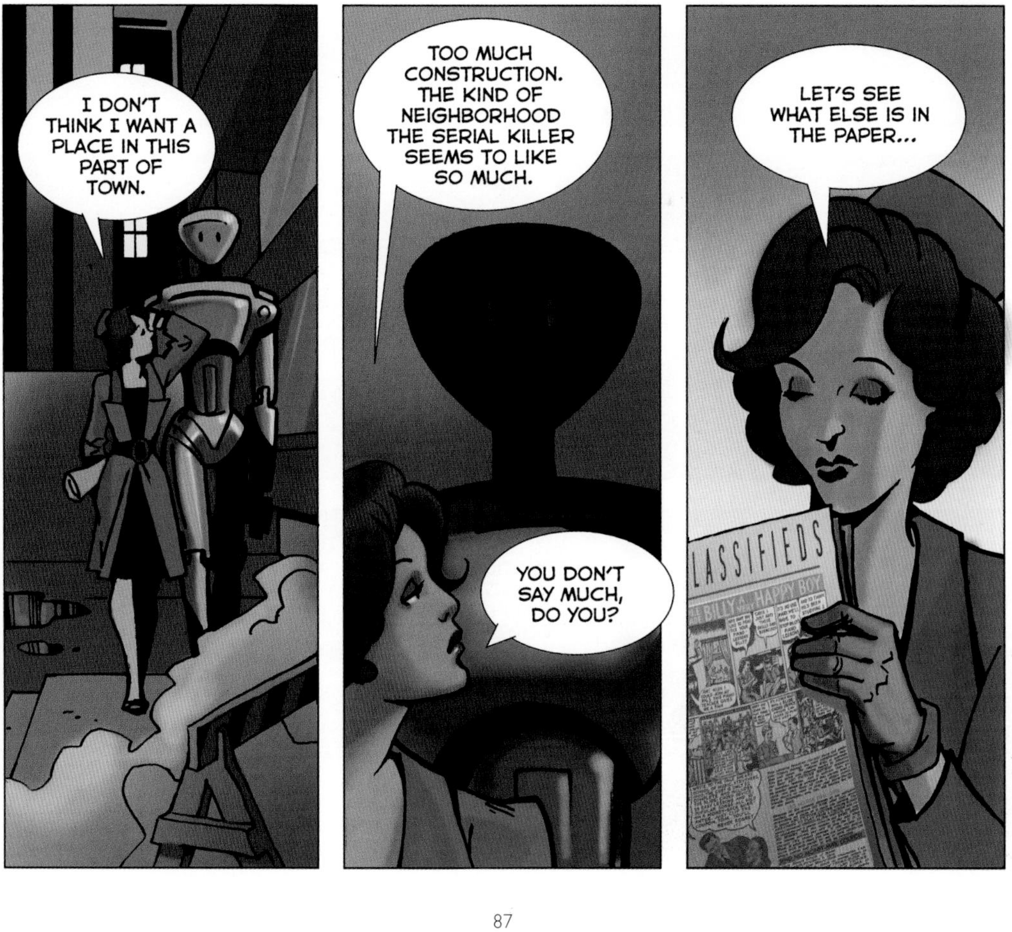
I DON'T THINK I WANT A PLACE IN THIS PART OF TOWN.
TOO MUCH CONSTRUCTION. THE KIND OF NEIGHBORHOOD THE SERIAL KILLER SEEMS TO LIKE SO MUCH.
YOU DON'T SAY MUCH, DO YOU?
LET'S SEE WHAT ELSE IS IN THE PAPER...
LASSIFIEDS

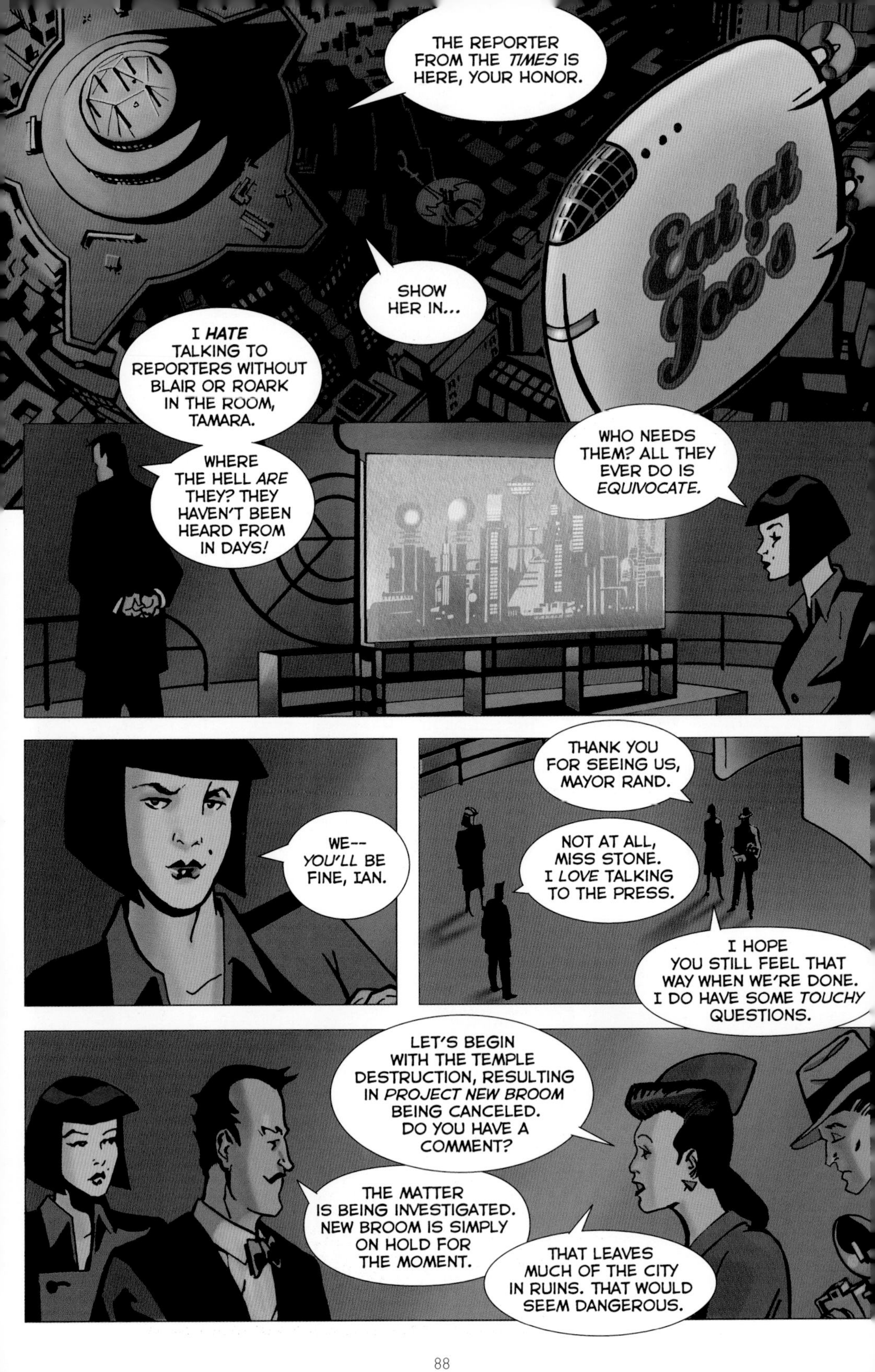
THE REPORTER FROM THE *TIMES* IS HERE, YOUR HONOR.
SHOW HER IN...
Eat at Joe's
I ***HATE*** TALKING TO REPORTERS WITHOUT BLAIR OR ROARK IN THE ROOM, TAMARA.
WHERE THE HELL *ARE* THEY? THEY HAVEN'T BEEN HEARD FROM IN DAYS!
WHO NEEDS THEM? ALL THEY EVER DO IS *EQUIVOCATE.*
WE-- *YOU'LL* BE FINE, IAN.
THANK YOU FOR SEEING US, MAYOR RAND.
NOT AT ALL, MISS STONE. I *LOVE* TALKING TO THE PRESS.
I HOPE YOU STILL FEEL THAT WAY WHEN WE'RE DONE. I DO HAVE SOME *TOUCHY* QUESTIONS.
LET'S BEGIN WITH THE TEMPLE DESTRUCTION, RESULTING IN *PROJECT NEW BROOM* BEING CANCELED. DO YOU HAVE A COMMENT?
THE MATTER IS BEING INVESTIGATED. NEW BROOM IS SIMPLY ON HOLD FOR THE MOMENT.
THAT LEAVES MUCH OF THE CITY IN RUINS. THAT WOULD SEEM DANGEROUS.

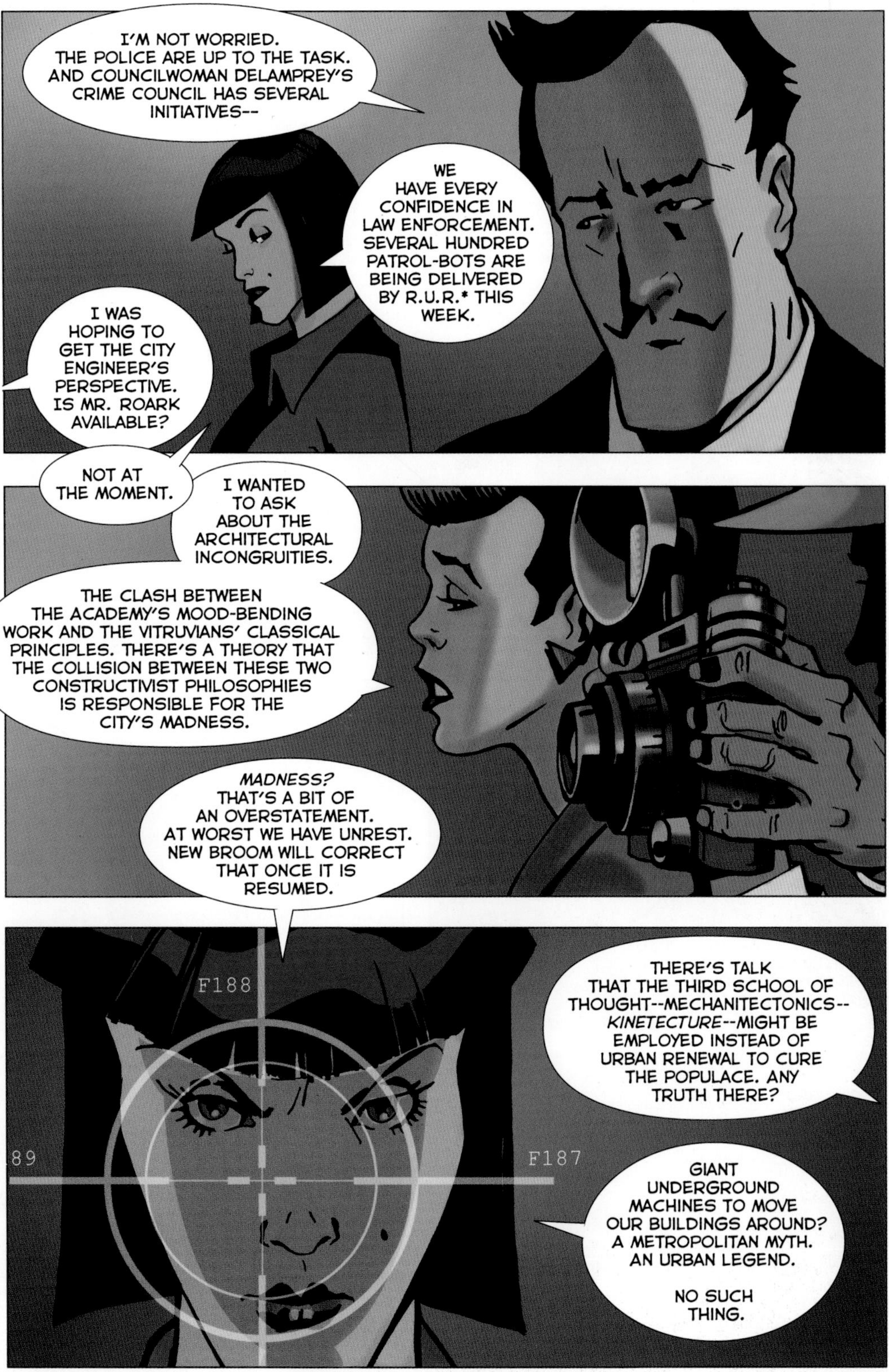
I'M NOT WORRIED. THE POLICE ARE UP TO THE TASK. AND COUNCILWOMAN DELAMPREY'S CRIME COUNCIL HAS SEVERAL INITIATIVES--
WE HAVE EVERY CONFIDENCE IN LAW ENFORCEMENT. SEVERAL HUNDRED PATROL-BOTS ARE BEING DELIVERED BY R.U.R.* THIS WEEK.
I WAS HOPING TO GET THE CITY ENGINEER'S PERSPECTIVE. IS MR. ROARK AVAILABLE?
NOT AT THE MOMENT.
I WANTED TO ASK ABOUT THE ARCHITECTURAL INCONGRUITIES.
THE CLASH BETWEEN THE ACADEMY'S MOOD-BENDING WORK AND THE VITRUVIANS' CLASSICAL PRINCIPLES. THERE'S A THEORY THAT THE COLLISION BETWEEN THESE TWO CONSTRUCTIVIST PHILOSOPHIES IS RESPONSIBLE FOR THE CITY'S MADNESS.
MADNESS? THAT'S A BIT OF AN OVERSTATEMENT. AT WORST WE HAVE UNREST. NEW BROOM WILL CORRECT THAT ONCE IT IS RESUMED.
F188
89
F187
THERE'S TALK THAT THE THIRD SCHOOL OF THOUGHT--MECHANITECTONICS--*KINETECTURE*--MIGHT BE EMPLOYED INSTEAD OF URBAN RENEWAL TO CURE THE POPULACE. ANY TRUTH THERE?
GIANT UNDERGROUND MACHINES TO MOVE OUR BUILDINGS AROUND? A METROPOLITAN MYTH. AN URBAN LEGEND.
NO SUCH THING.

** **R.U.R.**- ROSSUM'S UNIVERSAL ROBOTS. THE WORLD'S LARGEST MANUFACTURER OF MECHANICAL MEN.*

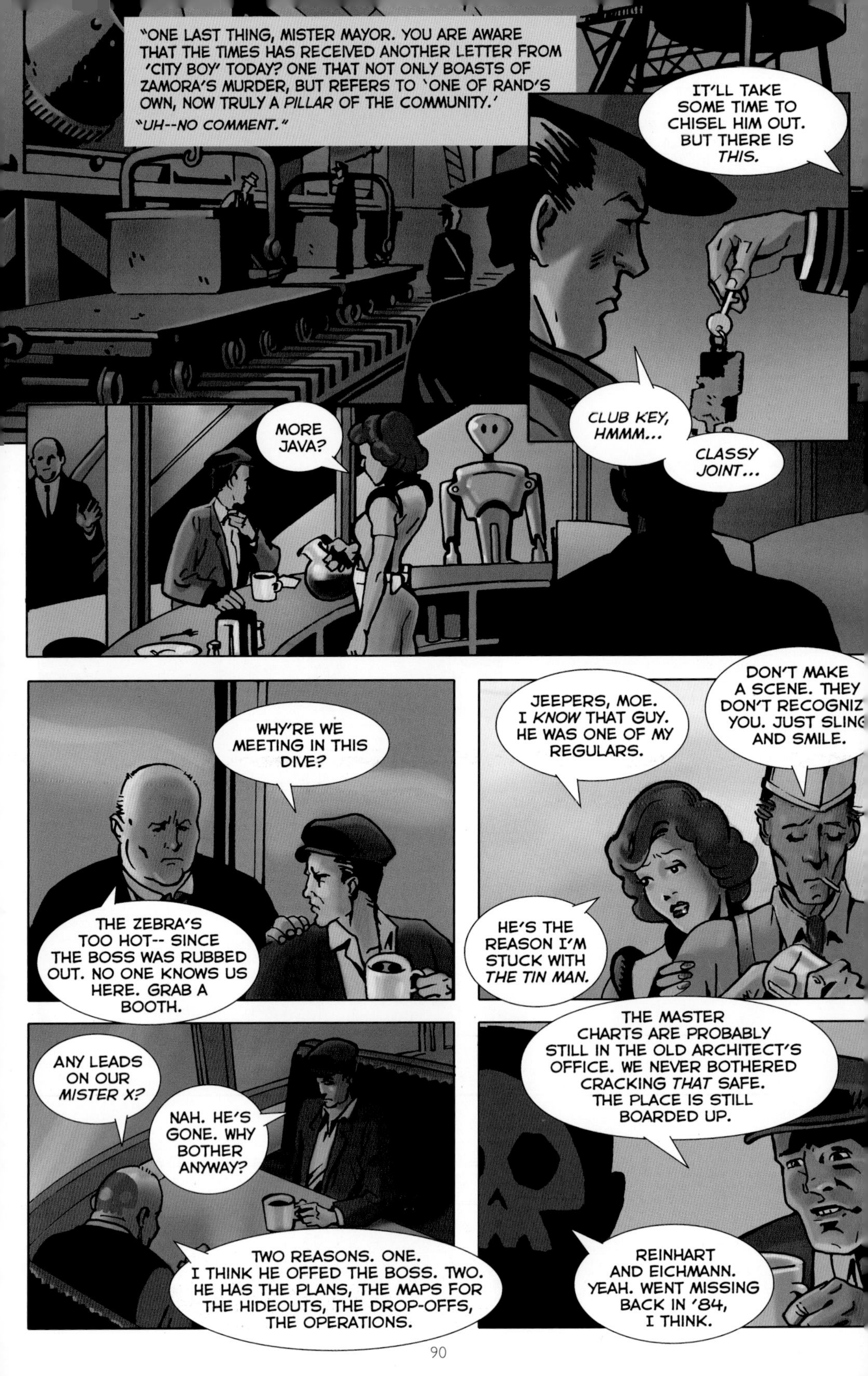

"ONE LAST THING, MISTER MAYOR. YOU ARE AWARE THAT THE TIMES HAS RECEIVED ANOTHER LETTER FROM 'CITY BOY' TODAY? ONE THAT NOT ONLY BOASTS OF ZAMORA'S MURDER, BUT REFERS TO 'ONE OF RAND'S OWN, NOW TRULY A *PILLAR* OF THE COMMUNITY.'
"UH--NO COMMENT."
IT'LL TAKE SOME TIME TO CHISEL HIM OUT. BUT THERE IS *THIS.*
CLUB KEY, HMMM...
CLASSY JOINT...
MORE JAVA?
WHY'RE WE MEETING IN THIS DIVE?
THE ZEBRA'S TOO HOT-- SINCE THE BOSS WAS RUBBED OUT. NO ONE KNOWS US HERE. GRAB A BOOTH.
JEEPERS, MOE. I *KNOW* THAT GUY. HE WAS ONE OF MY REGULARS.
DON'T MAKE A SCENE. THEY DON'T RECOGNIZ YOU. JUST SLING AND SMILE.
HE'S THE REASON I'M STUCK WITH *THE TIN MAN.*
ANY LEADS ON OUR *MISTER X?*
NAH. HE'S GONE. WHY BOTHER ANYWAY?
TWO REASONS. ONE. I THINK HE OFFED THE BOSS. TWO. HE HAS THE PLANS, THE MAPS FOR THE HIDEOUTS, THE DROP-OFFS, THE OPERATIONS.
THE MASTER CHARTS ARE PROBABLY STILL IN THE OLD ARCHITECT'S OFFICE. WE NEVER BOTHERED CRACKING *THAT* SAFE. THE PLACE IS STILL BOARDED UP.
REINHART AND EICHMANN. YEAH. WENT MISSING BACK IN '84, I THINK.

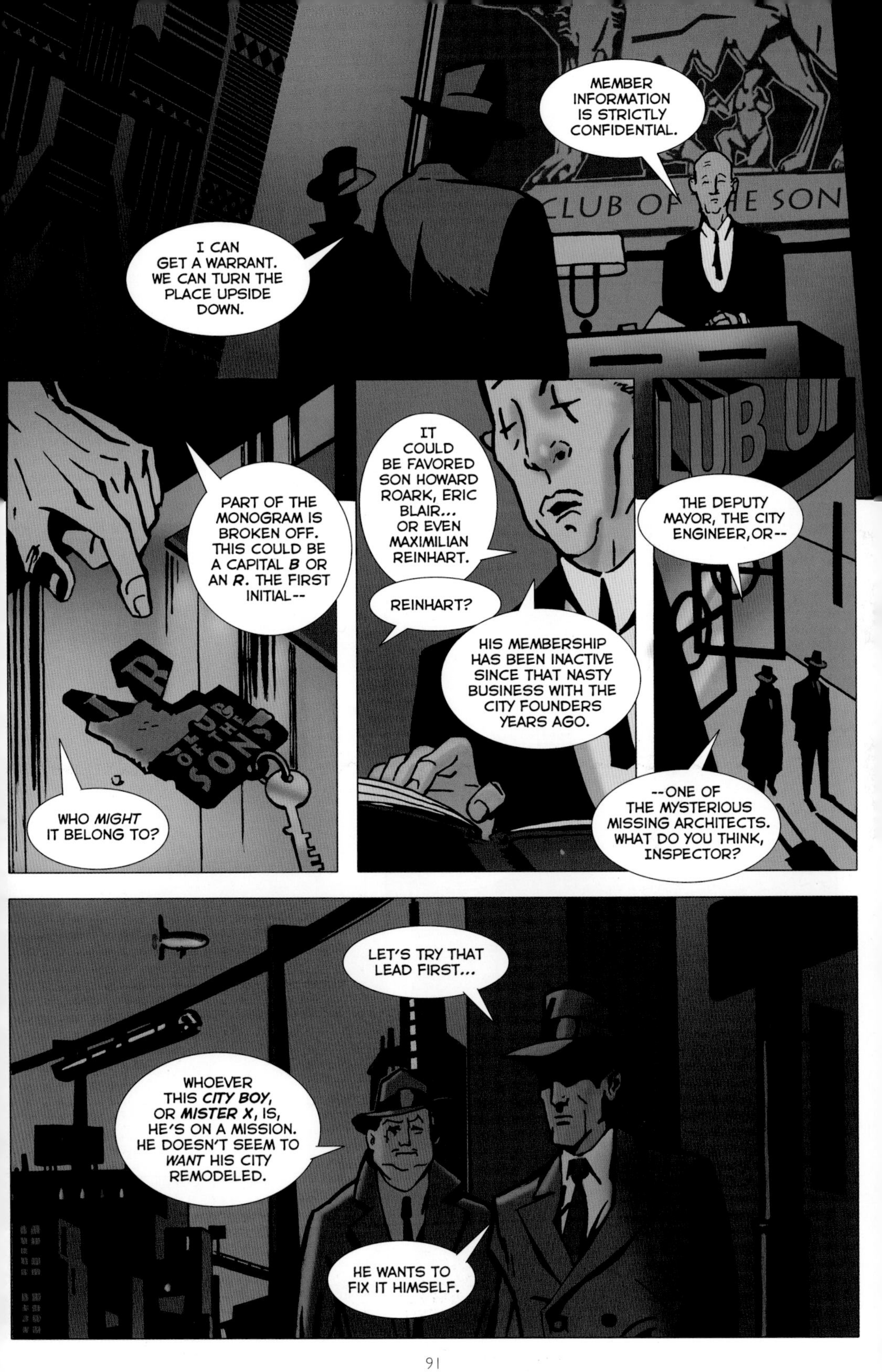
MEMBER INFORMATION IS STRICTLY CONFIDENTIAL.
CLUB OF THE SON
I CAN GET A WARRANT. WE CAN TURN THE PLACE UPSIDE DOWN.
PART OF THE MONOGRAM IS BROKEN OFF. THIS COULD BE A CAPITAL *B* OR AN *R*. THE FIRST INITIAL--
WHO *MIGHT* IT BELONG TO?
IT COULD BE FAVORED SON HOWARD ROARK, ERIC BLAIR... OR EVEN MAXIMILIAN REINHART.
REINHART?
HIS MEMBERSHIP HAS BEEN INACTIVE SINCE THAT NASTY BUSINESS WITH THE CITY FOUNDERS YEARS AGO.
THE DEPUTY MAYOR, THE CITY ENGINEER, OR--
--ONE OF THE MYSTERIOUS MISSING ARCHITECTS. WHAT DO YOU THINK, INSPECTOR?
LET'S TRY THAT LEAD FIRST...
WHOEVER THIS *CITY BOY*, OR *MISTER X*, IS, HE'S ON A MISSION. HE DOESN'T SEEM TO *WANT* HIS CITY REMODELED.
HE WANTS TO FIX IT HIMSELF.

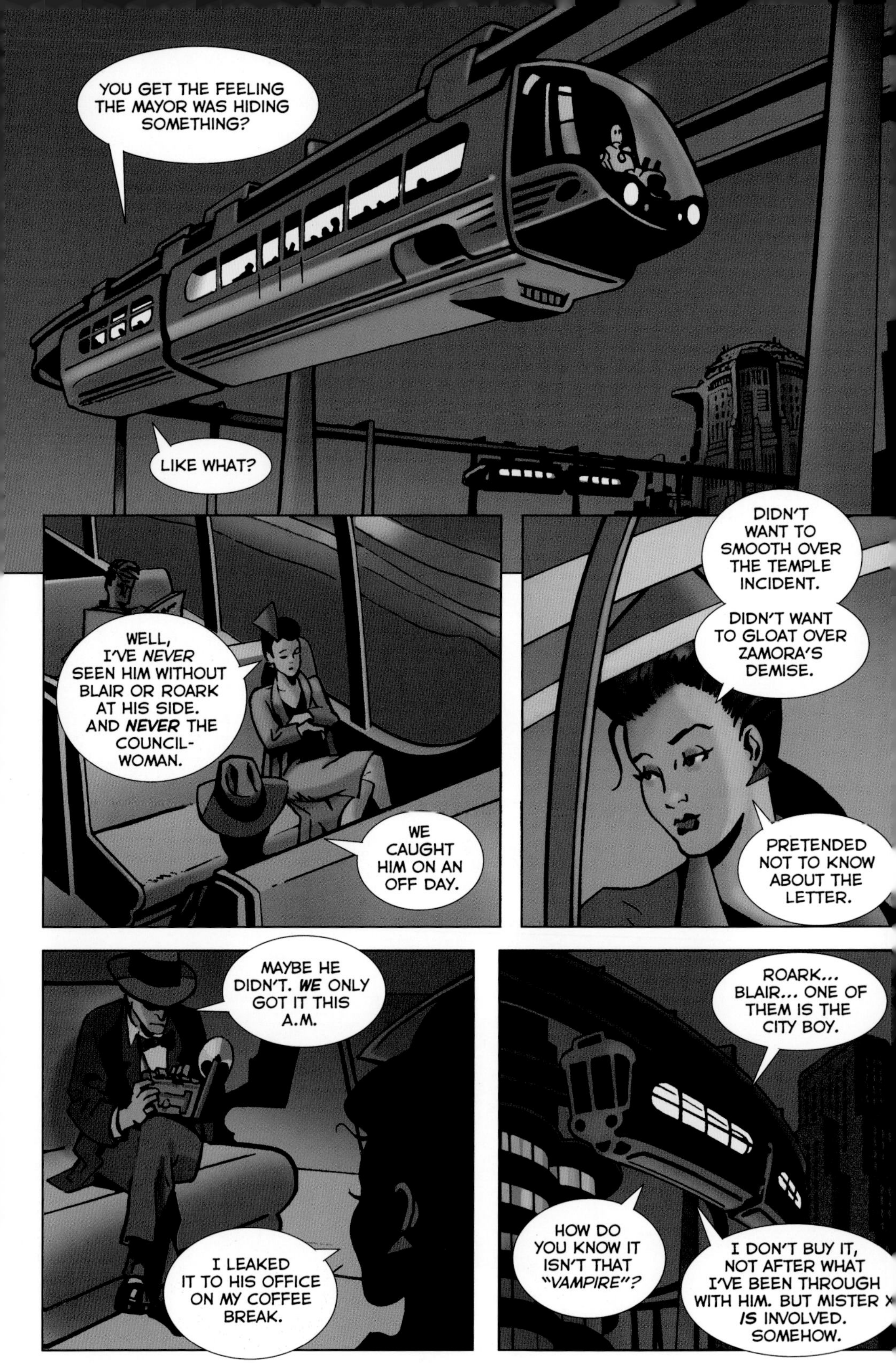
YOU GET THE FEELING THE MAYOR WAS HIDING SOMETHING?
LIKE WHAT?
WELL, I'VE *NEVER* SEEN HIM WITHOUT BLAIR OR ROARK AT HIS SIDE. AND *NEVER* THE COUNCIL-WOMAN.
WE CAUGHT HIM ON AN OFF DAY.
DIDN'T WANT TO SMOOTH OVER THE TEMPLE INCIDENT.
DIDN'T WANT TO GLOAT OVER ZAMORA'S DEMISE.
PRETENDED NOT TO KNOW ABOUT THE LETTER.
MAYBE HE DIDN'T. *WE* ONLY GOT IT THIS A.M.
I LEAKED IT TO HIS OFFICE ON MY COFFEE BREAK.
ROARK... BLAIR... ONE OF THEM IS THE CITY BOY.
HOW DO YOU KNOW IT ISN'T THAT *"VAMPIRE"*?
I DON'T BUY IT, NOT AFTER WHAT I'VE BEEN THROUGH WITH HIM. BUT MISTER X *IS* INVOLVED. SOMEHOW.

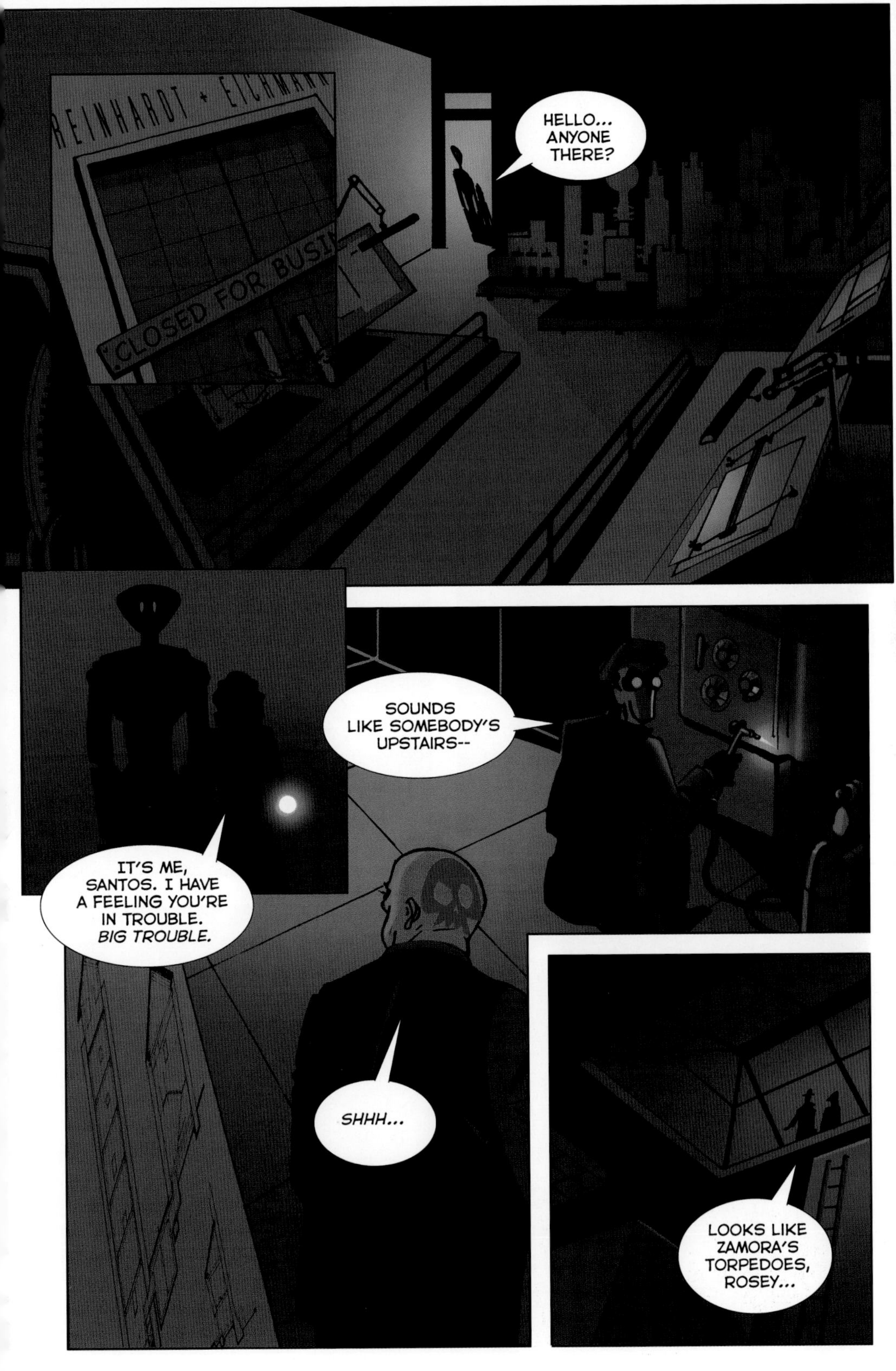
REINHARDT + EICHMANN
CLOSED FOR BUSI
HELLO... ANYONE THERE?
SOUNDS LIKE SOMEBODY'S UPSTAIRS--
IT'S ME, SANTOS. I HAVE A FEELING YOU'RE IN TROUBLE. *BIG TROUBLE.*
SHHH...
LOOKS LIKE ZAMORA'S TORPEDOES, ROSEY...

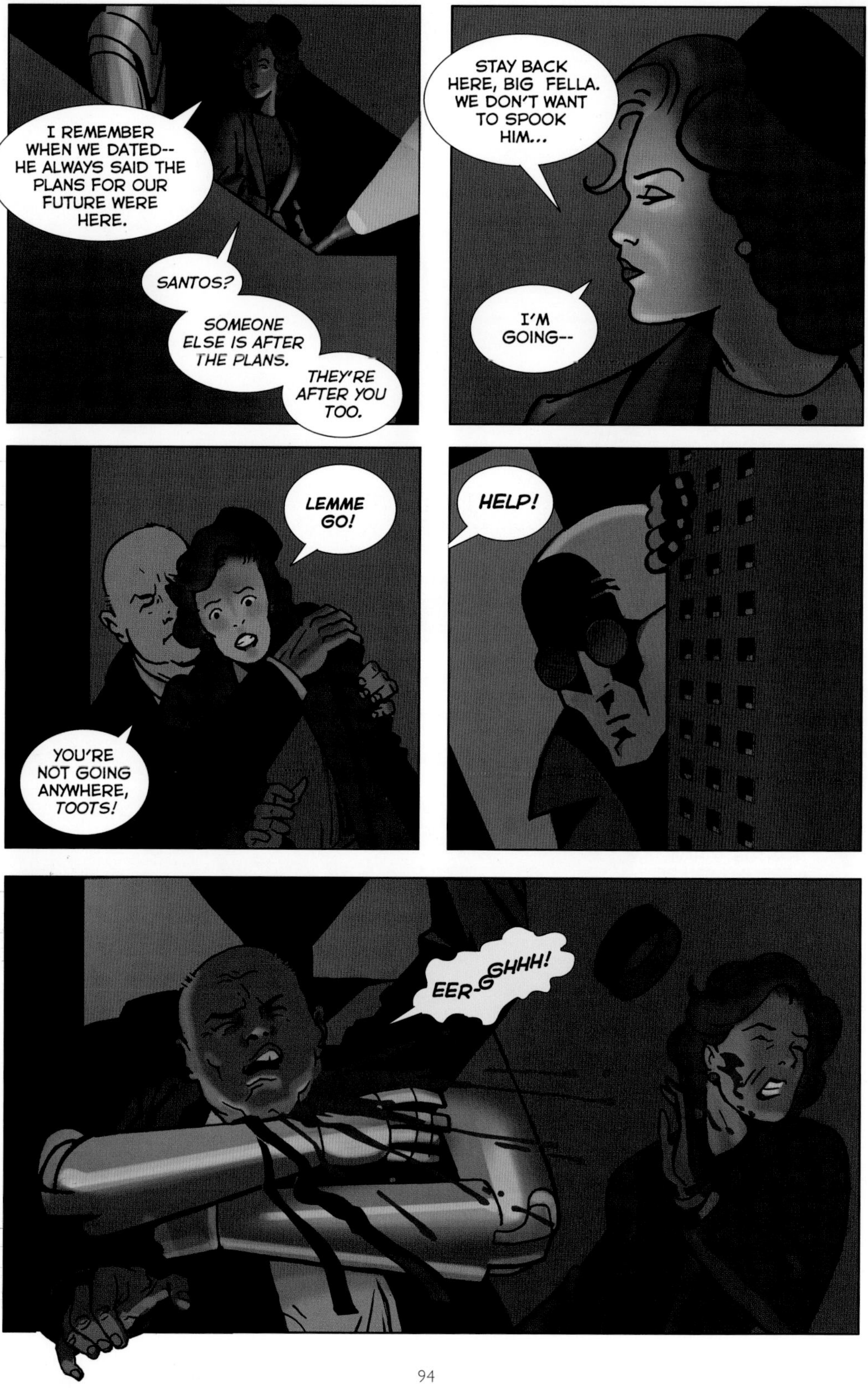
I REMEMBER WHEN WE DATED-- HE ALWAYS SAID THE PLANS FOR OUR FUTURE WERE HERE.
SANTOS?
SOMEONE ELSE IS AFTER THE PLANS.
THEY'RE AFTER YOU TOO.
STAY BACK HERE, BIG FELLA. WE DON'T WANT TO SPOOK HIM...
I'M GOING--
LEMME GO!
YOU'RE NOT GOING ANYWHERE, TOOTS!
HELP!
EER-GGHHH!

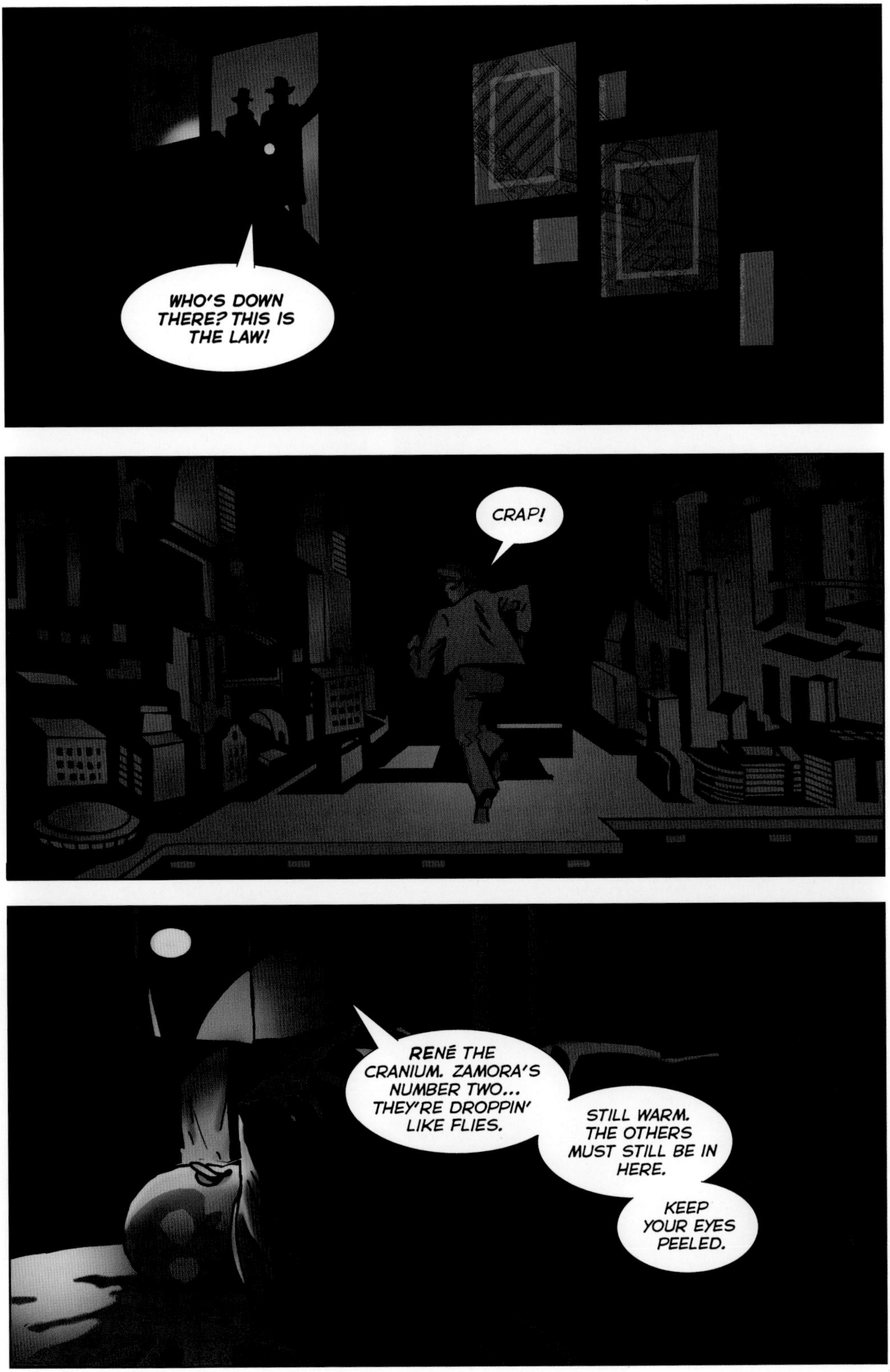
WHO'S DOWN THERE? THIS IS THE LAW!
CRAP!
RENÉ THE CRANIUM. ZAMORA'S NUMBER TWO... THEY'RE DROPPIN' LIKE FLIES.
STILL WARM. THE OTHERS MUST STILL BE IN HERE.
KEEP YOUR EYES PEELED.

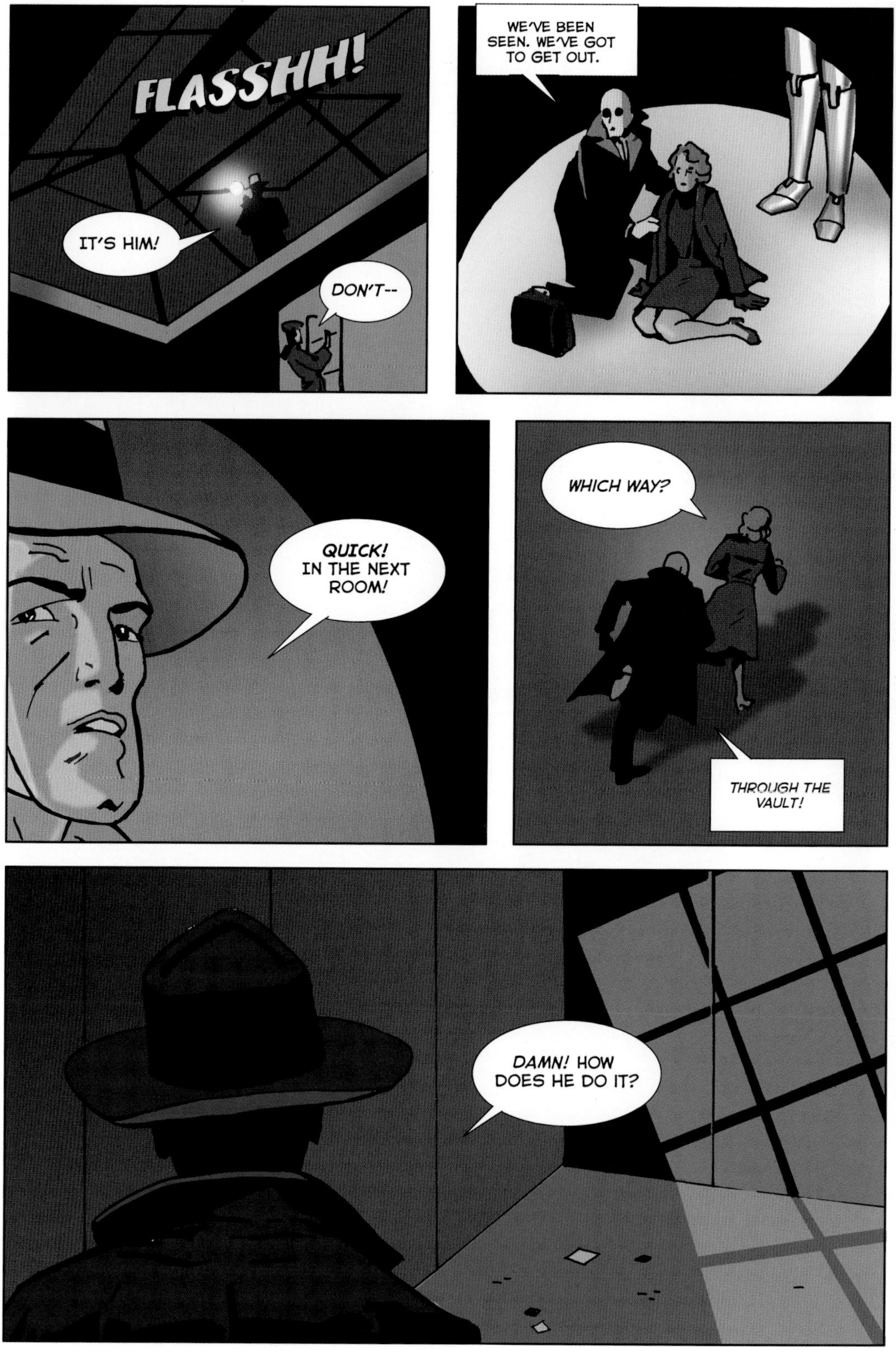
FLASSHH!
IT'S HIM!
DON'T--
WE'VE BEEN SEEN. WE'VE GOT TO GET OUT.
QUICK! IN THE NEXT ROOM!
WHICH WAY?
THROUGH THE VAULT!
DAMN! HOW DOES HE DO IT?

WELL, WELL. MISS STONE. WHAT ARE YOU DOING HERE? THIS IS A CRIME SCENE... BUT YOU KNEW THAT DIDN'T YOU?

INSPECTOR LOHMANN. JUST WORKING ON A STORY ABOUT THE VANISHED ARCHITECTS. I DON'T KNOW ANYTHING ABOUT A "CRIME SCENE."

A LITTLE LATE IN THE EVENING FOR RESEARCH IN AN ABANDONED BUILDING ON THE OUTSKIRTS OF TOWN ISN'T IT?

I DO MY BEST WORK AT NIGHT.

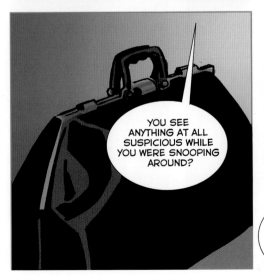

YOU SEE ANYTHING AT ALL SUSPICIOUS WHILE YOU WERE SNOOPING AROUND?

NO... NO. WHY? WHAT HAPPENED HERE?

YOU'LL BE BRIEFED AFTER THE INVESTIGATION. IN THE MEANTIME SUGGEST YOU LEAVE.

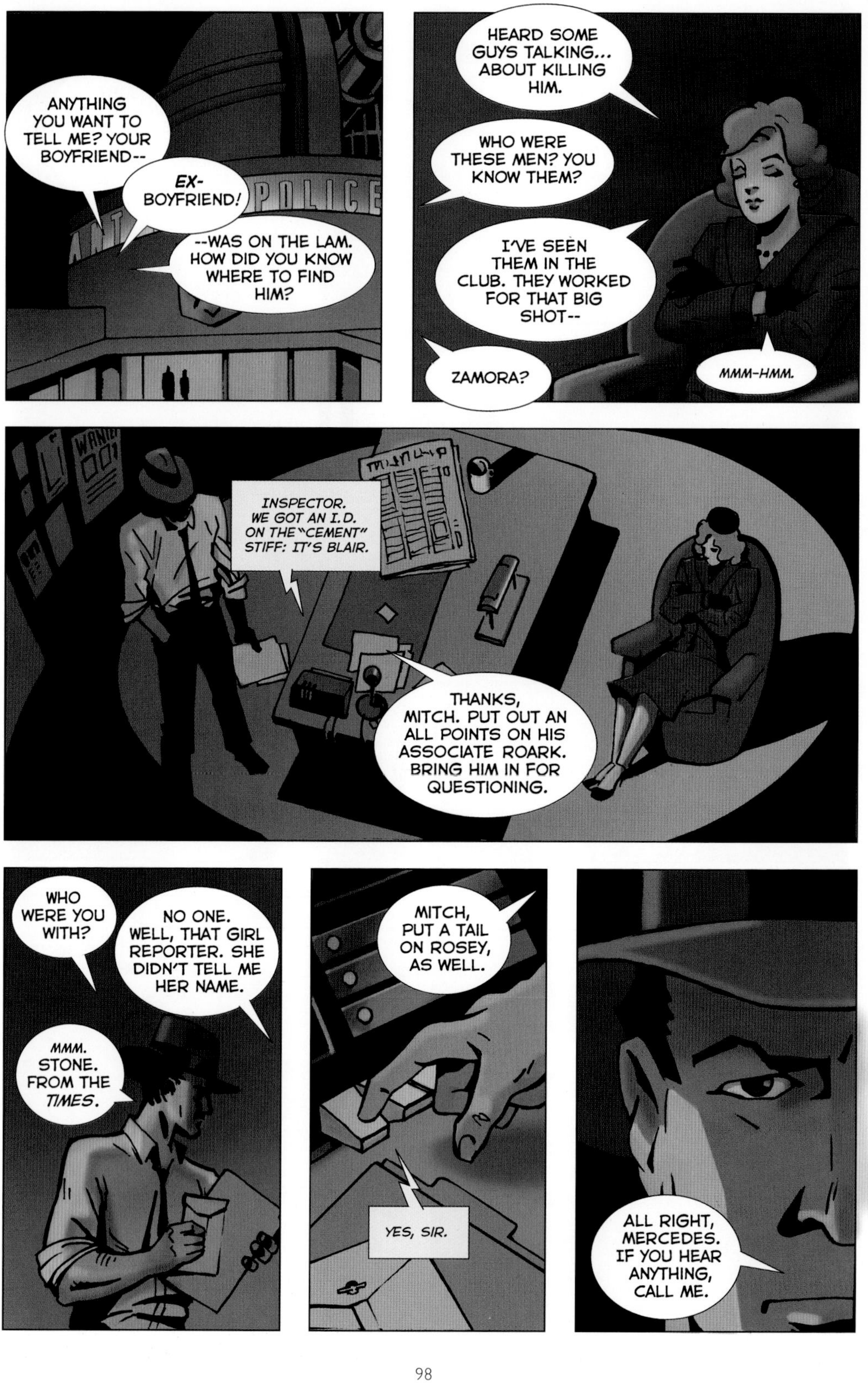
ANYTHING YOU WANT TO TELL ME? YOUR BOYFRIEND--
EX-BOYFRIEND!
--WAS ON THE LAM. HOW DID YOU KNOW WHERE TO FIND HIM?
POLICE
HEARD SOME GUYS TALKING... ABOUT KILLING HIM.
WHO WERE THESE MEN? YOU KNOW THEM?
I'VE SEEN THEM IN THE CLUB. THEY WORKED FOR THAT BIG SHOT--
ZAMORA?
MMM-HMM.
INSPECTOR. WE GOT AN I.D. ON THE "CEMENT" STIFF: IT'S BLAIR.
THANKS, MITCH. PUT OUT AN ALL POINTS ON HIS ASSOCIATE ROARK. BRING HIM IN FOR QUESTIONING.
WHO WERE YOU WITH?
NO ONE. WELL, THAT GIRL REPORTER. SHE DIDN'T TELL ME HER NAME.
MMM. STONE. FROM THE TIMES.
MITCH, PUT A TAIL ON ROSEY, AS WELL.
YES, SIR.
ALL RIGHT, MERCEDES. IF YOU HEAR ANYTHING, CALL ME.

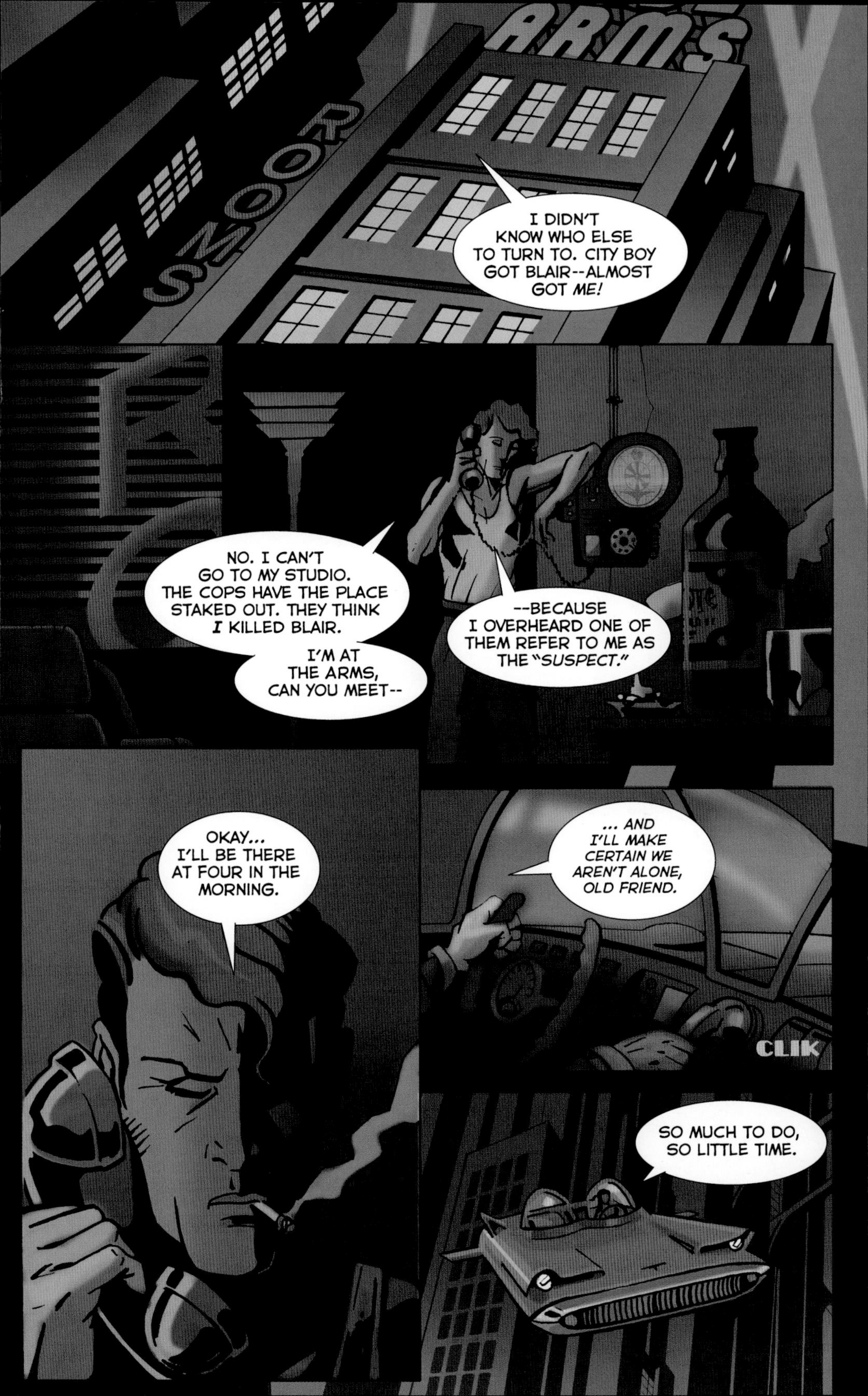

ARMS
SMOOR
I DIDN'T KNOW WHO ELSE TO TURN TO. CITY BOY GOT BLAIR--ALMOST GOT *ME!*
NO. I CAN'T GO TO MY STUDIO. THE COPS HAVE THE PLACE STAKED OUT. THEY THINK *I* KILLED BLAIR.
I'M AT THE ARMS, CAN YOU MEET--
--BECAUSE I OVERHEARD ONE OF THEM REFER TO ME AS THE "*SUSPECT.*"
OKAY... I'LL BE THERE AT FOUR IN THE MORNING.
... AND I'LL MAKE CERTAIN WE AREN'T ALONE, OLD FRIEND.
CLIK
SO MUCH TO DO, SO LITTLE TIME.

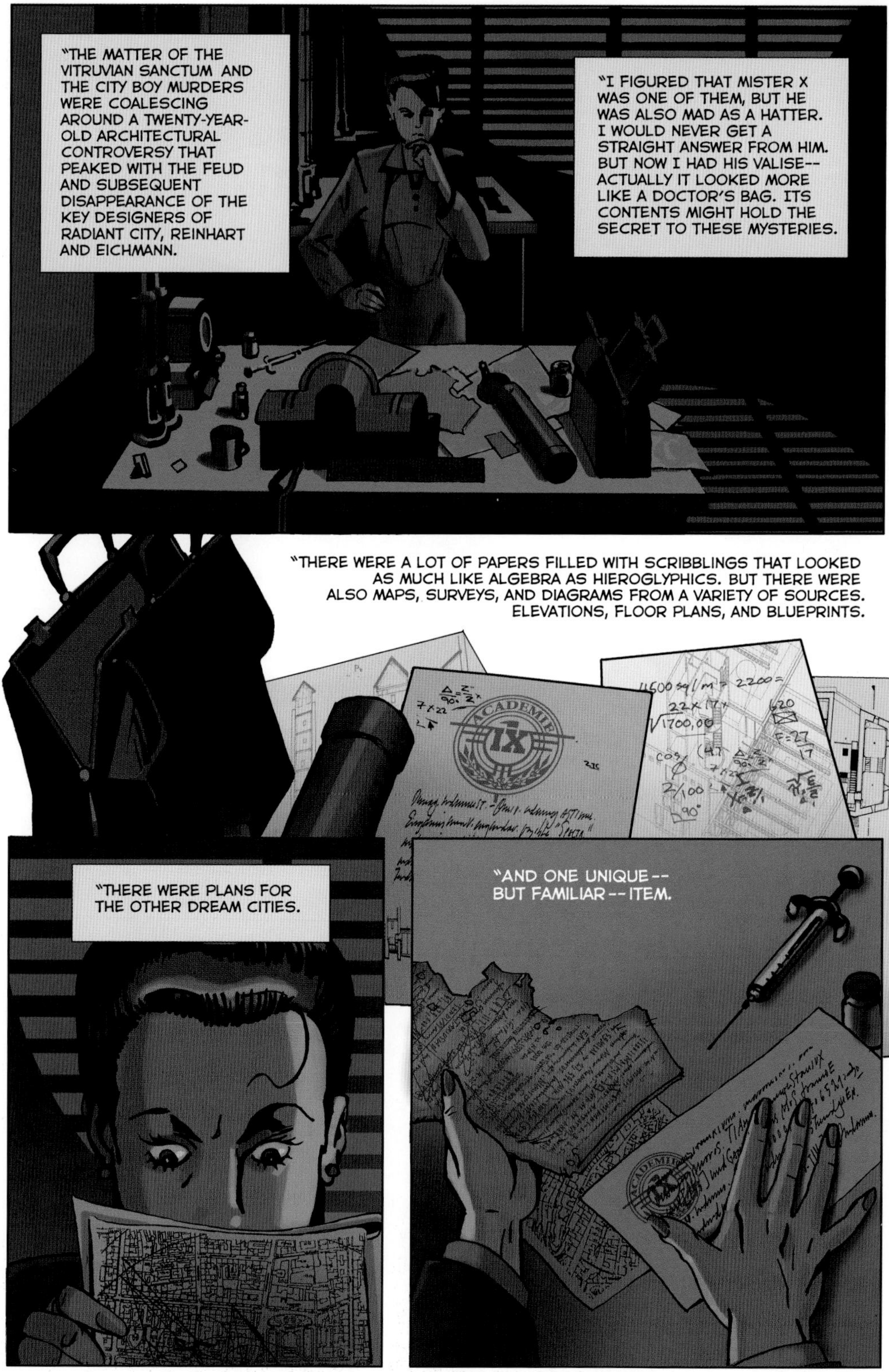
"THE MATTER OF THE VITRUVIAN SANCTUM AND THE CITY BOY MURDERS WERE COALESCING AROUND A TWENTY-YEAR-OLD ARCHITECTURAL CONTROVERSY THAT PEAKED WITH THE FEUD AND SUBSEQUENT DISAPPEARANCE OF THE KEY DESIGNERS OF RADIANT CITY, REINHART AND EICHMANN.
"I FIGURED THAT MISTER X WAS ONE OF THEM, BUT HE WAS ALSO MAD AS A HATTER. I WOULD NEVER GET A STRAIGHT ANSWER FROM HIM. BUT NOW I HAD HIS VALISE-- ACTUALLY IT LOOKED MORE LIKE A DOCTOR'S BAG. ITS CONTENTS MIGHT HOLD THE SECRET TO THESE MYSTERIES.
"THERE WERE A LOT OF PAPERS FILLED WITH SCRIBBLINGS THAT LOOKED AS MUCH LIKE ALGEBRA AS HIEROGLYPHICS. BUT THERE WERE ALSO MAPS, SURVEYS, AND DIAGRAMS FROM A VARIETY OF SOURCES. ELEVATIONS, FLOOR PLANS, AND BLUEPRINTS.
ACADEMIE
IX
"THERE WERE PLANS FOR THE OTHER DREAM CITIES.
"AND ONE UNIQUE -- BUT FAMILIAR -- ITEM.

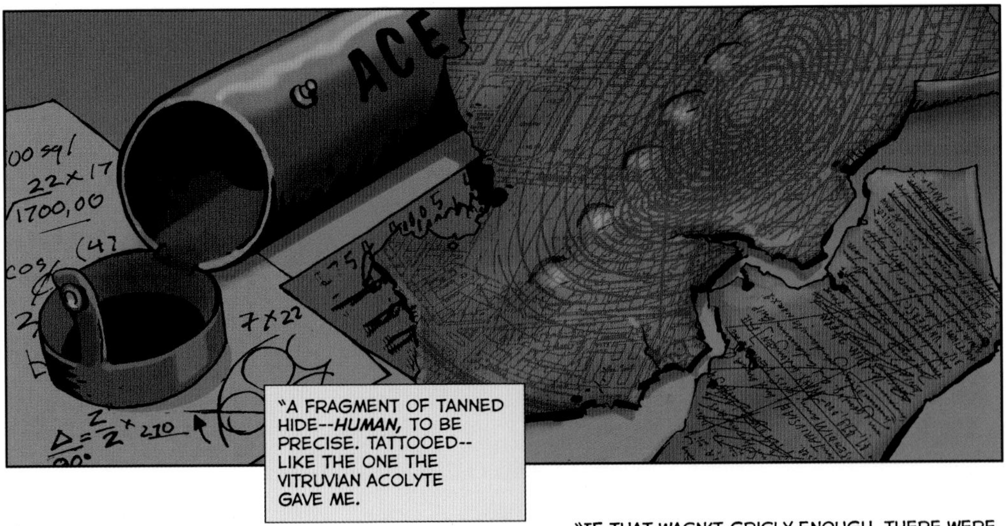
ACE
"A FRAGMENT OF TANNED HIDE--*HUMAN,* TO BE PRECISE. TATTOOED--LIKE THE ONE THE VITRUVIAN ACOLYTE GAVE ME.

"IT WAS, IN FACT, THE MISSING LEGEND.

"IT LOOKED TO DEPICT WHAT THE COUNCILWOMAN HAD DISMISSED AS URBAN MYTHOLOGY. GIANT MACHINES BENEATH THE CITY. OLD MACHINES. POWERFUL MACHINES.

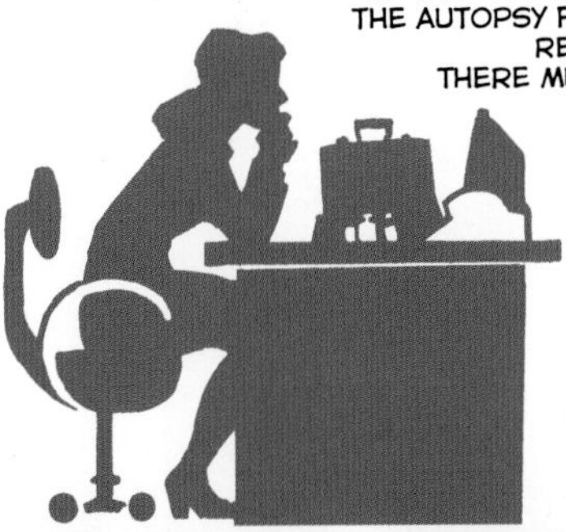

"IF THAT WASN'T GRISLY ENOUGH, THERE WERE THE AUTOPSY FILES FROM THE NINTH ACADEMY. REINHART, EICHMANN, NOSTRAND... THERE MUST HAVE BEEN A DOZEN OR SO.

"WITH MARGINAL NOTES.

"AND THEN THERE WERE THE DRUGS: *INSOMNALIN, METAMORPHINE, POLTERCAINE.* THEY WEREN'T FROM ANY PHARMACY, THAT WAS FOR SURE."

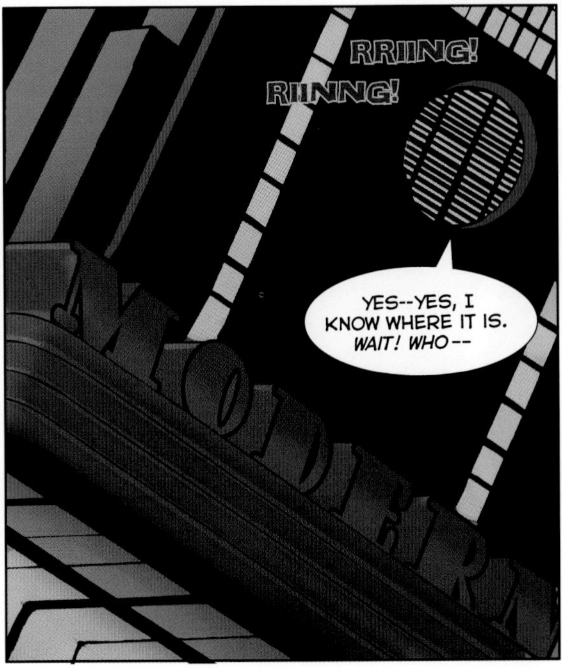
RRIING!
RIINNG!
YES--YES, I KNOW WHERE IT IS. *WAIT! WHO--*

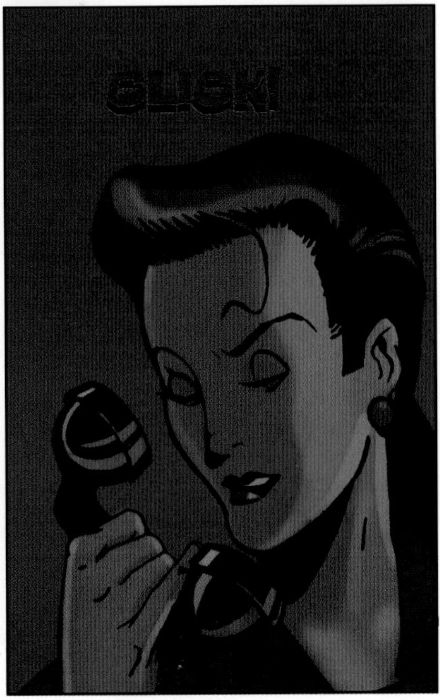
CLICK!

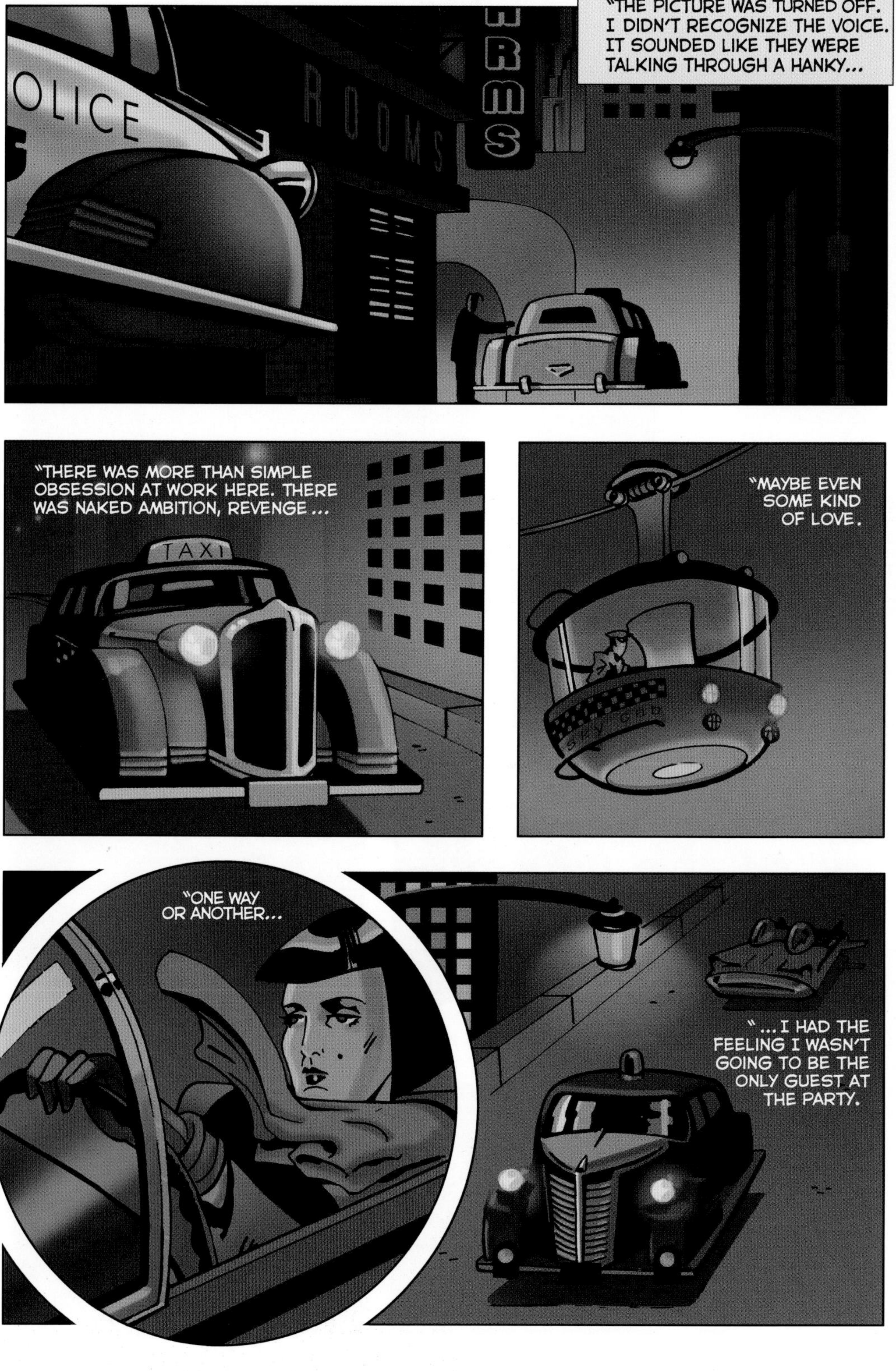
"THE PICTURE WAS TURNED OFF. I DIDN'T RECOGNIZE THE VOICE. IT SOUNDED LIKE THEY WERE TALKING THROUGH A HANKY...
OLICE
ROOMS
"THERE WAS MORE THAN SIMPLE OBSESSION AT WORK HERE. THERE WAS NAKED AMBITION, REVENGE ...
TAXI
"MAYBE EVEN SOME KIND OF LOVE.
sky cab
"ONE WAY OR ANOTHER...
"...I HAD THE FEELING I WASN'T GOING TO BE THE ONLY GUEST AT THE PARTY.

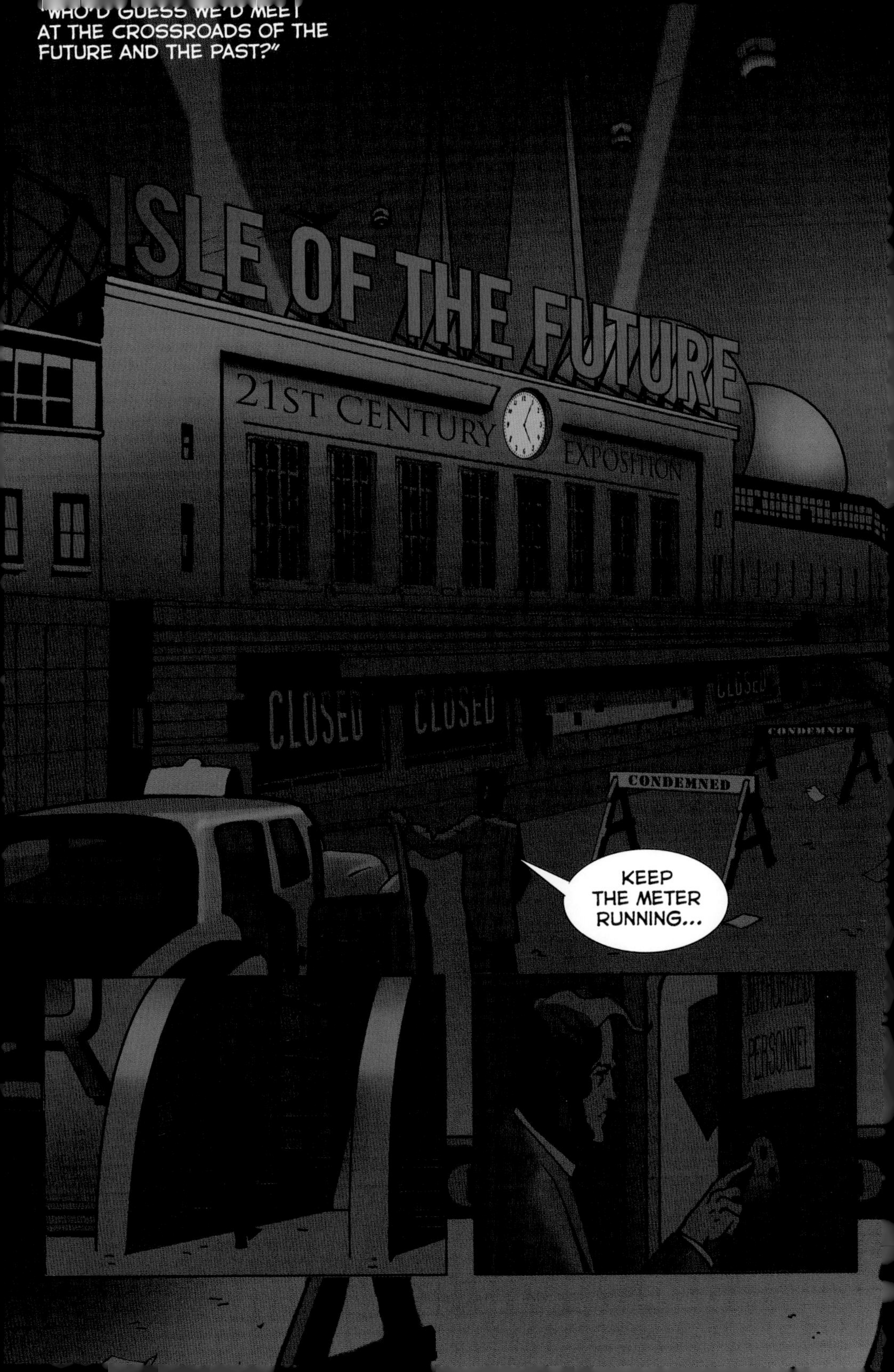
"WHO'D GUESS WE'D MEET AT THE CROSSROADS OF THE FUTURE AND THE PAST?"
ISLE OF THE FUTURE
21ST CENTURY EXPOSITION
CLOSED
CLOSED
CLOSED
CONDEMNED
CONDEMNED
KEEP THE METER RUNNING...
PERSONNEL

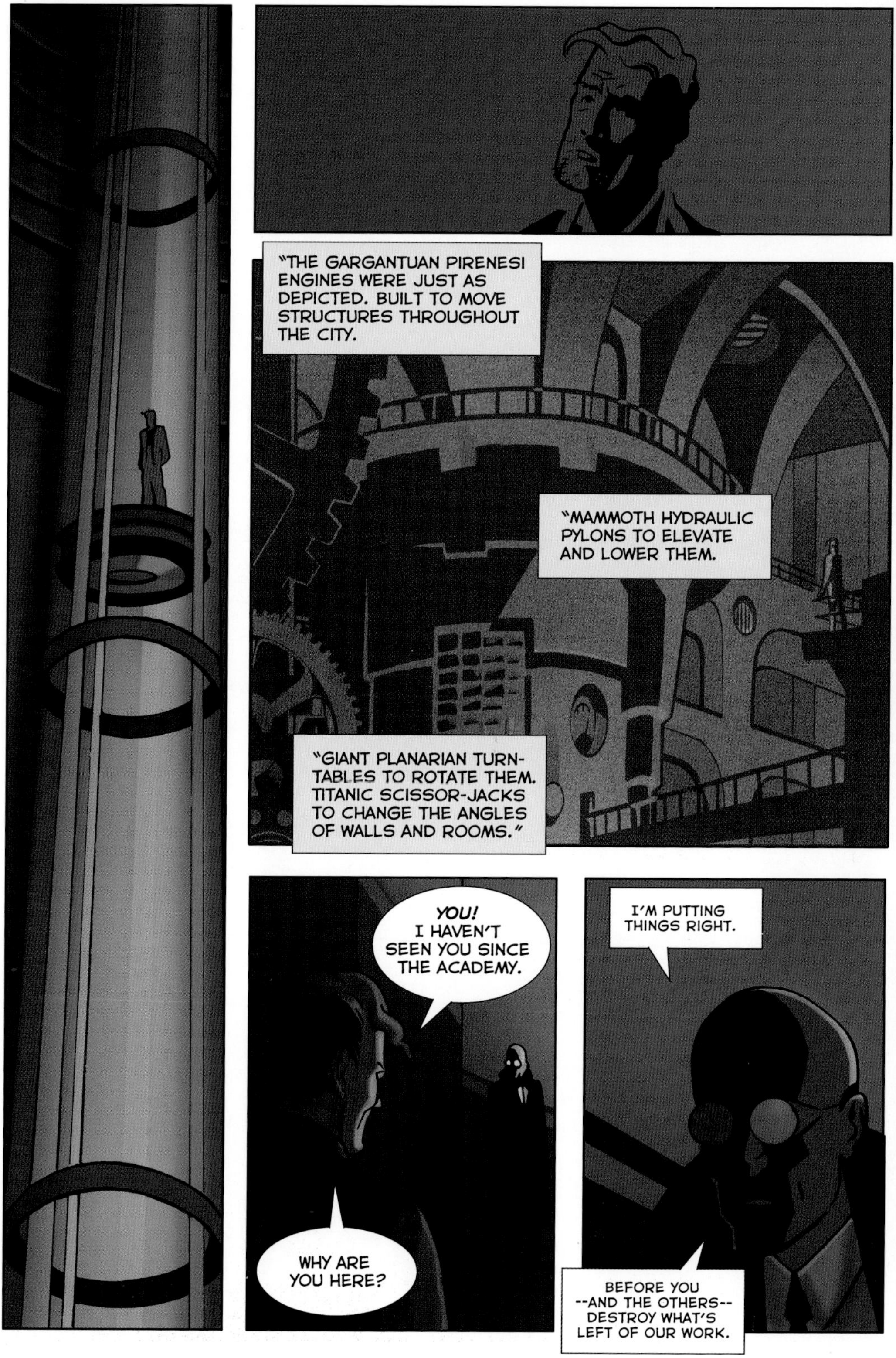
"THE GARGANTUAN PIRENESI ENGINES WERE JUST AS DEPICTED. BUILT TO MOVE STRUCTURES THROUGHOUT THE CITY.
"MAMMOTH HYDRAULIC PYLONS TO ELEVATE AND LOWER THEM.
"GIANT PLANARIAN TURN-TABLES TO ROTATE THEM. TITANIC SCISSOR-JACKS TO CHANGE THE ANGLES OF WALLS AND ROOMS."
YOU! I HAVEN'T SEEN YOU SINCE THE ACADEMY.
WHY ARE YOU HERE?
I'M PUTTING THINGS RIGHT.
BEFORE YOU --AND THE OTHERS-- DESTROY WHAT'S LEFT OF OUR WORK.

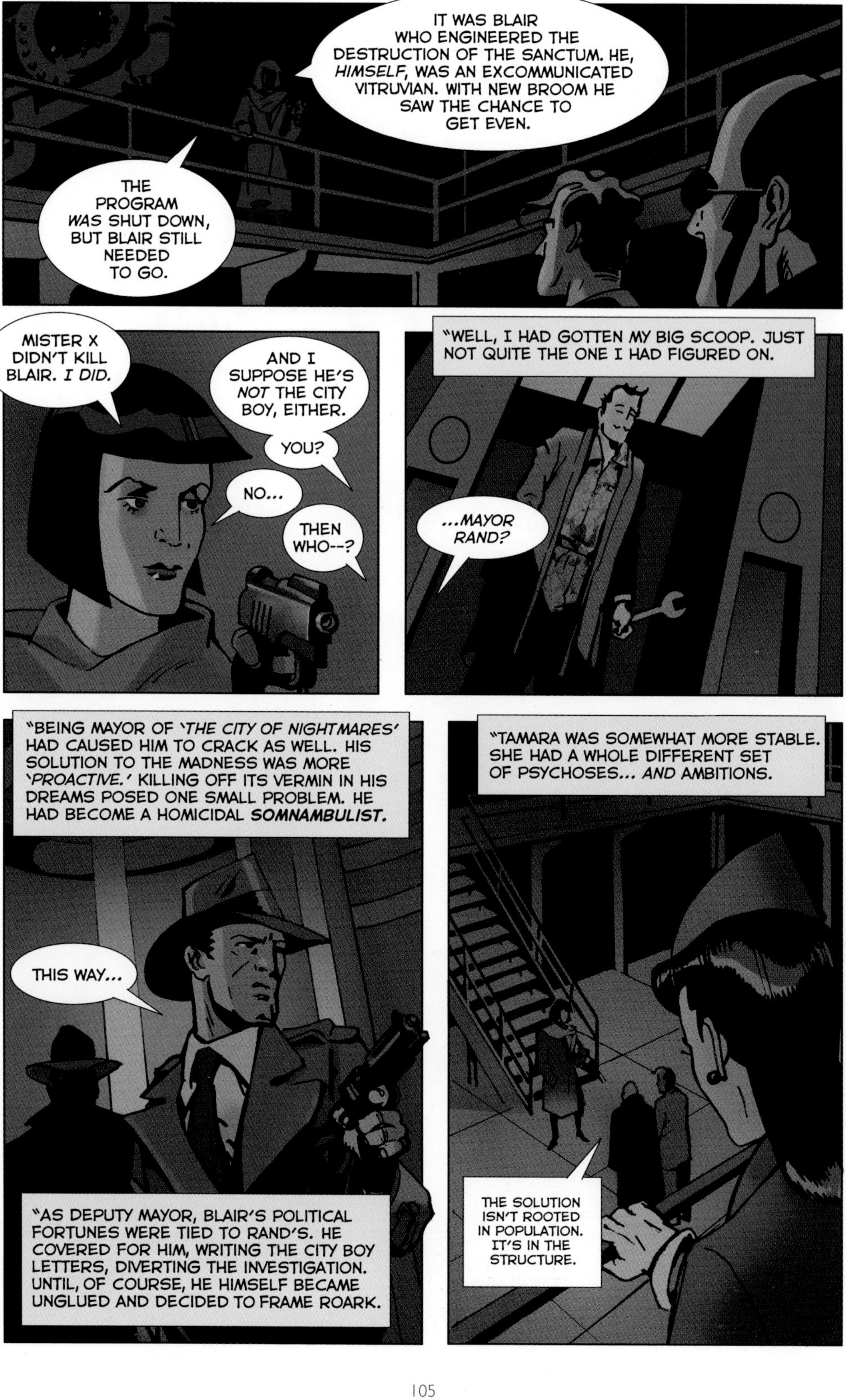
IT WAS BLAIR WHO ENGINEERED THE DESTRUCTION OF THE SANCTUM. HE, *HIMSELF*, WAS AN EXCOMMUNICATED VITRUVIAN. WITH NEW BROOM HE SAW THE CHANCE TO GET EVEN.
THE PROGRAM *WAS* SHUT DOWN, BUT BLAIR STILL NEEDED TO GO.
MISTER X DIDN'T KILL BLAIR. *I DID.*
AND I SUPPOSE HE'S *NOT* THE CITY BOY, EITHER.
YOU?
NO...
THEN WHO--?
"WELL, I HAD GOTTEN MY BIG SCOOP. JUST NOT QUITE THE ONE I HAD FIGURED ON.
...*MAYOR RAND?*
"BEING MAYOR OF '*THE CITY OF NIGHTMARES*' HAD CAUSED HIM TO CRACK AS WELL. HIS SOLUTION TO THE MADNESS WAS MORE '*PROACTIVE.*' KILLING OFF ITS VERMIN IN HIS DREAMS POSED ONE SMALL PROBLEM. HE HAD BECOME A HOMICIDAL ***SOMNAMBULIST.***
THIS WAY...
"AS DEPUTY MAYOR, BLAIR'S POLITICAL FORTUNES WERE TIED TO RAND'S. HE COVERED FOR HIM, WRITING THE CITY BOY LETTERS, DIVERTING THE INVESTIGATION. UNTIL, OF COURSE, HE HIMSELF BECAME UNGLUED AND DECIDED TO FRAME ROARK.
"TAMARA WAS SOMEWHAT MORE STABLE. SHE HAD A WHOLE DIFFERENT SET OF PSYCHOSES... *AND* AMBITIONS.
THE SOLUTION ISN'T ROOTED IN POPULATION. IT'S IN THE STRUCTURE.

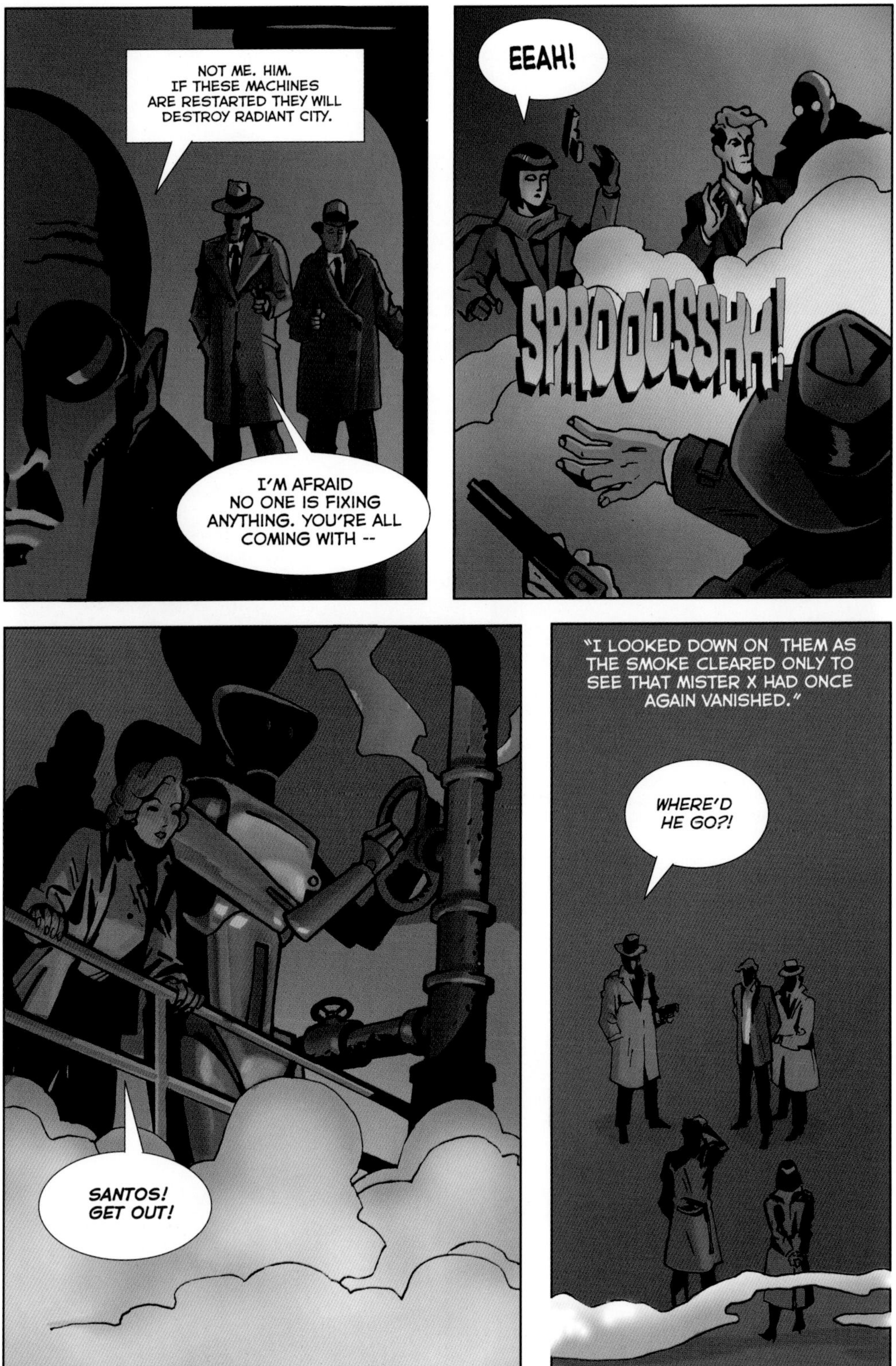
NOT ME. HIM.
IF THESE MACHINES
ARE RESTARTED THEY WILL
DESTROY RADIANT CITY.
I'M AFRAID
NO ONE IS FIXING
ANYTHING. YOU'RE ALL
COMING WITH --
EEAH!
SPROOOSSHH!
SANTOS!
GET OUT!
"I LOOKED DOWN ON THEM AS
THE SMOKE CLEARED ONLY TO
SEE THAT MISTER X HAD ONCE
AGAIN VANISHED."
WHERE'D
HE GO?!

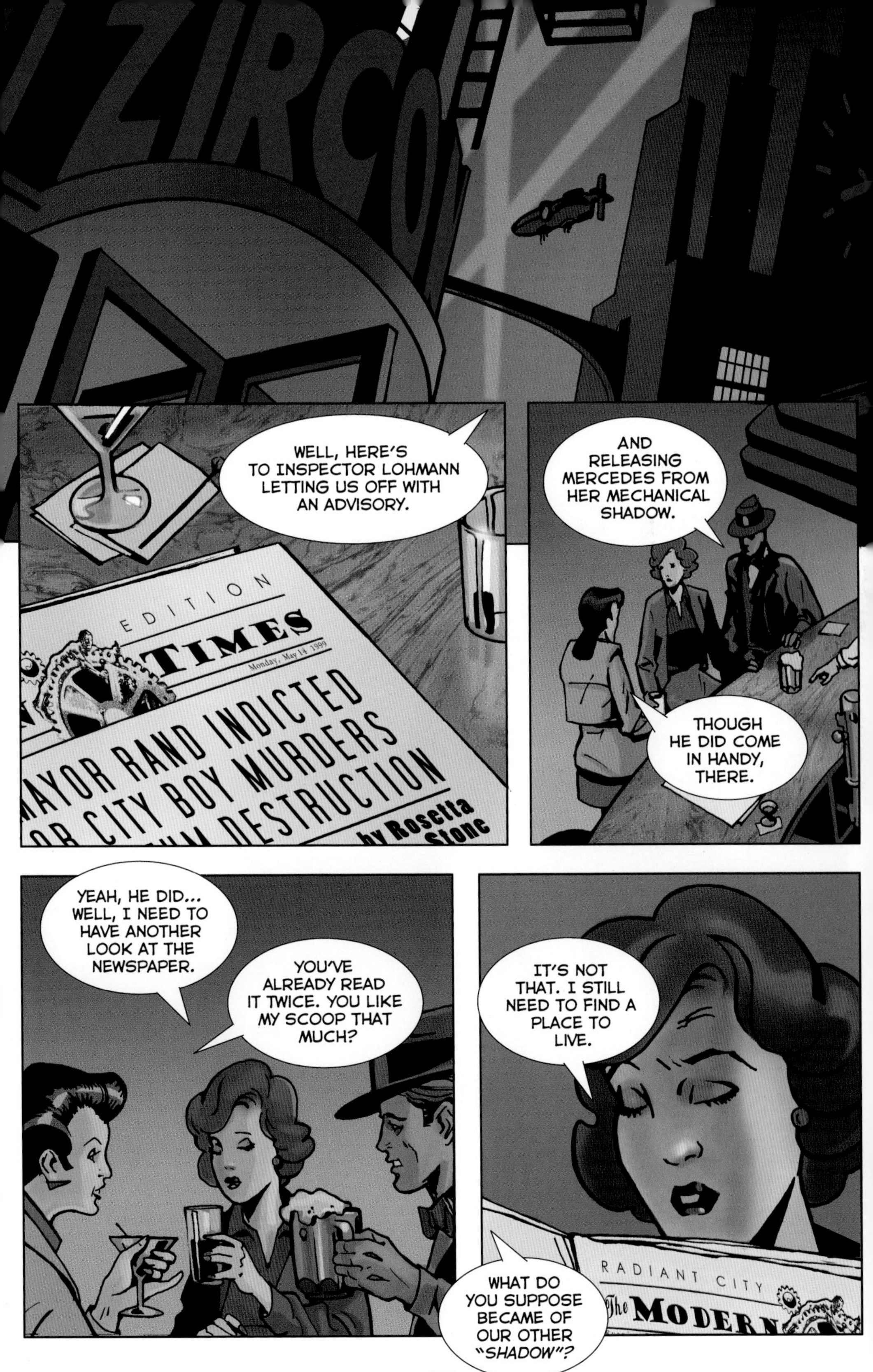
ZIRCO
WELL, HERE'S TO INSPECTOR LOHMANN LETTING US OFF WITH AN ADVISORY.
EDITION
TIMES
Monday, May 14 1999
MAYOR RAND INDICTED
OR CITY BOY MURDERS
DESTRUCTION
by Rosetta Stone
AND RELEASING MERCEDES FROM HER MECHANICAL SHADOW.
THOUGH HE DID COME IN HANDY, THERE.
YEAH, HE DID... WELL, I NEED TO HAVE ANOTHER LOOK AT THE NEWSPAPER.
YOU'VE ALREADY READ IT TWICE. YOU LIKE MY SCOOP THAT MUCH?
IT'S NOT THAT. I STILL NEED TO FIND A PLACE TO LIVE.
WHAT DO YOU SUPPOSE BECAME OF OUR OTHER "*SHADOW*"?
RADIANT CITY
The MODERN

"HE'LL TURN UP AGAIN. HIS WORK IS FAR FROM FINISHED."
RADIANT CITY
STAY AWAKE
MISTER X
CITY BOY
CONDEMNED
THE END

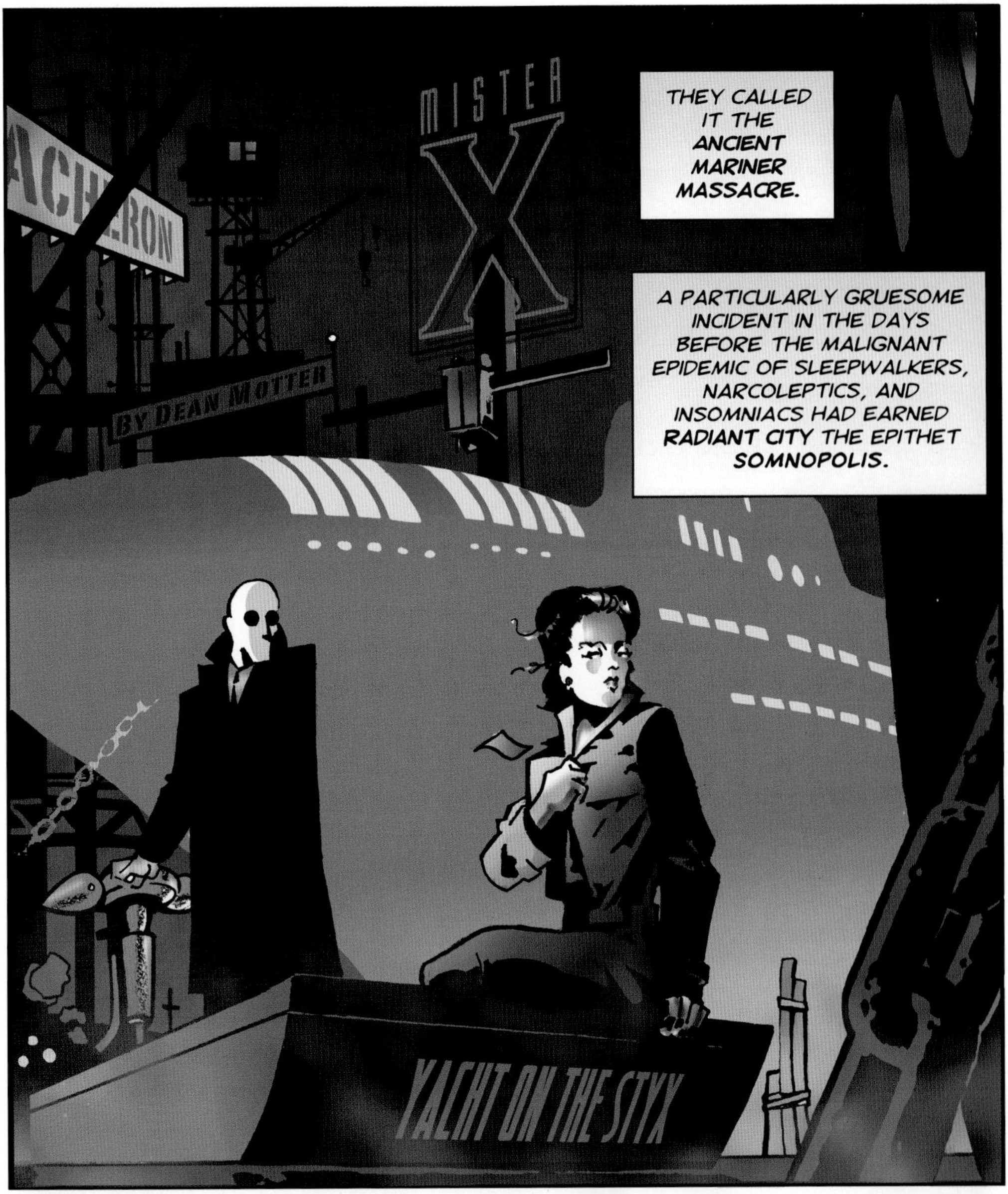
MISTER X
ACHERON
BY DEAN MOTTER
THEY CALLED IT THE ANCIENT MARINER MASSACRE.
A PARTICULARLY GRUESOME INCIDENT IN THE DAYS BEFORE THE MALIGNANT EPIDEMIC OF SLEEPWALKERS, NARCOLEPTICS, AND INSOMNIACS HAD EARNED RADIANT CITY THE EPITHET SOMNOPOLIS.
YACHT ON THE STYX

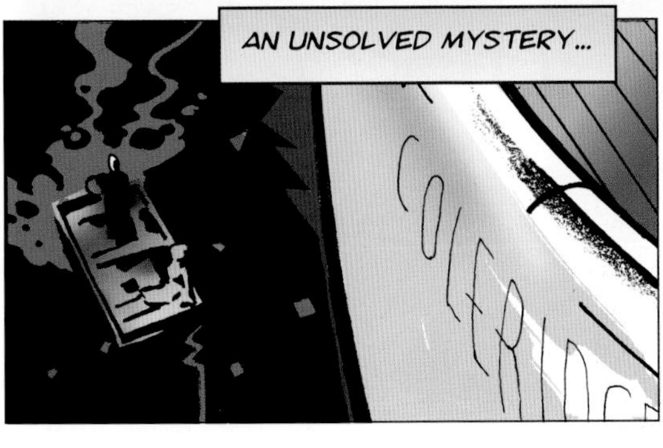
AN UNSOLVED MYSTERY...
COLERIDG

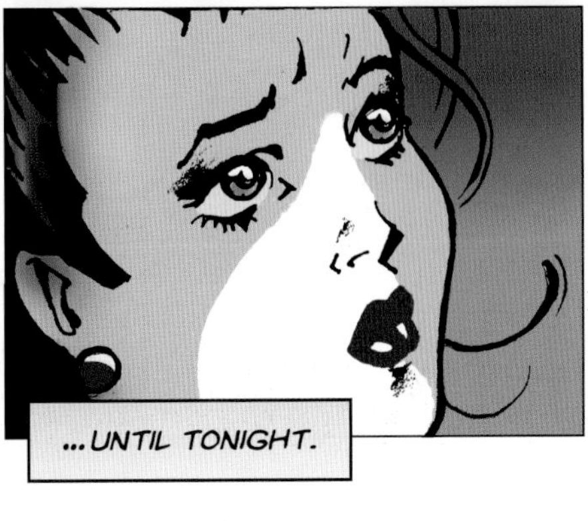
...UNTIL TONIGHT.

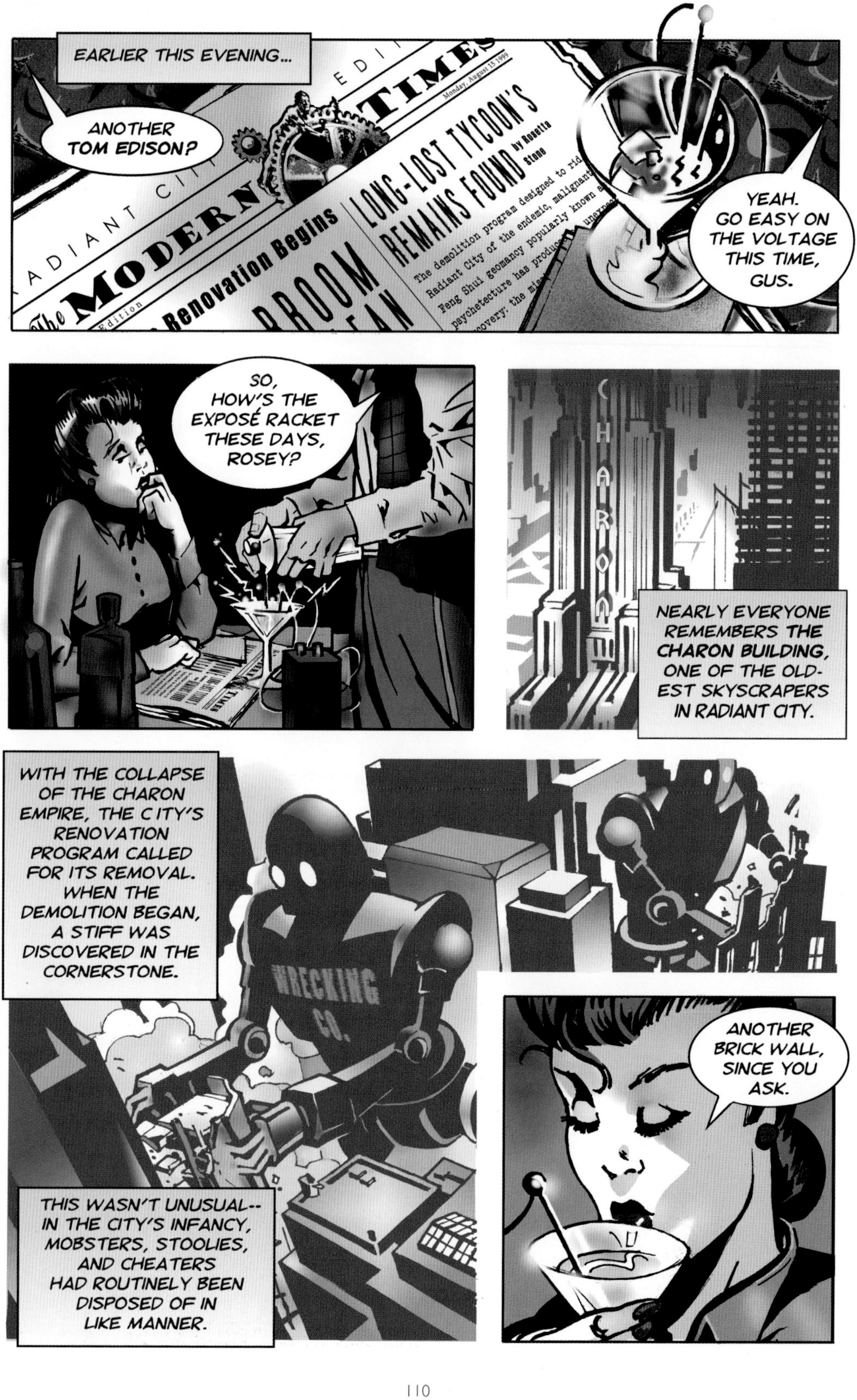
EARLIER THIS EVENING...
ANOTHER TOM EDISON?
The MODERN TIMES
Monday, August 15 1999
Renovation Begins
LONG-LOST TYCOON'S REMAINS FOUND
by Rosetta Stone
YEAH. GO EASY ON THE VOLTAGE THIS TIME, GUS.
SO, HOW'S THE EXPOSÉ RACKET THESE DAYS, ROSEY?
CHARON
NEARLY EVERYONE REMEMBERS THE CHARON BUILDING, ONE OF THE OLD-EST SKYSCRAPERS IN RADIANT CITY.
WITH THE COLLAPSE OF THE CHARON EMPIRE, THE CITY'S RENOVATION PROGRAM CALLED FOR ITS REMOVAL. WHEN THE DEMOLITION BEGAN, A STIFF WAS DISCOVERED IN THE CORNERSTONE.
WRECKING CO.
THIS WASN'T UNUSUAL-- IN THE CITY'S INFANCY, MOBSTERS, STOOLIES, AND CHEATERS HAD ROUTINELY BEEN DISPOSED OF IN LIKE MANNER.
ANOTHER BRICK WALL, SINCE YOU ASK.

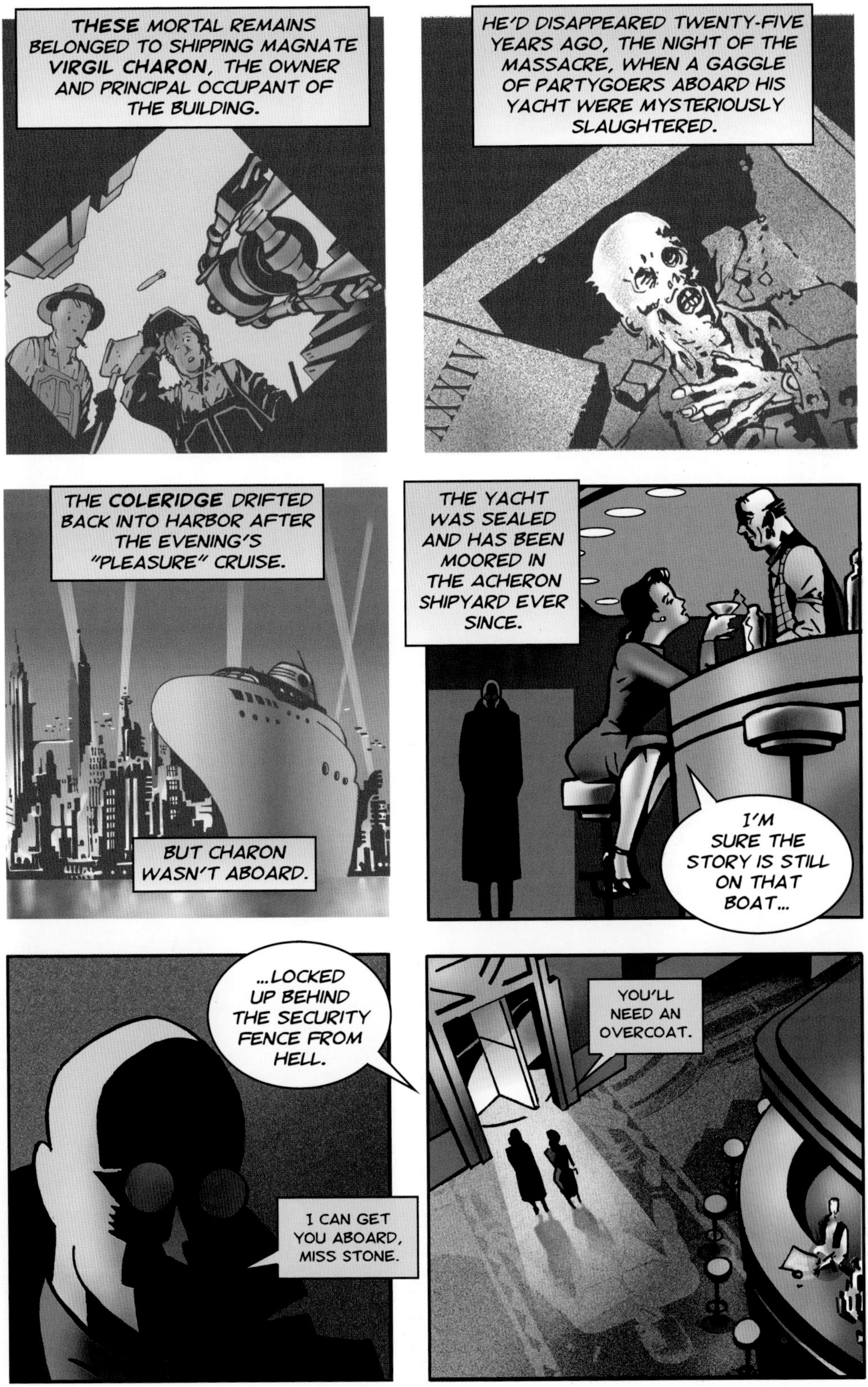
THESE MORTAL REMAINS BELONGED TO SHIPPING MAGNATE VIRGIL CHARON, THE OWNER AND PRINCIPAL OCCUPANT OF THE BUILDING.
HE'D DISAPPEARED TWENTY-FIVE YEARS AGO, THE NIGHT OF THE MASSACRE, WHEN A GAGGLE OF PARTYGOERS ABOARD HIS YACHT WERE MYSTERIOUSLY SLAUGHTERED.
THE COLERIDGE DRIFTED BACK INTO HARBOR AFTER THE EVENING'S "PLEASURE" CRUISE.
BUT CHARON WASN'T ABOARD.
THE YACHT WAS SEALED AND HAS BEEN MOORED IN THE ACHERON SHIPYARD EVER SINCE.
I'M SURE THE STORY IS STILL ON THAT BOAT...
...LOCKED UP BEHIND THE SECURITY FENCE FROM HELL.
I CAN GET YOU ABOARD, MISS STONE.
YOU'LL NEED AN OVERCOAT.

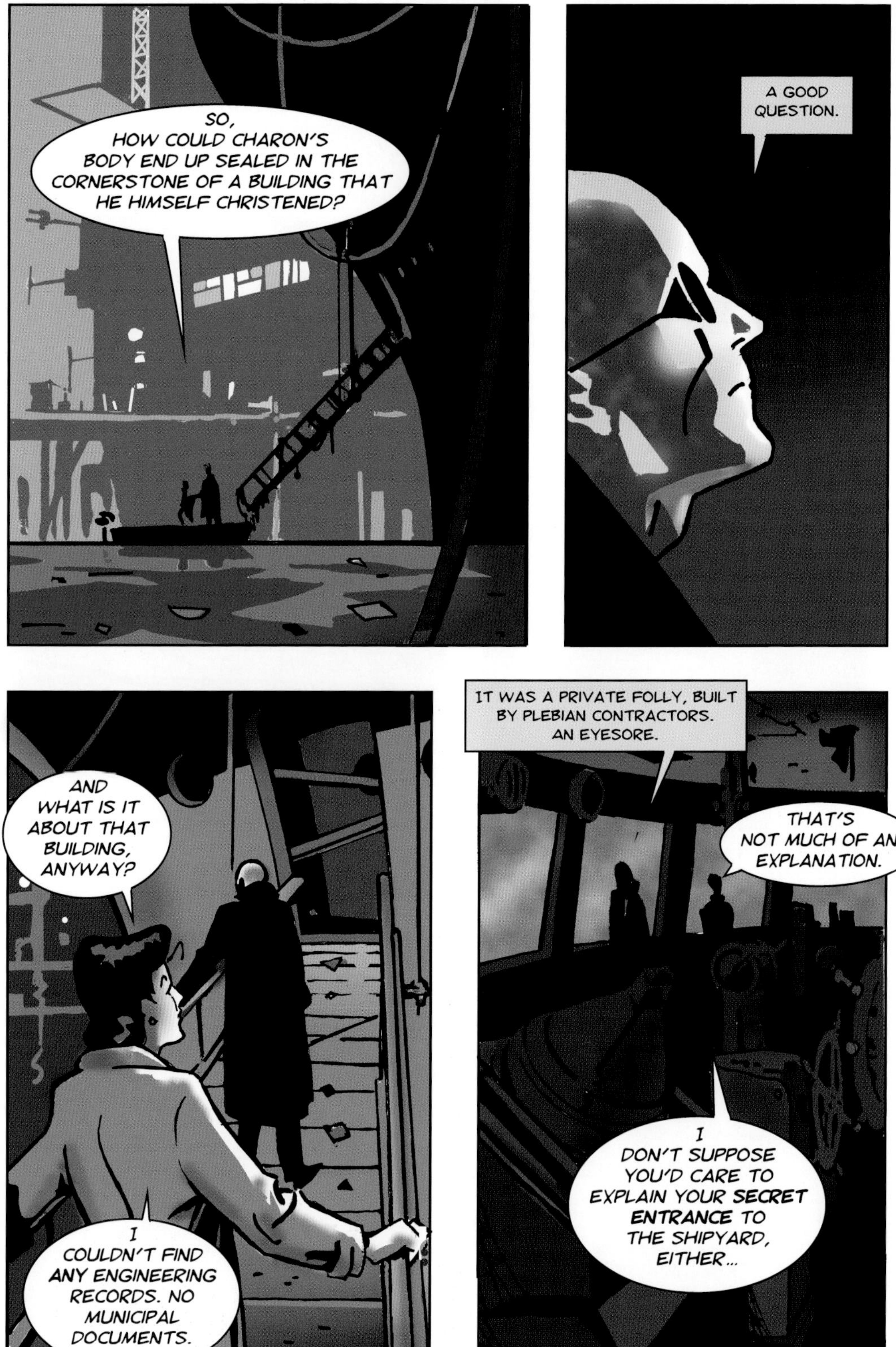
SO, HOW COULD CHARON'S BODY END UP SEALED IN THE CORNERSTONE OF A BUILDING THAT HE HIMSELF CHRISTENED?
A GOOD QUESTION.
AND WHAT IS IT ABOUT THAT BUILDING, ANYWAY?
I COULDN'T FIND ANY ENGINEERING RECORDS. NO MUNICIPAL DOCUMENTS.
IT WAS A PRIVATE FOLLY, BUILT BY PLEBIAN CONTRACTORS. AN EYESORE.
THAT'S NOT MUCH OF AN EXPLANATION.
I DON'T SUPPOSE YOU'D CARE TO EXPLAIN YOUR **SECRET ENTRANCE** TO THE SHIPYARD, EITHER...

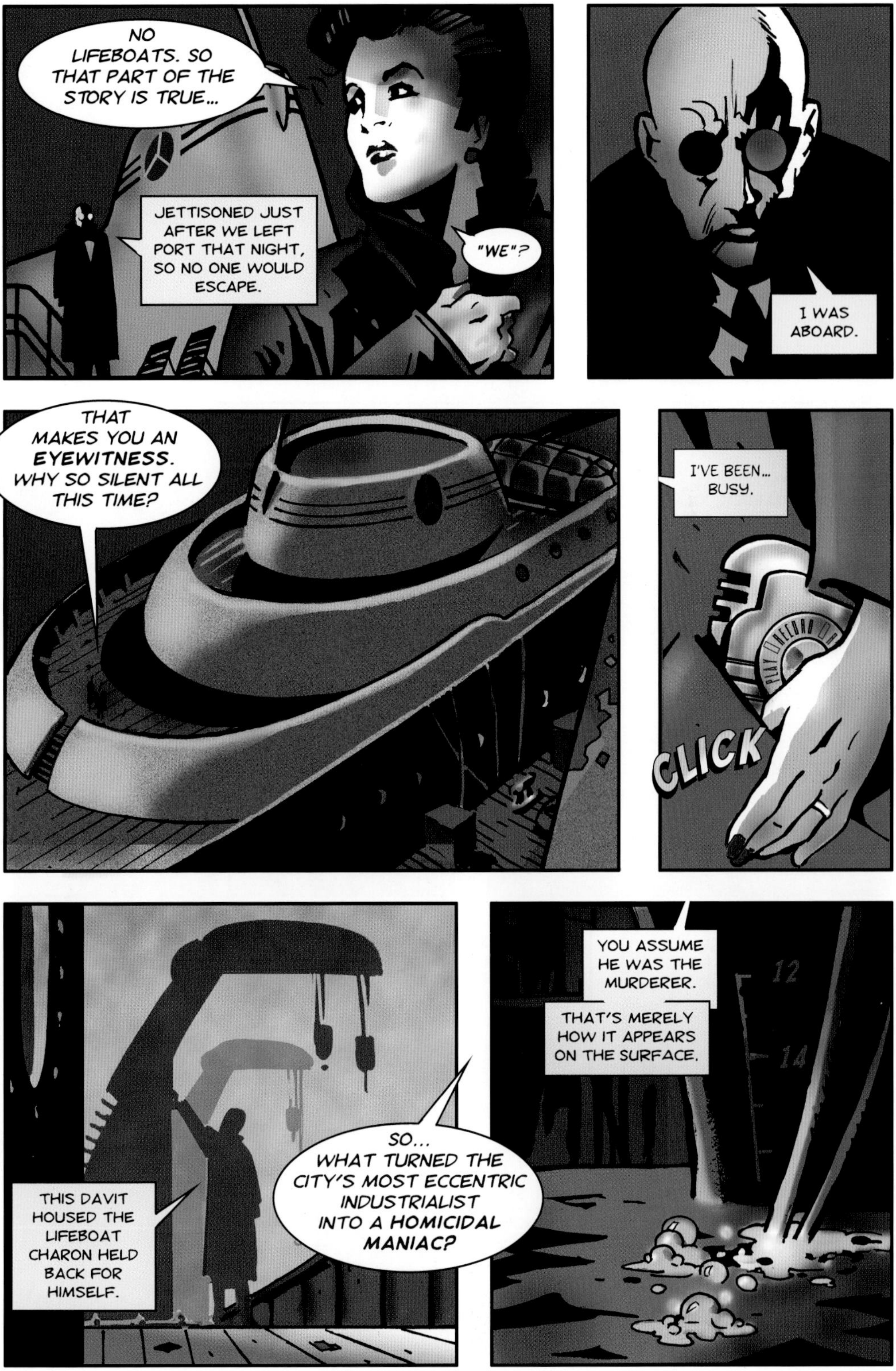
NO LIFEBOATS. SO THAT PART OF THE STORY IS TRUE...
JETTISONED JUST AFTER WE LEFT PORT THAT NIGHT, SO NO ONE WOULD ESCAPE.
"WE"?
I WAS ABOARD.
THAT MAKES YOU AN EYEWITNESS. WHY SO SILENT ALL THIS TIME?
I'VE BEEN... BUSY.
PLAY RECORD
CLICK
THIS DAVIT HOUSED THE LIFEBOAT CHARON HELD BACK FOR HIMSELF.
SO... WHAT TURNED THE CITY'S MOST ECCENTRIC INDUSTRIALIST INTO A HOMICIDAL MANIAC?
YOU ASSUME HE WAS THE MURDERER.
THAT'S MERELY HOW IT APPEARS ON THE SURFACE.
12
14

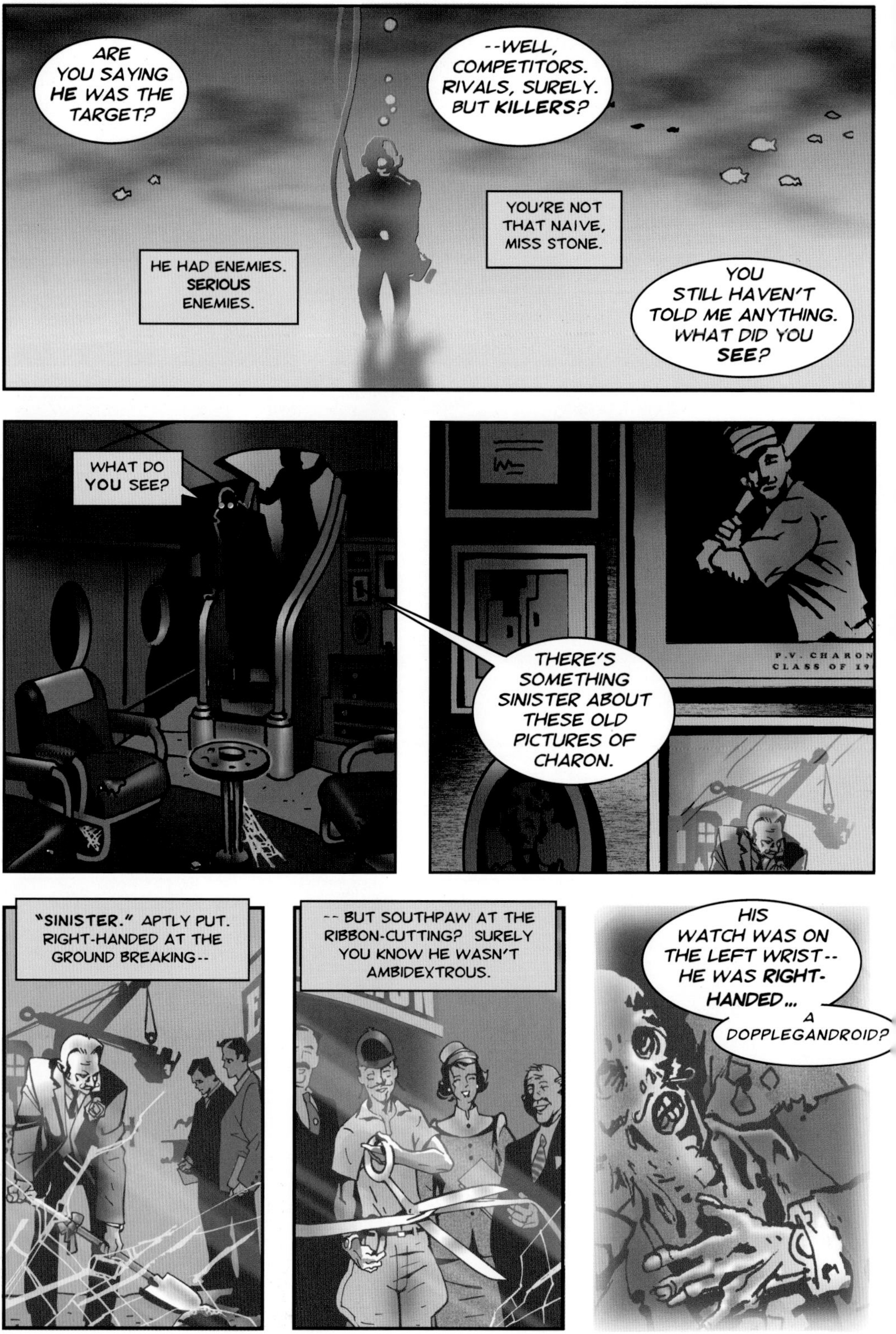
ARE YOU SAYING HE WAS THE TARGET?
HE HAD ENEMIES. SERIOUS ENEMIES.
--WELL, COMPETITORS. RIVALS, SURELY. BUT KILLERS?
YOU'RE NOT THAT NAIVE, MISS STONE.
YOU STILL HAVEN'T TOLD ME ANYTHING. WHAT DID YOU SEE?
WHAT DO YOU SEE?
THERE'S SOMETHING SINISTER ABOUT THESE OLD PICTURES OF CHARON.
P.V. CHARON
CLASS OF 19
"SINISTER." APTLY PUT. RIGHT-HANDED AT THE GROUND BREAKING--
-- BUT SOUTHPAW AT THE RIBBON-CUTTING? SURELY YOU KNOW HE WASN'T AMBIDEXTROUS.
HIS WATCH WAS ON THE LEFT WRIST-- HE WAS RIGHT-HANDED...
A DOPPLEGANDROID?

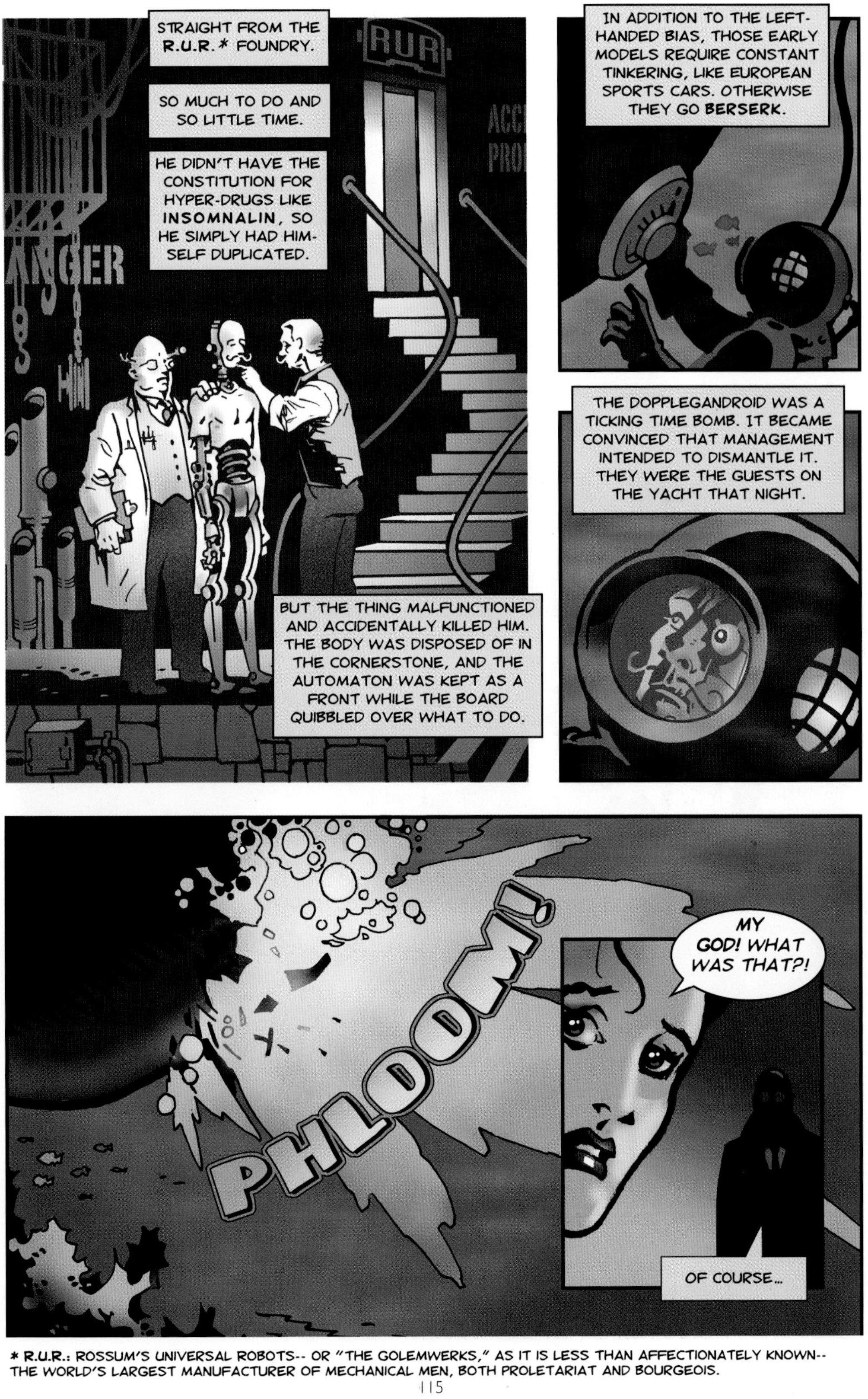
STRAIGHT FROM THE R.U.R.* FOUNDRY.
SO MUCH TO DO AND SO LITTLE TIME.
HE DIDN'T HAVE THE CONSTITUTION FOR HYPER-DRUGS LIKE INSOMNALIN, SO HE SIMPLY HAD HIM-SELF DUPLICATED.
RUR
BUT THE THING MALFUNCTIONED AND ACCIDENTALLY KILLED HIM. THE BODY WAS DISPOSED OF IN THE CORNERSTONE, AND THE AUTOMATON WAS KEPT AS A FRONT WHILE THE BOARD QUIBBLED OVER WHAT TO DO.
IN ADDITION TO THE LEFT-HANDED BIAS, THOSE EARLY MODELS REQUIRE CONSTANT TINKERING, LIKE EUROPEAN SPORTS CARS. OTHERWISE THEY GO BERSERK.
THE DOPPLEGANDROID WAS A TICKING TIME BOMB. IT BECAME CONVINCED THAT MANAGEMENT INTENDED TO DISMANTLE IT. THEY WERE THE GUESTS ON THE YACHT THAT NIGHT.
PHLOOM!
MY GOD! WHAT WAS THAT?!
OF COURSE...

* **R.U.R.**: ROSSUM'S UNIVERSAL ROBOTS-- OR "THE GOLEMWERKS," AS IT IS LESS THAN AFFECTIONATELY KNOWN-- THE WORLD'S LARGEST MANUFACTURER OF MECHANICAL MEN, BOTH PROLETARIAT AND BOURGEOIS.

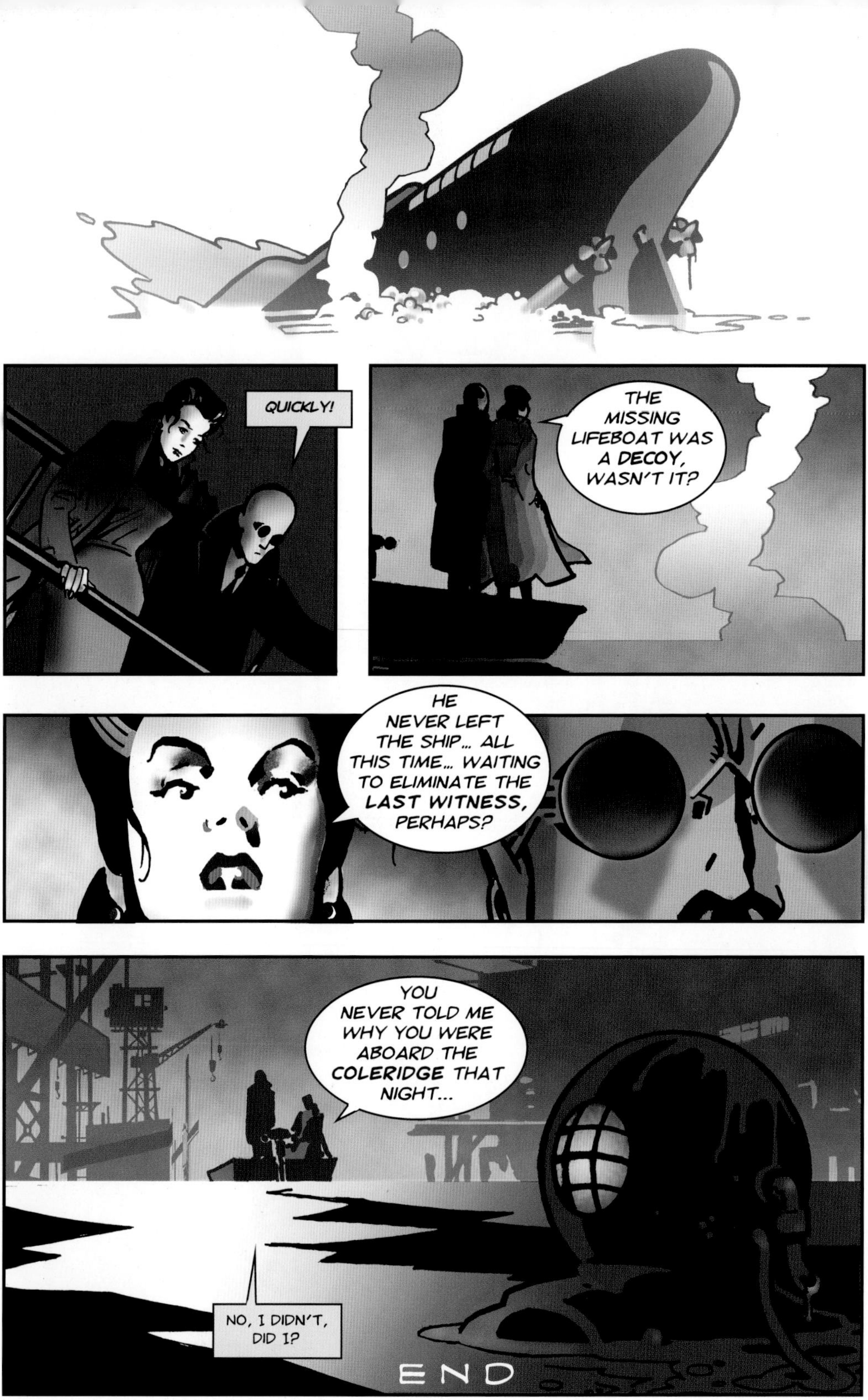
QUICKLY!
THE MISSING LIFEBOAT WAS A DECOY, WASN'T IT?
HE NEVER LEFT THE SHIP... ALL THIS TIME... WAITING TO ELIMINATE THE LAST WITNESS, PERHAPS?
YOU NEVER TOLD ME WHY YOU WERE ABOARD THE COLERIDGE THAT NIGHT...
NO, I DIDN'T, DID I?
END

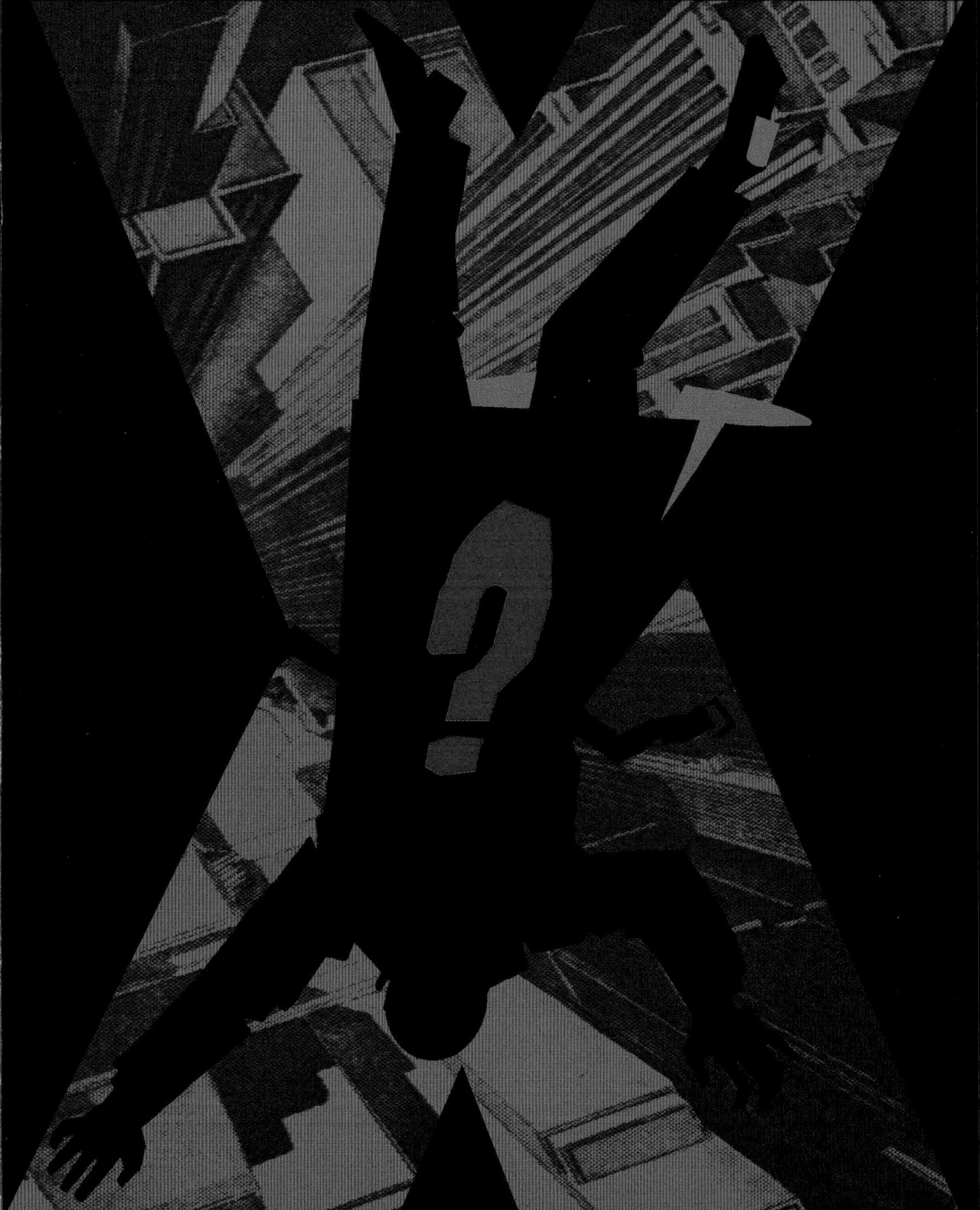

MISTER X

THE ARCHIVES

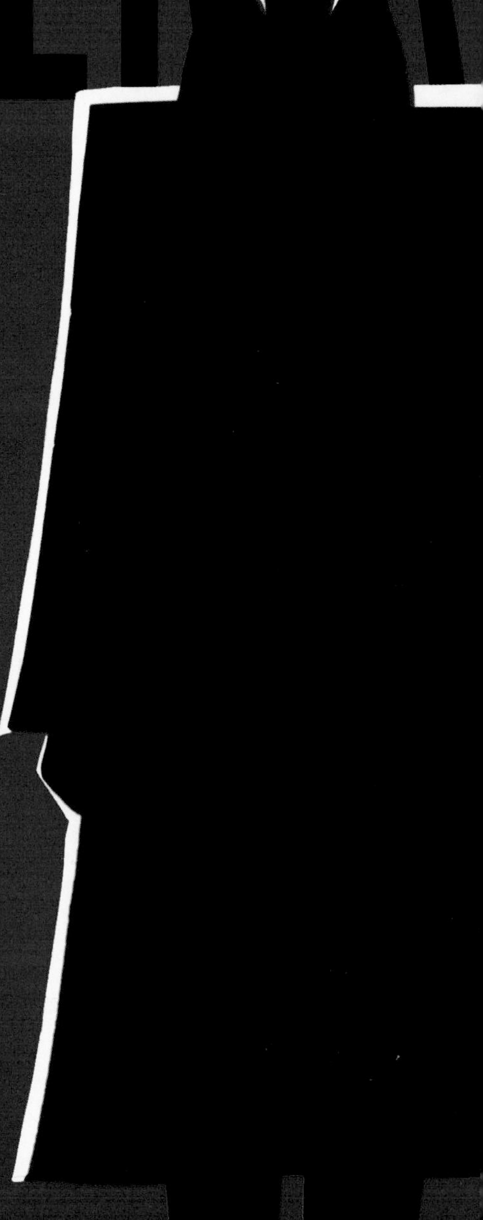

DEAN MOTTER

with

LOS BROS. HERNANDEZ

SETH

PAUL RIVOCHE

TY TEMPLETON

NEIL GAIMAN

DAVE MCKEAN

BILL SIENKIEWICZ

and more

THE COMPLETE FIRST SERIES IN ONE VOLUME

"Mister X changed the way comics looked, and it changed the way we looked at comics. And it told a hell of a story in the process."—Warren Ellis

DARK HORSE BOOKS

Available at your local comics shop. To find a comics shop in your area, call 1-888-266-4226. For more information or to order direct visit darkhorse.com or call 1-800-862-0052.

Mister X: The Archives © 2009 Vortex Comics, Inc. Mister X™ is a trademark of Vortex Comics, Inc. Dark Horse Books™ and the Dark Horse logo are registered trademarks of Dark Horse Comics, Inc.